Praise for *American Bloodlines*

"If those who cannot remember the past are doomed to repeat it, if we are on a terrifyingly fast track to becoming a people doomed, then voices like Lea's, those who will not comply, who will not roll over into the comfortable privilege of denial but instead insist on *history*, are an essential part of our collective resistance and any hopes of—someday—our national salvation."

—Gina Frangello, author of *Blow Your House Down: A Story of Family, Feminism, and Treason*

"In the urgent fight against historical amnesia, *American Bloodlines* does the heavy lifting. Sonya Lea's unflinching account of complicity in America's racial violence sets an example at a crucial time when this country—and, indeed, the rest of the world—must contemplate our acquiescence and our silences in the face of genocidal hate. *American Bloodlines* demonstrates that taking responsibility for past atrocities is an ethical obligation."

—Anna Badkhen, author of *Bright Unbearable Reality*

"Sonya Lea has given us a master class in weaving research with family narrative. She has created a book about reckoning with personal and cultural legacies of whiteness, white supremacy, and lynch culture that is incisive, insightful, and brutally devastating. Though *American Bloodlines: Reckoning with Lynch Culture* is a call to radical action, it is also a call to radical love. The book itself is an act of compassion."

—Kelly Sundberg, author of *The Answer Is in the Wound*

"Sonya Lea has written a courageous, insightful, necessary book—part memoir, part American (and Canadian) history, part reflection on the nature of racism and on what is involved in the work of bringing it to an end."

—Priscilla Long, author of *Where the Sun Never Shines: A History of America's Bloody Coal Industry*

"*American Bloodlines* is an insightful, propulsive, and vital work of homecoming and reckoning. Sonya Lea masterfully models how to engage in the project of reconciliation, truth-telling, and grace that is so urgently needed in this moment. Reading this work felt like an outstretched hand—a generous offering toward a more just collective future."

—Garrett Bucks, author of *The Right Kind of White: A Memoir*

"In this act of reckoning, this necessary labor, Lea faces violence directly—in all its bloody forms. Lea's admirable flow of research does not leave anyone she's affiliated with, whether by blood or heritage, to escape the attention of a fine-toothed anti-racist comb."

—Davis Shoulders, editor of *Queer Communion: Religion in Appalachia*

"*American Bloodlines* is both an interrogation of Sonya Lea's own whiteness and a lighthouse for others who may be nervous about taking on the same work. Lea argues boldly that the shame many of us harbor about our family histories and white privilege is actually a barrier to becoming anti-racist; only when we shed it can we have clear-eyed, compassionate conversations with ourselves about opposing 'the white supremacy that has formed us.'"

—Kristi Coulter, author of *Exit Interview: The Life and Death of My Ambitious Career*

AMERICAN BLOODLINES

AMERICAN BLOODLINES

RECKONING WITH LYNCH CULTURE

SONYA LEA

The author acknowledges the support of Canada Council for the Arts and the Alberta Foundation for the Arts.

A note to the reader: This volume contains references to domestic violence, sexual assault, and historical and contemporary instances of racial violence and oppression.

Published by The University Press of Kentucky,
scholarly publisher for the Commonwealth, serving Bellarmine University, Berea College, Centre College of Kentucky, Eastern Kentucky University, The Filson Historical Society, Georgetown College, Kentucky Historical Society, Kentucky State University, Morehead State University, Murray State University, Northern Kentucky University, Spalding University, Transylvania University, University of Kentucky, University of Louisville, University of Pikeville, and Western Kentucky University.

Editorial and Sales Offices: The University Press of Kentucky
663 South Limestone, Lexington, Kentucky 40508-4008
www.kentuckypress.com

Cataloging-in-Publication data is available from the Library of Congress.

ISBN 978-1-9859-0285-5 (hardcover : alk. paper)
ISBN 978-1-9859-0286-2 (epub)
ISBN 978-1-9859-0287-9 (pdf)

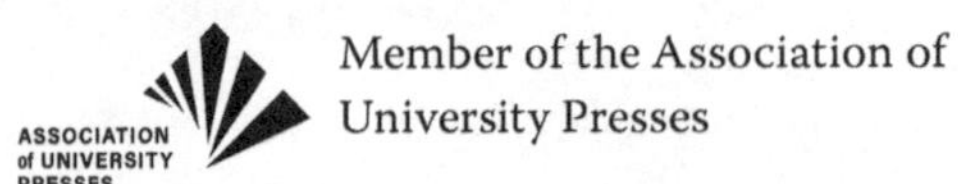

Member of the Association of University Presses

In memory of Rainey Bethea, and all those murdered and harmed by racial terror.

For our kin—ancestors, descendants, familial, and chosen.

Contents

1

The Legal Lynching of Rainey Bethea

In the summer of 1936, in Owensboro, Kentucky, Rainey Bethea, a young Black man, was jailed for the rape and murder of an elderly white woman and then tried by an all-white, all-male jury that took four and a half minutes to find him guilty. He was hanged near the banks of the Ohio River. According to most news reports and historical photographs, the white people in attendance made a brutal carnival of the observation of his death. Bethea's would become the last public execution in America.

We know little of Rainey Bethea before he is sentenced to hang. Court records sometimes list his first name as Railey. He is the son of Rainey Bethea Sr. and Beulah Bethea,[1] sometimes recorded as Ella. Brother of Prince and Bennie, stepbrother of David and Ora. Student. Farmhand. Citizen. Member of the Baptist Church. Orphaned at thirteen. Left home shortly after. Full-grown, he was five-foot-four, 128 pounds. Made his way in the spring of 1933 from Virginia or South Carolina (records differ) to Owensboro, Kentucky, where he would find work in the tobacco fields, work for families, rent apartments, attend Sunday school, learn to drink and smoke, get jailed for a year for snatching a purse, become known as a criminal—an identity he would hold forever in American history. At the time of his hanging, he was most often reported to be twenty-two, but his age is also listed as twenty-four or twenty-six years old.[2] Records vary about his name, birth date, family members, location—and really any details of his life—until he becomes a criminal in the eyes of white Owensboro.

Bethea arrived in an Owensboro of some twenty-three thousand people, nearly all of them white. There were fewer Black people in the town after 1916, when many African Americans who could no longer live under Jim Crow departed in the Great Migration.

Bethea lived in the homes where he worked—in a basement at the home of the Rutherfords on East Fourth Street and then in a little cabin behind the Wells family home two blocks away—and then he rented a room from Mrs. Brown on West Seventh, where he worked as a laborer. He was arrested in June 1935 on "breach of peace," a law white people disproportionately used against Black men.

Across the segregated South, and up to and throughout the civil rights movement of the 1940s to 1960s, many thousands of Black Americans went to jail for protesting segregation—and many of those who went to prison were sent there on the grounds that they were violating unconstitutional restrictions on speech. Often a white person need only initiate the claim that a Black person caused harm or appeared likely to cause harm to a white person or their property, or even that white people were afraid of such harm being done, for a charge to be laid.

Bethea was fined twenty dollars. Shortly after this incident, he was charged with stealing "two pocketbooks, four lipsticks, two compacts, 1 cigarette case and lighter, [and] two sets of keys" from the Vogue Beauty Shop. The state determined that the cash in those purses was "$5.50 in lawful money"—written in the margin of the court records, as if it was added to the charges later—and since the value of the property was then placed at over twenty-five dollars,[3] Bethea could be convicted of a felony, grand larceny, and sent to the Eddyville State Prison with a sentence of one year.

Eddyville, built in 1886, housed (and still houses) Kentucky's violent male prisoners, including death row inmates and the commonwealth's execution facility. The moving force behind the building of Eddyville was Hylan Lyon, a Confederate brigadier general, a plantation owner, and state prison commissioner. Very soon after its opening, the state penitentiary at Eddyville was full of Black men—about three and a half times as many Black men as in the population. They were there to make shoes and brooms in workshops that leased the labor of prisoners at five cents a day to private industry. In the time of Bethea's imprisonment, the ball and chain—a kind of shackle—would have been used as punishment. Eddyville was a precursor to the current prison-industrial complex, for it was a major profit-making enterprise for the state.

On December 1, 1935, Bethea was paroled from prison six months early. He returned to Owensboro, where he was paid seven dollars a week as a laborer. In less than a month, he was arrested for breaking into a house, but that charge was revised to drunk and disorderly. When he couldn't pay the one-hundred-dollar fine (equivalent to fourteen weeks of pay), he was incarcerated in the Daviess County Jail for four months. After he was let out, he wrote a letter to the Parole Board:

> Owensboro, Ky.
> May 4, 1936
> Dear Sir:
>
> I have lost my papers and i can't take any monthly reports and i won't [*sic*] you to send me some more if you please sir.
>
> From
> Rainey Bethea
> 408 W. 7th St.
> Owensboro, Ky.[4]

On Sunday, June 7, 1936, the body of seventy-year-old Lischia Edwards, a widow and mother to a University of Kentucky professor, was found dead in her upstairs apartment in Owensboro. Edwards had been raped and strangled. Edwards rented a room from Emmett Wells on East Fifth Street. When a neighbor hadn't heard her typical morning movements, he found assistance from other neighbors and broke into the room, where Edwards was discovered dead in her bed. People rushed to find her relatives at the Central Presbyterian Church. Others ran to Settle Memorial United Methodist Church to find the local doctor; Coroner Delbert Glenn was also pulled from the Methodist Church. All of this activity caused curiosity among the church's white parishioners. Before the police had been called, the doctor and the coroner were in the room and examining Edward's body. In testimony, Dr. George Barr said, "I went in the room, and she was dead, killed, and she was bruised about the face." Later the coroner called Barr back to examine Edwards at the funeral home, where the doctor reported vaginal swelling and blood loss that indicated a rape.

Glenn observed bruises on Edwards's neck, where she appeared to have been choked. He lifted the sheets to see a pool of blood around Edwards's hips. He also "investigated to see how they got in," including raising the windows, examining the screens, and parts of the roof, and walking through the backyard. It was only after this trampling through the scene that he asked the neighbors to contact the police, and soon after, Assistant Chief of Police Will Vollman and Patrolman Raleigh Bristow, followed by Commonwealth's Attorney Herman A. Birkhead and Owensboro chief of police R. P. Thornberry, arrived. The police inspected the crime scene and searched the room. Some of Edwards's jewelry was missing, and the killer was said to have left behind his muddy footprints. After the police left, Glenn reported that he found an Eddyville prison ring—a celluloid material prisoners used to mold rings from toothbrushes—this one initialed with an *R*, in the kitchen cabinet, near "where the person came in the window, I presume."[5]

The police searched their records for any criminals in the area, focusing on those whose name might match the *R* on the ring. They identified Rainey Bethea as a Black man who had a prison record and set out in search of him. A guard was placed at Bethea's residence, and the police looked for him all night.

Perry Ryan, a former assistant attorney general for the Commonwealth of Kentucky, who has published several books on hangings in Kentucky, including *The Last Public Execution in America*, wrote, "Pandemonium erupted in Owensboro when news of the murder broke. Doors and windows were locked, producing a suffocating effect in the hot weather. Many of the Owensboro women refused to go out after dark. In fact, some would venture out in the daytime only when it was absolutely necessary. Some of the men actually began wearing guns on their waists."

The *Owensboro Inquirer*, under the headline "Action Demanded," published a critical editorial the next day:

> Owensboro's most heinous crime was committed early Sunday morning when an aged and prominent woman was brutally assaulted and murdered. In the quiet of the Sabbath morning when all the neighborhood was wrapped in slumber, some

> dastardly degenerate crept into the room, choked her to death, assaulted her criminally and left her bruised and bleeding body lying on the bed.
>
> Owensboro citizens are demanding that those sworn to preserve the peace of the community and protect its people act and act quickly. Women and children of the city are living in a state of terror, fearing that the fiend, if uncaught, will commit other outrages in this city.

> How long are the citizens of Owensboro going to stand for such crimes? Are these crimes committed because officials and jurors are lax in their sworn duty?
>
> Not a stone should be left unturned that will help to point out the criminal. When and if he is caught, there should be no undue delay in his trial. Whether he is hanged or sent to the electric chair, there should be a minimum amount of delay. He was without mercy for his defenseless victim. Why should he be shown the slightest degree of mercy? The quicker such a beast is destroyed the better it will be for Daviess County.

By Monday, two new suspects were arrested, but they admitted no crime. The police locked them up in holding cells. Photos of a celluloid prison ring with the initial *R* began to circulate in local newspapers. A twelve-year-old boy came forward to say that the ring belonged to Rainey Bethea, a Black man who had worked for his parents. Police were still unsure and decided that Bethea could have chosen to make a ring with a first initial rather than for a surname.

Patrolman Vogel found fingerprints near the head of Edwards's bed, of which he noted that one finger seemed to resemble Bethea's fingerprints, which were on file at the police headquarters. The Owensboro police, in the throes of early belief in the infallibility of fingerprinting,[6] thought they'd caught their man. Vogel sent the files off to the FBI, but no one at that agency confirmed their accuracy. No one considered whether Bethea's cleaning of the room as a laborer for Edwards could have created those same fingerprints.

On Tuesday, the *Owensboro Inquirer* published a front-page report with a large photograph of Rainey Bethea, noting he was the prime suspect and that the police had not been able to locate him. "After evasively eluding the police for 30 hours after the murder, assault and robbery . . . Rainey Bethea, 32, the negro ex-convict hunted as her slayer apparently effected his escape from Owensboro," they wrote, aging Bethea almost ten years.

On Wednesday, the police determined that they had enough evidence to convict Bethea. They dispatched descriptions of Bethea to police throughout the region. The two suspects who had been jailed were released. The complaint was filed:

> AFFIDAVIT
>
> This affiant R. P. Thornberry states that he has reasonable grounds for believing that Rainey Bethea has committed the crime of willful [*sic*] murder. That said crime was committed in manner and form as follows: That, in Daviess County, Kentucky, on or about the 7 day of June, 1936, that said Rainey Bethea did unlawfully, maliciously & feloniously kill, slay, and murder Mrs. Lischia R. Edwards by striking, beating, and choking her with his hands, fists and feet, upon her body, arms, limbs and person from which striking beating and choking the said Lischia R. Edwards did then and there die against the peace and dignity of the Commonwealth of Kentucky.
>
> /S/ R. P. Thornberry, Subscribed and sworn to before me by R. P. Thornberry the 10th day of June 1936.

A warrant was issued, and the angry white people in the region began a search for Rainey Bethea.

By Wednesday afternoon, a house painter saw Bethea by the banks of the Ohio and reported that Bethea proclaimed, "The law is after me." This would be the first of a half dozen reports by white observers and officials declaring that Bethea had made confessions to them. Two officers arrested Bethea, pointing their pistols at him, and shouting from the top of the riverbank, "Come up here, boy."[7] Oddly, Bethea was sent in the car of an *Owensboro Inquirer* journalist to travel to the police station. Local reporters said that this happened because law officers and the city police judge Forest Roby were concerned about mob violence.

At the arraignment, Judge Roby sent Bethea to the jail in Louisville. White journalists reported that Bethea appeared drunk at the time of arrest, that he was interrogated by police, and initially admitted nothing. Suddenly, en route to Louisville, the officers said Bethea had confessed. The police reported to the newspapers that "he said he choked her [Edwards] and did not know at the time of the assault if she was alive or dead." This was pertinent information because, for the sexual assault to be punishable by a public execution, Edwards would have had to have been alive at the time of the assault, and in addition, hangings were not possible sentences for murder; they were only eligible for crimes of rape.

An archaic Kentucky law had been brought out of hiding in 1920 when Will Lockett, a Black man, was convicted and sentenced to die for raping a nine-year-old white girl from Lexington. Even though Lockett was electrocuted, Kentuckians believed the sentence was too lenient. In the wake of the white community demanding more punishment, the Kentucky General Assembly amended the death penalty statute to allow juries to sentence a rapist to hang in the county seat where the crime was committed.

The law did not specify whether the hanging should be public or private. Soon after the law's change, eight Black men were hanged publicly for allegedly raping white women. One white man was hanged, a sentence imposed after he raped a pregnant white woman.

The *Louisville Courier-Journal* covered the transport of Bethea on June 11, emphasizing that the white public was tricked by the law, under the headline "Negro Admits Daviess [County] Crime":

> Rainey Bethea, 22, Negro, spirited away from the Owensboro City Hall Wednesday afternoon as a threatening crowd of 200 milled outside, confessed in Louisville Wednesday night that he assaulted and killed Mrs. Elza Edwards, 70, in Owensboro last Saturday. . . . His safe departure from Owensboro was effected [*sic*] through subterfuge. The officers said they focused the attention of the mob there on one automobile, and then slipped the Negro into another and got out of town before the crowd grew aware of the switch.[8]

A deputy jailer "positively identified the negro as Bethea," said the *Owensboro Inquirer.* "A scar on the left side of his head, said to have been caused by a beating given him by police when he protested arrest previously, was the chief identifying mark." Proclamations of Bethea's guilt came then from the marks of white men on his body. The evidence for Bethea at this time was still the prison ring left at Edwards's home—which was one of his places of work—and that he was a Black man with a criminal record.

When Bethea made his first confession, he signed a statement indicating that the stolen rings were hidden behind the curtains in his room. A search found nothing. The next day, Bethea denied his guilt, admitting that he was drunk when he confessed.

Bethea was escorted to the county jail. The jailer was said to have found blood on Bethea's underwear when he was asked to disrobe. Not even a day after Bethea's denial of his confession due to drunkenness, a white jail guard said that Bethea had confessed privately to him. This time, Bethea was to have said that the jewelry and a dress were found in a barn across from Edwards's home. The jailer reported that Bethea said that he had been drunk the night he tried to steal Edwards's jewelry, that she'd been asleep, and that when she woke up, he decided to rape her. The jailer continued, "When he was finished, Mrs. Edwards said, 'I know you.' He [Bethea] claimed that she was still alive when he left." With these words, the jailer confirmed the notion that the right circumstances had occurred for a death sentence to be given.

In all, there would be five such confessions. The local press and citizens had one thing in common with the judge, police, and lawyers—everyone was certain of Bethea's guilt. No one cared that the confessions came without counsel. Miranda rights were forty years away.

A circuit judge called a special session of the grand jury in ten days, on June 22, 1936, the earliest date possible by law. The temperatures would rise to 107 degrees by then.

Felony prosecutions were heard in circuit court, and the commonwealth's attorney for Kentucky oversaw these proceedings. Herman A. Birkhead was the commonwealth's attorney in the Sixth Judicial District, including Daviess County. Birkhead knew that a grand jury did not decide guilt or innocence. The purpose of a grand jury is to decide whether the prosecution has enough apparent evidence of guilt to take a case to trial. Grand jury proceedings generally occur in secrecy, and the prosecutor has near-complete control over what happens. The goal is to encourage witnesses to speak freely and let the grand jurors see and hear all the information the prosecutor may have about a case without many restrictions. If the crime of murder had been charged, Bethea would have been electrocuted at the Eddyville prison. Birkhead deliberately sought an indictment against Bethea only for the crime of rape so that the legal question of a private punishment might never arise. Judge George S. Wilson had been a partner of Birkhead's before becoming a circuit judge and being appointed to hear the Bethea trial. Twelve white men were selected for the jury. They were businessmen of that small town, including a realtor, a pharmacist, and three grocers. Judge Wilson's instructions to them began like this:

> We have a fine people, gentlemen. We do not want for anything . . .
>
> And yet, gentlemen, right in the heart of it we have the most horrible crime that has ever been committed in any community. When we think of the good relation that has existed between the white and colored people, we cannot recall that there has ever been any clash between them. If reports that we read in the papers are true, a strange colored man from another locality drops into our community and remains here, except for a short time when he was sent away by the court, until a most horrible crime is committed.

Birkhead told them, "I expect to prosecute for rape, and if he [Bethea] is convicted, he will be hanged in Daviess County."

Bethea was not assigned counsel throughout his questioning, but once Judge Wilson set a trial date, he appointed four Owensboro lawyers to represent him throughout the legal proceedings. The four white attorneys included an anti–death penalty advocate, along with the judge's twenty-three-year-old son, who was ordered by his father to represent Bethea, though it was widely considered an unethical practice for a judge to preside at a trial in which his son represented one of the parties. Three of the four attorneys were in their twenties.

The trial was set to begin three days after the indictment was returned—the minimum amount of time permitted by law. This meant that Bethea's lawyers had little time to find people in the community who might testify on Bethea's behalf; only about thirty-six hours remained to mount a defense. Bethea's lawyers also requested a change of the venue, due to pretrial publicity, and were denied. Ryan reports that "the attorneys were required to present affidavits signed by two people who were willing to state that the defendant could not obtain a fair trial due to excessive publicity. Two people were located who signed affidavits, but the two later tore up their statements, leaving counsel for the defense with nothing upon which to base their motion."

But longtime Owensboro journalist Keith Lawrence says that it would have been common for the Black community to have avoided association with Bethea. "This [talk of Bethea] led in some cases to members of Owensboro's Black community seeming to align with whites, so that they might avoid being seen in the same light as Bethea," Lawrence said.[9]

In 1936, everyone in Owensboro expected a death penalty, and though Judge Wilson tried to protect Bethea's body from an Owensboro mob during the trial and hearing, that concern didn't extend to the prejudice in the justice system. A week before the jury trial began, Owensboro sheriff Florence Thompson forecasted her ability to become a hangman when she told County Attorney Sidney B. Neal as well as Birkhead that she did "not want her sex to be considered in determining the charge upon which Bethea will be tried. 'I'm ready to do my duty,' she said."[10]

Thompson had been appointed sheriff just days after the funeral of her husband, Sheriff Everett Thompson, an event that happened just two months prior to the Bethea trial. In the early twentieth century in America and other countries, "widow's succession" was a common political practice whereby politicians who died in office were succeeded by their widows. A mother of four children, Florence Thompson suddenly needed a reliable financial means to care for them. On the day of her husband's funeral, she was sworn in to fill her husband's term. By the end of that year, she had been elected by a landslide to the position of sheriff, which she held for another two years.

After the judgment of Bethea, a national debate began due to the anomalies of the moment. Not only had all other states banned public hangings by the 1930s, making this punishment an aberrant sentence, but Owensboro had the double image of a white victim in Edwards and a white defender of the law in Thompson. White newspapers and communities assumed Bethea's guilt, so their attention now moved toward a misogynistic interpretation of Thompson's role. As a white widow and mother who had a proper place in southern society, Thompson had both respectability and privilege. Historian Carrie Pitzulo, author of the essay "The Skirted Sheriff," says, "Newspapers across the country pondered the appropriateness of a female sheriff—a mother—overseeing an execution. The effects of this widespread coverage can be seen in the hundreds of letters Thompson received from people expressing their views on the case and her role in it, with all sides claiming her as a moral agent."[11] In the press Thompson was derided for refusing to allow a man to do the job. To others, she was a mother simply trying to take care of her children. But as a woman, she became part of a gendered national discussion that raised interest in the case and eventually influenced the number of people who attended the hanging as well as affected Owensboro's concern—the impression in the media that Kentucky was a degenerate place.

Florence Thompson's image replaced Bethea's as the central focus in newspaper stories, which asserted the mores of the era in their comments about Thompson. The *Atlanta Constitution* noted her domestic skills, saying, "She cares for her home and children. 'Getting the children's breakfast, looking after our home and taking care of my duties at the courthouse keep me busy. It keeps me from worrying,' she said."[12] Still, Thompson hadn't yet stated whether she would hire a hangman or act as the executioner. Her evasiveness only further inflamed white readers and journalists. Pitzulo says,

> She embodied the type of femininity that demanded protection in the Jim Crow South. . . . White women had always been necessary players in the South's culture of racial violence. They filled the crowds that cheered on male lynch mobs and filled leadership roles in both the movement to demonize black men and the movement to protest lynching. To some observers, Thompson's involvement in the execution could be seen as a usurpation of white-male privilege, and she symbolized the ways in which women were gaining power and moving into the public sphere in new ways, especially given the displacement so many men experienced in the midst of the Great Depression.[13]

Prior to the trial, in the few hours they had to mount a case, counsel Bill Kirtley interviewed Bethea. Bethea told him that his confessions had been coerced and that he should plead not guilty. William Wilson, another of Bethea's attorneys, couldn't find anyone who would testify on his behalf. "We couldn't find anybody in town hardly who knew him," Wilson said. "People just would not testify. Well, there was nothing they could testify about."[14] It's not known if Wilson walked through the successful Black business and residential district of Owensboro called Baptist Town or solicited people there to testify.

The menace of a lynch mob draped like a suffocating humidity over the day of the trial. Ten state police officers outfitted with tear gas stood guard outside the courthouse. Armed guards were posted at every door. Crowds gathered at 7:00 a.m. for the 9:00 a.m. trial start. Those admitted were searched upon entry. Though the most severe heat wave in Owensboro's history had already begun, hundreds of white people stood outside throughout the trial. Bethea was brought into the courtroom in the polo shirt and trousers in which he had been arrested.

The *Owensboro Inquirer* posted three headlines that day, with two large images. The first is of a crowd of white people dressed in hats and suits, or summer dresses, milling by the courthouse steps. The other is of a packed courtroom, from the vantage point of the floor in front of the judge. There's a long wood table and four empty wood chairs, the kind you used to see in legal offices. The faces in the crowd are all white, stock-still, rapt, waiting. They're as unified as a ghostly apparition at a somber ritual. The scene at the courthouse foretold the spectacle that white people would make of Bethea's hanging.

Since Birkhead said he wanted no one seated who was against the death penalty, over one hundred men had been brought in to determine the jury. The first twelve white men interviewed were selected for trial. Seven of them were farmers or retired farmers. "Each was asked if he had an [*sic*] scruples against the death penalty," the reporter for the *Inquirer* said. Imitating the language used in the newspapers prior to the trial, County Attorney Neal read a statement:

> This is one of the most dastardly, beastly, cowardly crimes ever committed in Daviess County. Justice demands and the commonwealth will ask and expect a verdict of the death penalty by hanging.

On the morning of the trial, Bethea unexpectedly decided to plead guilty. Wilson reported that Bethea said, "All I want is time to make peace with my maker."[15]

Due to Bethea's guilty plea, the judge instructed the jury, "The jury will, therefore, find the defendant, Rainey (Railey) Bethea, guilty as charged in the indictment and fix his punishment at confinement in the penitentiary for not less than ten (10) years nor more than twenty (20) years, or at death, in the discretion of the jury."[16] Instead, the Commonwealth of Kentucky asked for the rape law to be used. Birkhead argued for the death penalty by an execution in public view and asked for a chance to present the prosecution's case to the jury. Had the judge chosen to sentence Bethea, the accused would not have been hanged. This decision to favor Birkhead's proposition didn't just affect the death penalty decision; it also offered a chance for white people in the community to witness a gruesome death.

The trial of Rainey Bethea, including the impaneling of the jury, lasted just over three hours. In jury selection, the defense did not question any member of the jury. The defense made no opening statement. The defense called no witnesses, nor did they cross-examine the twenty-one witnesses the prosecution called. The defense made no closing statement. The defense counsel spoke not one word to the jury on behalf of their client. Criminal records from the case demonstrate that *no* defense was mounted during the trial.

One of the key pieces of evidence—the prison ring marked with an *R*—brought twelve-year-old Robert Rutherford to the stand. The son in a family whose home Bethea had worked in claimed he had seen the ring on Bethea, but he would state at trial that it had been "two summers ago" in 1934, a full year before Bethea was sent to the Eddyville prison for pickpocketing.

Four and a half minutes after the jury retired, Judge Wilson was reading their verdict—guilty with a punishment of death. "The court now pronounces Rainey Bethea, that you shall be hanged by the neck in this county until you are dead, and may God have mercy on your soul," the judge said.

The *Owensboro Messenger-Inquirer* reported that "It was when the negro was being rushed from the courthouse that he displayed fright. He was almost dragged down the pavement to the automobile as the police shoved the crowd back on either side. . . . A few cries of 'catch him' were heard as the car sped from the court-house."[17] Bethea was hurriedly transported to Louisville for safekeeping while the trial's audience was asked to remain seated, and Judge Wilson waited for "the sound of a police siren which was a signal . . . that the negro was safely on his way [and] court was adjourned."[18]

One might ask how the holding of a full trial might have inflamed the already near-riotous citizens of Owensboro. The description of the statements made by witnesses, the opening and closing statements made by the prosecutor, the very dramatic moments of the trial scene and the ways they were reported placed not only Bethea in harm but also the Black residents of Owensboro. Other institutions were complicit in this demonizing and calls for violence, including the Owensboro media.

After the trial, the headlines of the *Owensboro Inquirer* read:

> **BETHEA IS SENTENCED TO HANG JULY 31**
> **FOR ASSAULT OF MRS. ELZA EDWARDS**
> **Scenes in Courthouse Yard and Courtroom at Trial of Rainey Bethea Today**
> Daviess County Jury Gives Its Verdict in Trial That Consumed Only Three Hours
> Negro Enters Plea of Guilty After First 12 Men Called Qualify for Jury Service;
> Judge George S. Wilson Orders All Evidence Given to Jury;
> Commonwealth's Attorney H. A. Birkhead Demands Death Sentence;
> Slayer Rushed From Courthouse under Guns of State Police and Whisked Away to Louisville Jail
>
> NO INDICATION OF APPEAL OF VERDICT

The newspaper chose to publish the photograph of Bethea with a mustache, looking more mature than the images taken at the jail with the police officers, where he looks young and fearful and alone.

In contrast to the white newspapers, the *Chicago Defender* published under the headline "Youth Doomed to Death upon Thin Evidence" the following piece:

> Louisville, Ky. July 3—(Special)—Upon strikingly flimsy evidence, Rainey Bethea, 22, was sentenced to be hanged on July 31 by an Owensboro jury for the alleged robbery, assault and murder of a 70-year-old Owensboro woman on June 7. Despite

> the doomed youth's denial of having made any confession of the crime, Kentucky papers have played large headlines to the effect that Bethea had entered a plea of guilty to the crime of which he is accused.
>
> The National Association for the Advancement of Colored People, and other social agencies have taken up the fight to gain justice for the prosecuted youth.
>
> The only link connecting Bethea with the heinous crime was the location of several pieces of jewelry Bethea admitted had been in his possession before he was arrested but said that it had been given him by a companion with whom he worked.
>
> During an interview at the jail here shortly after his arrival on June 10 Bethea denied any part in the crime. Daily papers reported, however, that he had alternately confessed and denied the charges.[19]

While white people worried about whether a white woman should pull the lever, Black communities saw Bethea as a victim of state violence and began to organize. Two Black lawyers, Charles Ewbank Tucker and Stephen A. Burnley, came forward to work on an appeal for Bethea, and Charles W. Anderson Jr., Harry E. Bonaparte, and R. Everett Ray joined their team. Tucker was a lawyer, a civil rights advocate who led early demonstrations and sit-ins in Kentucky, and a pastor (later a bishop) in the Louisville AME church. His name appears on several Kentucky appellate cases as counsel for Black citizens who appealed death sentences. Also notable was Anderson, who was a partner in the law firm of Anderson, Thomas & Walker. He became Kentucky's first Black legislator that year, running against Tucker. Because Kentucky enforced higher education segregation laws, Anderson worked to legislate the Anderson-Mayer State Aid Act, which provided funding for Black Americans to seek higher education out of state. Anderson also was responsible for enacting a new Senate bill which repealed the portion of Section 1137 requiring hanging for the crime of rape, passed two years after the trial, in 1938.

Bethea's new legal team filed a motion for a new trial on July 11 and were denied by Judge Wilson as having filed a week past the end of the court's term. The term had concluded just nine days after Bethea's trial, with the same haste that the white community had insisted on from before the arrest. Still, the attorneys for the defendant filed a motion that the verdict was flagrantly against the law and evidence, that the defendant was denied a fair trial, that the confessions were a result of intimidation and coercion, that the court erred in its instructions to the jury, and in a condemnation of the defense counsel said that

> the defendant was denied his constitutional right of benefit of proper counsel and that even though three attorneys were appointed by the court to defend him, not one question was asked of the Jury—the first twelve men being accepted by the Defense, that the defendant was not even put upon the stand to explain his side of the case, that no questions were propounded to any witness by defense counsel and that further said defense counsel never spoke a word to the Jury on behalf of defendant and that while counsel were present in body—they were absent in spirit.[20]

Sheriff Thompson oversaw her deputy in creating a scaffold using railroad ties to build a tall deck structure upon which the gallows would be set. This was done so the thousands expected at the hanging wouldn't have to strain themselves to see. The location was selected at the county's garage lot near the Ohio River because Thompson didn't want the crowds ruining the flowers at the Daviess County Courthouse.

The same day as the motion for a new trial was filed and summarily denied, Sheriff Thompson received a letter from the US marshal for Indiana, introducing her to a farmer by the name of Phil Hanna, who was making himself available to conduct hangings across Kentucky. Kentucky had a long history of hangmen being used for government-sponsored lynchings. Hanna provided a service that included hoods sewn by his wife, a custom-made trap door with a trigger handle, and his own signal for the person pulling it. He thought himself to be a humanitarian, though several of his hangings were reported to be brutal affairs. By the time he was hired for Bethea's killing, Hanna had come to officiate sixty-nine hangings around the country. Phil Hanna suffered from algophobia, involving fear and hypersensitivity to pain, often diagnosed today as being related to multiple exposures to traumatic events. Hanna was apparently motivated to become a hangman after seeing a botched hanging at twenty-two years old; he then studied hangings to develop a more efficient method. Ryan states, "Ironically, while he [Hanna] would himself supervise the hanging of a man, he could not bear to watch someone slaughter a chicken,"[21] but Hanna's extreme fear and anxiety could have as likely emerged from his chosen hobby. It's now known that he attempted to diffuse his anxiousness with alcohol, and that algophobia is related to substance abuse. Hanna wouldn't take money for his cruel expertise, but he asked for the weapon used in the crime in exchange for his services.[22] Hanna waited for the gallows to be prepared and consulted with Sheriff Thompson while the town grew expectant for the execution to happen in a few weeks after the appeal.

On July 20, Bethea's new legal team filed in the Kentucky Court of Appeals, and when the appeal was denied, as the lawyers expected, it paved the way for a habeas corpus hearing in the federal courts. A writ of habeas corpus reports an unlawful imprisonment to a court and requests that a prison official is to bring the prisoner to court, to determine whether the detention is lawful. In this statement to the courts, Bethea said that in his transport to Louisville, he was beaten by officers and that he was threatened with being turned over to the mob if he didn't admit the crime. Bethea also asserted that he was forced to sign a confession against his will, and "that he did not have the benefit of counsel to prepare and present his defense and that no defense was made in his behalf; that although he asked that he be permitted to testify in his own behalf, at the trial, and to deny his guilt, and requested that certain witnesses be summoned to testify on his behalf, it was not permitted, and no witnesses were called on his behalf."[23] Likewise, Bethea stated that he was innocent of the crimes, and his lawyers also noted: "Your petitioner did not plead guilty at any time, nor was he permitted to take the stand in his behalf, and that he was not at any time told or confessed to anyone that he is guilty of said charge; that he has not had his day in court."[24] The legal team said that Bethea's right to an appeal to the Court of Appeals of Kentucky "was cut off, denied, sacrificed and barred to him, by the attitude and effort and action of one of the attorneys appointed to defend him."

Judge Elmwood Hamilton of the US District Court for Kentucky called off the July 31 hanging and asked the jailer to deliver Bethea for an August 5 habeas corpus hearing.

The *Chicago Defender*, under the headline, "Kentucky Town in Holiday Mood for Hanging," printed a sardonically told story from the *Louisville Herald-Post*. The author was Molly Clowes, a white, self-trained journalist, who often wrote of issues related to the poor and dispossessed, and who would go on to become an editor for the *Louisville Courier-Journal*, the first woman to hold such a position on a major metropolitan daily newspaper:

> Daviess County officials rushed the Negro to Louisville immediately [after] the sentence was passed, to avoid the possibility of mob violence. This is a commendable precaution, since there is no possible comparison between the publicity and cash value of a lynching arranged on the spur of the moment and participated in anonymously by all sorts of rabble, and a hanging invested with the full majesty of the law, well publicized in advance and conducted with the personal supervision of a female martyr to duty.[25]

The Black community continued to press for justice for Bethea, and for other places in Kentucky to repeal the law that was created to hang mostly Black men in town squares.

At the habeas corpus hearing in Louisville, attorney for the commonwealth, Herman Birkhead, made an appearance and brought along several witnesses, mostly to deny that Bethea had been threatened by officers, the jailer, or any other members of the legal system. Bethea was called as the first witness, but no transcript was taken of his words. There was no documentation of what happened at the hearing, only a description in the local newspaper the next day.

In a moment demonstrating the power of whiteness in the courtroom, one of Bethea's court-appointed counsels, Kirtley (the same lawyer who said Bethea told him he wanted a guilty plea), remarked in his testimony at the hearing that he now thought "it would have been better for Bethea if he had been left in Owensboro." When Bethea's Black lawyers insisted he explain, Kirtley became angry and said, "Well if he had been kept there, he would not have been bothered with you lawyers." This was a statement about the authority and control that the white legal system knew it could invoke, and it alluded to an offering of Bethea's body to a white mob and whatever actions would expedite a Black man's death.

The *Owensboro Messenger-Inquirer* journalist Lawrence Diemandes "Birdie" Gasser, who wrote into history what happened in the trial and hanging, was also a witness for the commonwealth. He testified that there had been no danger of mob violence during the trial, and that Bethea would have been safe even without the state police controlling the mob outside the courthouse. "The people had too much respect for law and order to resort to violence," Gasser said, without apparent irony.

On the stand, Bethea denied that he had signed any confessions. When shown his written confession, Bethea stated that he did not know what he was signing. Bethea pleaded "guilty" he said because "I was scared of that mob. They told me if I opened my mouth, that mob would get me."[26]

The *Messenger-Inquirer* also reported that the "negro lawyer R. Everett Ray" had argued that Bethea's lawyers had done nothing for him. "What could they do after he pleaded guilty in open court? What would you have done?" Judge Hamilton repeatedly asked Ray during his closing statement. Ray said that he would have pleaded with the court for a lesser penalty than death. Ray also argued that Bethea's trial counsel didn't question the jurors, cross-examine the prosecution's witnesses, or address the jury. Ray noted that Bethea's counsel failed to make a motion for a new trial, and this had cost Bethea his right to appeal to the Kentucky court. The Scottsboro case of 1932 was referenced in the closing, a rape case verdict that had been overturned by the Supreme Court due to the absence of preparation time for the lawyers. The judge was not moved, pointing to the presence of four lawyers, but Hamilton did not address the fact that the court-appointed lawyers hadn't spoken a word in Bethea's defense. Further, Judge Hamilton said habeas corpus did not extend the right to an appeal.

The judge dismissed the petition for habeas corpus, replying in a final statement, "It is time every man, white or black, learned that there is not argument for mitigation of punishment that juries will entertain." However, this proved untrue. After Owensboro was humiliated in the international press for the hanging, the law was repealed, and ever since that moment, there has been not one death verdict in the county.

Governor "Happy" Chandler signed the death warrant that week. A Kentucky State Police captain Jesse Stone said that all the cameras found at the hanging would be "smashed." Chandler overruled the cop.

Bessie Etherly, the secretary of the Louisville branch of the National Association for the Advancement of Colored People, wrote to the governor entreating him to prohibit a public spectacle in Owensboro. Chandler sent Etherly's letter on to Thompson, asking the sheriff for restraint, but that was not to be the outcome. Years later, when asked about the hanging in Owensboro, Chandler said, "I didn't care for 'em takin' pictures of it." Images made a record, one that might affirm that the day had been a ghastly performance of a kind of punishment that never had been interested in justice.

Sheriff Thompson took the first offer that came her way for who to conduct the execution—Arthur Hash, a former Louisville police officer. In his appeal to her by letter, Hash had stated, "Please do not give this letter to anyone for publication if you accept or regect [*sic*] my services, as I am not hunting Publicity. I only want to help you. Please let me hear from you at once, and if you accept my offer I will go to see Bethea, and if he wants anything I will get it for him, and I will also get a Preacher to visit him, and etc. but, he will never know that I am the one to send him to meet his maker."[27] Thompson believed him to be trustworthy since he took no fees for agreeing to pull the lever and wanted no publicity. She kept this agreement, until the day before the hanging, refusing to tell the eager white public whether she would execute Bethea. Pitzulo says, "It is likely, however, that the intense media scrutiny was unintentionally of her own making. If she had announced Hash's role early on, much of the fascination with the skirted sheriff would have quickly faded."[28]

Thompson reported to the *New York Times* that she'd consulted "her priest and several protestant ministers as to her duty. She said the clergymen had told her that the Negro's death was sanctioned by the laws of God and man."[29] But Thompson didn't check out Hash's background. The retired cop had fourteen arrests, almost five times as many as Bethea (although the white man had no prison sentences), including drunk and disorderly conduct, drunkenness, mayhem, and two grand larceny charges. In a few days, Hash would prove to be just one of the elements of the government-sponsored lynching that brought shock and humiliation to the white citizens of Owensboro.

In Louisville, a priest had been visiting Bethea in jail. On July 29, the Associated Press was present when Father Herman Lammers of the Cathedral of the Assumption Church baptized the young Black orphan. The white Catholic priest made plans to stand beside Bethea when he was hanged.

The hanging was to be at sunrise on Friday. Hanna was to supervise the hanging, and Hash was to pull the trigger that would cause the fall. The white-supervised gallows were completed, the white state police had been ordered, the white hangman was hired, the white man to pull the lever had been found, the white-managed hotel rooms were filled. The death warrant was issued. Thousands of white people began to pour into Owensboro by passenger train, freight train, bus, car, airplane, and on foot. Hundreds of white journalists arrived from all over America, lured by the hope of seeing a Black man hanged by a white woman. The *Chicago Times* sent a special truck rigged with a developing room and telephoto lenses for long focal views. White men and white women arrived in the town. White children and white babes in arms were there. It was said that the people of Owensboro could hardly sleep for the town's murmur. Owensboro resident Medora Withers said, "People came to Owensboro, truckloads of people, sitting on the bed of the truck with their feet hanging over, hayride or picnic style. It was warm weather, and we were sleeping with the window up, and you could hear this muffled shuffle and voices all during the night. It was an eerie feeling."[30] Twenty thousand people in all, filling the streets from the site near the Ohio River all the way to the edge of Baptist Town, threatening the lives of the Black community by their very presence.

That Thursday night, some white people brought cots and slept outside near the gallows. Vendors arrived selling popcorn and cold bottles of Coca-Cola in buckets of ice to the waiting crowd. Other white people held "necktie" parties, one of them attended by the sheriff's daughter. The *Louisville Courier-Journal* said, "Kentucky is already famous for her hospitality. Her Derby parties are known all over the country. Her hanging parties should have an even wider fame. Most people are interested in horse-racing, but all people are interested in death."[31] Hanging parties were not known to be held for the death of a white person.

On this Thursday, Bethea wrote a letter to be delivered, along with his body, to his only remaining family member. He'd been promised by the authorities that he might be buried at the only home he knew, with his sister in South Carolina, six hundred miles southeast.

> Dear Sister
>
> This is my last letter and I have told them to send you my body and I want you to put it beside my father and I am saved and dont you worry about me because I goin to meet my maker and you must pray to meet me some day in the outher world so you must pray heard sister that we will meet someday and don't you worry at all becuse I saved looking to meet you someday in the outher world So good by and pray that we will meet agin some day.
>
> Mrs. Ora Fladger, R.F.D. #3, Box 135, Nichols, S.C.

Two white police officers left the jail in Louisville with Bethea at about 1:00 a.m. and made their way to Owensboro. They reported that Bethea did not admit his guilt, and that he had commented, "I'll die happy. I have made my peace with God."

The *Louisville Times* described the scene: "Hotels were overflowed. Restaurants and drug stores catered to crowds jamming doorways. Boisterous parties . . . were in progress in most of the rooms. Through the night a crowd had swarmed the streets."[32] The *Louisville Courier-Journal* said, "Persons from out of town poured in, automobiles rolled through the streets of this town . . . and concession stands sprang up to serve those who would wait all night for a vantage point around the lot that holds the gallows."[33] Except for those Black citizens required to work in hotels and restaurants, newspapers reported that Owensboro's Black residents had temporarily vacated the town or were "at home in hiding."[34] The *Owensboro Inquirer* said, "Upon the pedestal, the gallows, fifteen feet tall, loomed against the sky last night, its waterproof-covered rope looped under the crossbeam. Early comers by scores staked out places in the vacant lot and prepared to wait all night for the hanging."[35]

Just after 4:00 a.m., the enclosure to the lot had to be opened to allow people to stream in closer. White people climbed into trees, up light poles, and onto the roofs of buildings. They were hoping to see a white woman executioner hang a Black man.

A white FBI agent drove Thompson in a black car to within view of the scaffold, where they waited. Ryan says Thompson was worried that Hash might not be able to do the job of pulling the trigger, and she'd have to step in. Perhaps it was an intuition, because when Hash showed up on the gallows wearing a white Panama hat and a white suit, he was drunk. The news reported that the "throng [was] surprised. . . . The action of Mrs. Thompson amazed the crowd which had expected her to hang Bethea personally."[36] Of her decision, Thompson later told reporters, "I did not want people pointing out my children and saying, 'Their mother was the one who hanged a negro in Owensboro.'"[37]

At 5:21 a.m., two white deputies walked Bethea toward the gallows, with Father Lammers in his stiff white Roman collar following. At the steps, Bethea took off his shoes, replaced his socks with the new ones he'd brought, and left the old things behind. No one asked Bethea about this act; his views were ancillary and unnecessary to the moment that had been created. Some people from the crowd yelled, "Hang him!" while Bethea remained at the steps. Others said there were shouts of "Take him up where we can see him!"

Bethea was taken by the officers up the steps, where he stood on the X marked on the trapdoor, as he had been instructed. Eleven white men stood on the gallows with him—the hangman, the trigger-puller, officers of the law, the priest.

The priest held up his hand to silence the crowd. Bethea had chosen not to speak, but Hash, drunk and out of his mind, kept asking Bethea to say something. Instead, Bethea ignored him and gave his last confession to the priest. A black hood was thrust over Bethea's head. At that moment, Bethea spoke, saying that he wanted to talk to the priest again, but that request was ignored. Hanna placed the noose over Bethea's neck. Hash was visibly unsteady as he held the lever that would trigger the trapdoor. Hanna stepped away and gave the prearranged signal. Hash did nothing. One can't help but imagine the terrifying silence of that pause in the dark. Hanna finally shouted, "Do it now!" One of the deputy sheriffs leaned onto the lever.

The trapdoor dropped.

Bethea fell.

A descent of eight feet.

His head fell against his shoulder.

The white people watched as his heart continued to beat.

The *Chicago Tribune* reported that Dr. Tyler of Owensboro said that the "neck was broken cleanly by the drop. He expressed surprise that the heartbeat continued for more than sixteen minutes."[38]

Hanna climbed down the scaffold and cut the hood so Lammers could anoint the body.

The white men placed Bethea's body in a reed basket. Then it was placed in the undertaker's vehicle, which moved inch by inch through the dense crowd.

Hash stumbled down the steps and said, "I'm drunk as hell. I'm getting away from this town as soon as I can," before he disappeared into the crowd. The Louisville media later reported that the hangman Hash had been arrested fourteen times in the past four years.

The Catholic church offered Bethea a funeral service, and Bethea's body was taken to St. Stephens Catholic Church, where a requiem mass was said by Father Leo J. Denise at 8 a.m. Three hours after Bethea died, the town ignored its promise to send his body to his sister. Instead, town officials buried him in a pauper's grave.

The press left to file their stories, and what's told about that day varies widely, depending on who was reporting, whether they were white or Black, and what region their paper represented. The *Chicago Tribune* reported, "As the doctors stepped away, souvenir hunters ripped the hangman's hood from Bethea." The *Fort Worth Star-Telegram*, under the headline, "10,000 Watch Hanging, Tear Hood from Body," said that "Bethea still breathed when a few persons from the crowd . . . scrambled for fragments as mementoes of the spectacle." The Associated Press filed a story saying that the crowd of white people "some jeering, others festive, but generally orderly—watched a prayerful black man put to death today on Daviess County's 'pit and gallows,' authorized by Kentucky law for the hanging of a rapist. . . . From the crowd came scattered shouts of 'Take him up! . . . Up on the scaffold where we can see him! . . . Let's go!'" Under the banner "20,000 See Hanging, Crowd Cheers at Kentucky Public Execution," the *San Francisco Examiner* wrote, "As the red sun rose from the Kentucky hills, a hulking Negro youth of 22 spun to his death at the end of a rope today. Twenty-thousand men, women and children cheered. Feeling good on hot dogs, lemonade, and good Kentucky whiskey, they cheered and whooped as a woman sheriff—from a distance—took an 'eye for an eye' in the name of the law."

From Chicago—"Death Makes a Holiday: 20,000 Revel Over Hanging." From Evansville, Indiana—"Ghostly Carnival Precedes Hanging." From Louisville—"'Did You Ever See a Hanging?' 'I Did,' Everyone in this Kentucky Throng Can Now Boast." *Time* magazine described the "admiring spectators" who "charged from every side, eager hands clawed at the black death hood. In a moment it was torn to shreds. The lucky ones stuffed the bits of black cloth proudly into their pockets." The piece condescendingly described "soft-hearted Sheriff Thompson," noting she was an "added attraction" to the hanging, and quoted her saying, "I suppose I will spend the rest of my life forgetting—or trying to forget."[39]

Florence Thompson's daughter, Lillian (Thompson) Lee, reported that she saw a journalist with the *Chicago Sun* boarding a train before the hanging. Ryan said, "The next day, the *Sun* falsely reported that Sheriff Thompson had fainted on the scaffold, which of course was completely untrue. Lillian believed that 'He had already written his story.'"[40]

The Owensboro news media and some white onlookers insist that when the lady sheriff didn't show up to act as executioner, there was anger in the press's unmet expectations, which then was taken out on the crowd, with the reporters lying about the audience's unruly behavior. In an editorial on the Sunday after the hanging, in an effort to place the blame on the press who had been deprived of their headlines, the *Owensboro Messenger-Inquirer* called out the "girls and boys" of the press under the headline "Panderers Galore." "Ambitious and irresponsible reporters and photographers who swarmed into Owensboro for the Bethea hanging dipped their ready hands into the cloaca of evil designs and plastered over the name of this city the dirty results of their pandering," the editors began. Accepting little responsibility for the scene that had been created by their orchestration of the hanging, they blamed the visitors from "Illinois, Tennessee, Missouri and some other states" and defended their Southern pride in faulting the "scurrilous attack upon [the city] by lurid writers and glib-tongued talkers in northern and eastern states for they delight to distort any news from Kentucky into weird barbaric tales. We have learned how best to protect our women from rapist-murderers, white or colored."

Owensboro had determined that the issue wasn't what happened in what other cities called the "carnival of sadism," but the immoral ethics of the press that had caused its national humiliation. In an excoriating editorial, Owensboro blamed the horrific press on the throng that "was composed largely of people who journeyed to Owensboro from distant places" and said that to the "sensation seeking star scribes of quacks of American journalism it was entirely too tame an affair. This is the reason that some of them reported it as they wanted it to be—not as it was."[41]

The *New York Times* reported on the polemic discourse:

> A furor of indignation has followed Kentucky's recent . . . public hanging. The press has been deluged with letters from horrified subscribers. . . . The leading Kentucky dailies have reproduced editorials from all over the United States, ridiculing Kentucky mannerisms and morals and denouncing the "carnival of sadism." . . . In their own columns they have demanded that the law . . . be amended, all but the press of Owensboro, that is, which protests that the good people there have been slandered.

Black newspapers tended to focus on the systemic racism and the injustices to Black people rather than on the smaller controversies of the lady sheriff or the humiliated locals. The *Chicago Defender* sent a white correspondent to cover the hanging, since a Black person could hardly have approached the scene.[42] The journalist described the scene at dawn, the "vendors of brightly striped candy, sugar cane slices, watermelon, peanuts, popsicles, ice cream, beer, and hot dogs . . . this throng of gay, 'fun-seeking' citizens. . . . I asked a comely studious looking young lady who wore glasses did she think Bethea was guilty of ravishing and murdering a 70 year-old white woman. She shot a piercing glance of surprised anger at me. 'Ni****s doan hev to be guilty down heah, stranger!' she said in a voice whose music cut like daggers. 'Ni****s er bahn to be lynched when we feels like heven' some spoht!'"[43]

The *Pittsburgh Courier* took a righteous stance, writing, "Ours is the task of ennobling and lifting up the lives of the savages who surround us. . . . Do not be saddened by the execution of Rainey Bethea. Let [the hanging] impress upon you your own moral superiority, your opportunity to give leadership to your country."

The Louisville Council of Churches wrote a letter to the hometown *Courier-Journal*, asking for a repeal of the rape law: "Women with young babes in their arms held the innocents high so that they could get the moral lesson of the thrilling moment. The crowd cheered as the trap was sprung. The newspapers described the scene as a 'picnic hanging' and a 'hangman's holiday.'"

Following the hanging, Thompson received a death threat in a letter signed "Sympathizers of the negro boy." The sheriff asked L. E. Cranor, the US marshal for the Western District of Kentucky, to intervene, who wrote back to her, "Don't be alarmed just be careful. I think it's the work of some fool negro woman that is only trying to scare you." These words were from a federal law enforcement agency, the same agency that had been responsible for upholding slavery through the Fugitive Slave Act.

The Owensboro citizens continued to take umbrage to the ways in which they were being portrayed in the national press. Shortly after the hanging of Bethea, a local campaign began with an intention to alter the perception of the western Kentucky community. Its focus didn't have to do with repealing a racist law but, instead, with condemning those journalists who they believed had lied about what happened. The Owensboro Lions Club set up a "vindication" committee to counteract the terrible publicity the town received by "unscrupulous news reporters."[44]

By the time the cameras stopped clicking and the newsmen flew home, Kentucky had been humiliated in the national press, the onlookers' violence both disputed and affirmed in accounts of this day. The state soon ended hangings in town squares, a practice that affected mostly Black people. Kentucky's Governor A. B. "Happy" Chandler signed a bill repealing the requirement that death sentences for rape be conducted by hanging. Chandler later expressed regret at having approved the repeal claiming, "Our streets are no longer safe." Chandler was not speaking of Bethea's streets.

2

Regular White People

I never knew the story of Rainey Bethea until my grandmother died. The account of the last public execution in America came to me through my family, and it is with my family that I'm still reckoning with its truths.

I was forty-two, and with my husband, was raising two teenagers when I flew on my own from our home in Seattle to my paternal grandmother's funeral in the place where I was born: Owensboro, Kentucky. Both the maternal and paternal sides of my family are Kentuckians, nearly all of them farmers, and I am the sixth generation to be born in that state. The day of the memorial service for Grandmaw, after Mass and a community meal at the parish hall, a neighbor and a friend of my family handed me a sheaf of papers. I didn't look at the pages until I was on the plane home, and there in the plastic-covered booklet—an oral history recently taken by a neighbor and titled, "A Celebration of Frances Ralph"—was confirmation. Two of those twenty thousand who came to watch the public execution were my grandparents, teenage newlyweds, Sherrel and Frances Ralph. Granddad and Grandmaw had attended the hanging just one week after their wedding, when he was eighteen years old and she was nineteen. (My father would be born one year later.) There, typed on the page, were my grandmother's words: *We were so close to him we heard his neck pop.*

In the days prior to Bethea's 1936 hanging, my grandmother Frances Margaret Moran, soon to be married, would have been walking home from work as a welder for General Electric, settling in for the last of her evenings with her single women friends who lived in a rooming house near that downtown street where the gallows were being erected. She would have been planning a wedding ceremony at St. Peter's Catholic Church, as well as a move to a home that would allow her and her fiancé, Sherrel Ralph, to become tenant farmers. Frances would have walked that street with the other townspeople, eating ice cream on those long, hot summer days, and thinking of where they'd like to be when the body fell.

Grandmaw's statement wasn't incongruent with who I knew her to be. But there had been no family conversations about this public hanging in Kentucky or of our family's involvement. I shoved the papers into my bag. On the way back from that funeral mass, I wanted to order a whiskey from the flight attendant, but I'd given up drinking five years earlier. Frances's language pointed me back toward other incidents that I didn't want to remember in my family and in myself. Alcohol had been a way that I coped with not liking who I had become and what I had seen in my family life.

Months after the funeral, I was at my desk in our home overlooking the forests of Tiger Mountain near Seattle creating a file with the name *Rainey Bethea*. I searched online for information about the public execution and trial and soon came across Perry Ryan, assistant attorney general for the Commonwealth of Kentucky and the author of several books on hanging in that state, including *The Last Public Execution in America*. When I first learned of the story of the legal lynching of Rainey Bethea, I believed that the last public execution in America had never been discussed in my family, though both my sisters can recall knowing of the event before I did. I read Ryan's version of the trial and execution, and then I wrote him a letter, asking him about the inconsistencies in the reporting of the execution. When I questioned Ryan about race in this case, he said, "There are numerous examples of 'color-coded' justice and railroadings in the history of American jurisprudence. I just could not report, with honesty, that the Bethea hanging was one of them." Instead of searching for other accounts, particularly those of Black historians, I deferred to Ryan's judgment. White, male, and establishment authority had been the basis for my education, those typical of white supremacist systems and communities.

After speaking with Ryan, I placed into boxes in my garage what had become by that time nearly a year of research. I had noticed that there were no markers about Bethea's hanging in the Owensboro town square and that it seemed that Rainey Bethea's life and the story were absent from the education of most Kentuckians. I thought what happened to Bethea might be easy to forget.

As a girl, I'd been told stories about moonshine whiskey, tobacco farms, cornfields, and barbecue festivals. In my family, I'd rarely had a conversation about race. When I learned about Bethea's legal lynching, I couldn't say *lynching.* I used *public execution* to be in alignment with the white historians I'd read who reported on the event. I wasn't sure whether a legal lynching was possible, and Ryan had warned me when I first used the term that it was "a common mistake . . . an oxymoron" because he believed the legal system, by its definition, could not lynch.[1]

The US is known around the world for being the most violent industrialized nation. That a person can be justified in killing another is a particularly American thought. There's a long moral and legal assertion of "no duty to retreat" that's included frontier gunfighters, independent farmers, encroaching rail barons, and users of stand-your-ground laws. But murders, whether they be mass shootings that now happen at a rate of more than one each day, or the record-breaking rising homicides of the COVID-19 era, are not lynchings.[2] Early on in my research, I found no definition of lynch culture, but in the US, there are prolific histories of how lynching behavior functioned everywhere and in plain view.[3] In a lynching, a community comes together to terrorize or punish someone they feel has violated a legal, moral, or social standard.

Lynching is murder endorsed through a kind of kinship. In a legal lynching, the justice system takes on the role of the mob. The ugliest form of white supremacy bends the justice system so that it is *legally* used not only to take a person's life but also acts as harm to the entire community. The twentieth century redefined lynching whereby those in power sped up criminal justice actions so that no mob would be required. Historian George C. Wright, professor and senior adviser to the University of Kentucky president, as well as the author of *Racial Violence in Kentucky, 1865–1940: Lynchings, Mob Rule and "Legal Lynchings,"* explains this systemic issue when he says, "Ultimately it is important to distinguish between legal lynchings and extralegal mob murders because nothing should obscure the fact that legal lynchings were the most brutal form of racial violence," though, he says, "dying on the gallows or in the electric chair probably seemed like an act of compassion when compared to the slow, torturous burnings that mobs extracted on some of their victims. Regardless of the method used in putting a person to death, it was the role of the state which in theory was committed to establishing and preserving an ethical system of justice that made legal lynching especially hideous."[4] Due to America's penchant for incarcerating Black people, Bethea's legal lynching certainly wouldn't be the country's last.[5]

Lynch culture is embedded in every action that upholds a system that makes it easier to punish Indigenous, Black, and people of color (IBPOC) and other marginalized groups rather than create and sustain a culture of justice. We tend to think of lynch culture as something that happens *out there*, usually in the past, and not in our communities and families. Not only do we consciously or unconsciously enact lynch culture, but we also are used as instruments of a white supremacist system to forward lynch culture in our beliefs, thoughts, and actions. To take responsibility for our actions, especially in a carceral society, we must also observe where the deception lies in the system and in the players who insist on violence against Black people as well as access to the very threat of violence. I wanted to know how lynch culture was created. In my nation, in my community, in my family, and in me.

In my childhood, what could be grown and made on western Kentucky land was nearly mythological. The Ralph family farm was situated near Reed, Kentucky, between the Ohio River and the Green River, fifteen miles west of Owensboro. Angel Mounds, one of the most significant archaeological sites for precontact ancient cultures, was just across the Ohio to the north, but I wouldn't know about that place until my forties. I loved the verdant emerald of the Ohio Valley and imagined its slope along those cone-shaped hills, long, long miles from The Knobs of the Outer Bluegrass, known for deep-rooted forests and erosional remnants of once mighty glacial ice sheets, down into the Western Coal Fields, and across the sinkholes, springs, and caverns of the Mississippian Plateau to the lakes, ponds, sloughs, and swamps of the western tip, which slid across the Madrid Fault.

My paternal grandfather worked on his father's farm, and then after he married, he was a tenant farmer for an investor from New York. Granddad was a big man, with large shoulders and hands, and unlike Grandmaw, he smiled wide and often. Our son carries his easy grin and sense of humor.

My grandmother helped in the fields, preserved food, cooked a hot meal for the school, and raised her kids. For fifteen years she'd been a grid welder for GE, enjoying the freedom of a paycheck as well as the independence of having a job. Soon after they had children, Grandmaw knew their days of tenant farming had ended: "When the lady that heired [*sic*] [the farm] died, and . . . then it went down to her children . . . I told Sherrel we had better find somewhere to get out of here because them kids will sell that place overnight."[6] The owners sold the land to Alcoa to build a smelter making 310,000 metric tons of flat rolled aluminum every year for use in cans. My grandparents bought their own land with loans. They weren't dirt poor, but the family story goes that when the Catholic church asked for payment for the pews in which the families sat for Sunday mass, my grandfather could afford to reserve the bench just in front of the last row. That farm served their children and their families until the 1980s, when Granddad sold his share, and his sons lost the rest to drought and debt. Industrial plants near their little clapboard home and barn made the region another kind of place, one that spouted coal fire into the sky from a pair of the world's tallest chimneys, burning seven million tons of carbon a year on the Abraham Lincoln Memorial Parkway. But before the land was given to waste—airborne formaldehyde from those paper and aluminum plants having replaced many family farms—it was beautiful to me. If I wander in the cornfield or watch the storms light the sky with silver blades, it's still a wondrous place.

My paternal grandmother was wild, a force, and she commanded her family. Frances Moran Ralph was four-foot-ten, black haired, sharp minded, iron willed, and in motion. She had a grandfather who was a stowaway from Ireland and a father who was a drunk, ten children she birthed, and plenty others she took care of. My middle name, Lea, was her mother's, which meant I got the southern double-identifier, *sahn-ya-lee*, always. One story I heard growing up was that my maternal great-grandmother Jessica Birkhead had introduced my father's side to Catholicism. The Ralphs were country religious—the priests ran things, and the rural people obeyed the doctrine. Frances's last two children died at birth—both after Grandmaw had asked (many times) to have a tubal ligation to prevent pregnancy and been denied by the priest. She birthed her last child after my mother was pregnant with me. My earliest memories are of going to church with my grandmother, a doily of lace bobby-pinned to my head, the Mass still in Latin. On the kitchen wall of my grandparents' little clapboard house, bookending a crucifix, there were portraits of Pope John Paul and JFK.

The church was central in all affairs, determining power, resources, reproduction, and social status. The community's religious leaders determined not only control of resources and recognition by the group but also a share in the political power.

Grandmaw taught me how to make dinner and tend strawberries, and she once killed a large black rat snake with an axe in the laundry closet, right in front of us kids. Her entire family raised corn and tobacco, and she smoked a lot of cigarettes. I hardly ever saw her without a cigarette in her hand or a butt smoldering in a brass ashtray, and late in her life, when she was in the hospital for emphysema, she'd leave her oxygen tank in the room and grab a smoke outside. I'd grown up being wary of her. She was kind to me, but she had a sharpness. When I was born, my teenage aunt, her eldest daughter, left her family to help take care of me—or so they'd told the others—but my father let me know that he'd wanted to keep his sister safe from my raging grandmother, who was prone to strike before reasoning.

As the eldest grandchild on both sides, I was often sent to stay with my grandparents, so my mother, who had four children over four consecutive years, could have a rest. In first grade, Grandmaw taught me to make biscuits at the little kitchen counter, my feet up on a step so I could pat the dough with my hands and push the wood-handled butcher knife to make a tray of uneven squares. Farm duties were utilitarian, not necessarily for wonder or beauty or sweetness. I was tasked with filling glasses with ice and bringing the tea pitcher around for the men coming home for lunch between their work in the field, and if I wasn't quick with the pour, she had words for me. The kitchen was where I first heard her speak the n-word, and even then, I knew from my schooling the racial slur was not one for me to repeat. Still, the sound lodged in my brain like a parasite.

After an early supper, I would often walk the fields of the farm with my grandfather. Here at my desk, I still have the arrowhead that I lifted from the fields one summer night when the light slid gold on flaxen sheaves of corn and the fireflies hadn't started their glow. When I held up the carved stone to show him, he looked down and told me Kentucky was named for "the blood red ground," a nomadic place of hunting for the Shawnee. I expect that he didn't know this was a Kentucky legend, one meant to convey that Indians never lived in this place—they only ever passed through—making the land free for the taking.[7]

Owensboro, Kentucky, is situated near a crook on the Ohio River and lies in a fertile valley where, at the beginning of the Common Era, the Moundbuilders—the Fort Ancient people, a sister culture of the Mississippians—made giant earth sculptures of birds and serpents. This place once had burial mounds as vast as the pyramids at Giza. The Fort Ancient people thrived here for almost a century along the Ohio during the Late Prehistoric period. Annual spring floods regularly replenished the nutrients in the soil and allowed cultivation of crops that included maize (corn), beans, and squash. They were a precontact civilization of one thousand people who observed a solar calendar, created negative-paint pottery for effigies, utility, and trade, made ceremony at the mounds, built palisade boundaries, and consolidated groups for protection. The oral history of the Shawnee, or *Shaawanwaki*, names the Fort Ancient people as their ancestors.[8] The Shawnee spoke the Algonquian language and hunted bear, deer, and buffalo in the winter. The land was thick with trees—sycamores, sweet gums, cottonwoods, hickory, black walnut, tulip poplars, sugar maples, redbud, sassafras, pawpaws, dogwood, black and white oak, and honey and black locusts. The Shawnee lived in wood lodges constructed throughout the Ohio Valley and traveled along the river.

Beginning in the mid-1600s, Europeans came to the land of Kentucky, first the Spanish, then the French, and then the English, traversing the Ohio by canoe and later by flatboats that moved goods and livestock from Pittsburgh to New Orleans. The Seneca called it the Good River (Ohi:yó), with land from its banks rising up into the fertile, rolling hills of Kentucky (kẽtaʔkeh, for "at the field").[9] The first European explorers brought infectious diseases to the tribes who traded with the Shawnee villages. A buffalo trace on the high clay banks of the Ohio River was a site where the English encroached and, in so doing, fortified a settler myth of dominion. Owensboro is also known for a history of violence that springs from settler colonialism, genocide, and racial terror—a founding story that's emblematic of America.

For two hundred years, white American historians argued that American Indians never lived in Kentucky. Instead, they portrayed Kentucky as either a middle ground used by all tribes for hunting, or a territory at the center of many dark and bloody disputes. The land speculator John Filson created this lie in his book, *The Discovery, Settlement, and Present State of Kentucke*, published in 1788. The book claimed that

American Indians had no valid claim to Kentucky because it was originally settled by an ancient white race that greatly predated the Indigenous tribes. Filson's tome became an invitation to colonize and—in the case of this crooked river land on the Ohio—offered maps to claim settlements.

The Shawnee tribe were murdered and displaced by encroaching settlers, and they sent out raiding parties hoping to drive settlers off their land. The Shawnee Nation fought in land skirmishes against the Kentucky militia, who destroyed their villages and crops. But the Europeans continued to come to the place they called the Yellow Banks, named for the color of the clay along the high shores. Lewis and Clark wintered here in October 1803, before their expedition. A Virginian named Bill Smothers built the first frontier cabin here at the turn of the century, a place on the river used as a public house to sell venison, bear meat, and buffalo robes. Early historians described him in loving detail as a teller of tall tales, a man of intelligence who valued the truth above all, but he detested his neighbors and was tried for stabbing one. By 1817 the town on the Yellow Banks had been named for one of their Indian-killing colonels—Owensborough, for Abraham Owen, formerly a Virginian of Welsh descent, and a fighter in the Revolutionary War as well as in many Indian wars and skirmishes. The town quadrupled in size from Reconstruction to the early twentieth century, and its name was changed to Owensboro.

Bloodshed dominated the region in this era of early settler encroachment. The Shawnee tribe, like the precontact Fort Ancient culture before them, built multifamily dwellings along the river and created important political, religious, and trade centers. By the early 1800s, in a resistance, Tecumseh's confederacy united the American Indian people with ties to Ohio Territory lands. But in 1830, so that white slave owners could take over tribal land, President Andrew Jackson signed into law the Indian Removal Act, which forced Kentucky's tribes to walk a thousand miles west of the Mississippi River, on a devastating journey known as the Trail of Tears.

Occupied for thousands of years by Indigenous people, western Kentucky would in a hundred years become home to immigrating Germans, Scots, Irish, Welsh, and English, and these ethnicities would soon be bound together by legal and cultural definitions that privileged them in homeownership, business ownership, and cultural networks. Rich landowners gave the poor people of European descent advantages over Africans and Native peoples. A multiclass alliance of European people came to identify themselves by their whiteness, a concept of race that exists merely to defend privilege.

A decade after I learned of my grandparents' presence at Bethea's legal lynching, I began to research Kentucky, to see how my family history had been constructed. My father had given each of us children a chronology of the maternal and paternal sides of his family. I signed up for Ancestry.com and began to coordinate the documents my father had given me with the information I found online. Soon, there were photos of ancestors and grave sites, birth and death records, and storytelling that went back generations. The Ralph/Rolfe side of my family, my paternal grandfather's line, had come to America at the time of the Revolution and had moved onto land occupied by the Shawnee or Chickasaw tribes. At the time of European immigration, Thomas Samuel Ralph from Essex, England, moved to Virginia and fought in the Revolutionary War. His sons, John and Will, moved to Kentucky, eventually owning vast amounts of land, from Deserter Creek to the divide between Panther Creek and Rough River. In 1782, around the same time as the Ralphs' move to Kentucky, Indigenous tribes such as the Delaware, Wyandot, Miami, Ottawa, Chippewa, and Mingo had formed a confederacy with the Shawnee to help fortify their residency in Kentucky. My fourth great-grandfather was spoken of as "the forefather of all the Ralphs in Kentucky" but rarely talked about as the colonizer who had stolen that land. Most of the stories I'd learned about this side of the family had to do with Andrew Jackson Ralph's well-loved custard ice cream recipe or of the Ralphs being divided in the Civil War. I now learned that my granddad's great-grandfather Will, who fought with the Union, said that he would "scratch himself out of the grave" if he were buried at the Ralph Cemetery with all the Democrats who wore the gray in that war. But I also discovered a family history that placed an exact value on what my family had stolen:

> John and Will settled in Kentucky when there were very few neighbors and therefore had to rely upon each other [and] their trusty rifles. They were forced to fight together against Indians, panthers and other wild animals. They built small cabins on the land where the Ralph Cemetery is now located. The Ralph's

> [*sic*] being a close family and not being ones to ramble or move are still living on some of the original 10,000 acres reported to have been taken from the Indians years ago.[10]

The arrowhead from my granddad and the "blood red ground" he said Kentucky was named for began to have a different meaning.

In 2017, fifteen years after I first heard the name Rainey Bethea, I returned to the research again. I visited the public library in Seattle and spoke with several librarians about the reportage that might be available in books, journals, and newspapers. Lynchings existed as early as the frontier era when vigilantes won public support to be considered legitimate.

"In a world where legally constituted authorities could exert only slight influence, and law enforcement depended on the will of the people, the line between mob and posse was uncertain," notes Christopher Waldrep in *The Many Faces of Judge Lynch: Extralegal Violence and Punishment in America*. Frontier criminals, multistate murder sprees, unsolved crimes, limited faith in local law enforcement and the courts, unsettled laws, rival forces, and Revolutionary zeal gave force to punishments that had the power to legitimize extralegal violence.[11]

I immersed myself in accounts of lynchings across the US, including those in Kentucky. During the lead-up to the Civil War, abolitionists reported that slavery encouraged lynching across the South. The legal process that led to the end of racialized slavery in America did not address the inventions of white supremacy that had sustained the institution. Black people might be free from involuntary labor under the law, but that did not mean southern white people recognized them as fully human.[12]

As a child, I'd learned on family vacations that due to its strategic position on the Ohio River, Louisville had been the center of planning, supplies, recruitment, and transportation for numerous campaigns. Louisville was a bulwark for Union troops, and the Confederacy never managed to attack the city, though battles in western Kentucky threatened the state. What I'd never been taught was that the enlistment of Kentucky slaves into Union regiments (Kentucky had the second-largest African American Union enlistment, behind only Louisiana) meant that Union support among Kentuckians had greatly diminished by the end of the Civil War. But during the war, owners could receive compensation when their enslaved property joined the Union forces. The Emancipation Proclamation of 1863 freed enslaved people in the states that were in rebellion, but in border states like Kentucky, slavery continued to be legal.[13] The federal law stated that no man was to fight as a slave, so for slaves in the border states, enlistment meant freedom. In a cruel truth, the only reparations ever paid by the American government were to enslavers who could file a claim against the federal government for the loss of the services of an enslaved person who had enlisted. Congress passed acts during the Civil War that bestowed loyal Union enslavers money for enslaved people who enlisted or were drafted into the US military.

In *South to America: A Journey below the Mason-Dixon Line to Understand the Soul of a Nation,* Imani Perry says of this moment: "Black people escaping slavery flooded into the city. Locally enslaved people freed themselves as well. Slaveholders panicked and grew embittered that their human wealth had taken possession of themselves. This is the source of the quip, 'Kentucky did not join the Confederacy until after the Civil War.' The human coffers were emptied."[14] The Emancipation Proclamation did not apply to the roughly 425,000 enslaved people living in Tennessee, Delaware, Kentucky, Missouri, and Maryland—states that had not seceded or were occupied by Union forces.[15]

After the Civil War, lawless groups of white supremacists formed under the guise of being "social clubs" for former Confederate soldiers; these clubs then transformed into paramilitary organizations that drew thousands of members from all sectors of white society. Six Confederate veterans formed the first Ku Klux Klan, including Confederate General Nathan Bedford Forrest as their Grand Wizard, and infiltrated the campaign for a Democratic president in 1868, creating racial terror against Black people and Republicans throughout the South.

As an adult, I'd lived in Kentucky and Tennessee, states where Forrest remained a revered figure celebrated with monuments and markers in parks, in government offices, and along roadways. But it would take me a much longer time to learn of the effects in my home state of Jim Crow, a time when Kentucky utilized Black Codes to restrict Black residents' freedoms, for example with vagrancy laws, which found punishable offenses like "rambling without a job" and "keeping a disorderly home." In 2024, some of these laws were called up once again by a biased

Supreme Court that determined the Constitution does not protect people who find themselves without a home against any American city's cruel and unusual punishment through displacement or jailing.

Starting in 1866, Kentucky passed many segregation laws, laws that prevented Black people from testifying against white people, laws that required white people to be present at the signing of Black contracts, and a miscegenation statute that wouldn't be repealed until 1955. Just as during slavery, Black children were sent out as "apprentices" to their former owners until they reached adulthood. These were continuations of Slave Codes (sometimes the only difference was that the word *slave* had been removed) meant to guarantee that Black people remain dominated by white people.

By 1910, public executions were increasingly being perceived as barbaric. Kentucky eliminated the nineteenth-century practice when its General Assembly voted to implement death sentences by execution behind bars. But in 1920, a lynch mob uprising formed in Lexington, Kentucky, when Will Lockett, a Black World War I veteran, was accused of killing Geneva Hardman, a young, white girl.[16] When virulent white people tried to storm the courthouse, the Kentucky National Guard and the state police opened fire on them, shooting more than fifty people, killing six. After Lockett was executed at Eddyville, the backlash was so severe that Kentucky amended its laws to allow the public execution of rapists in the county of the offense. By 1920, many in the state believed that in cases of rape, private execution by electric chair was "too humane."[17] Kentucky's racist laws and its lack of racial justice was an outgrowth of white attitudes in the state throughout the twentieth century. Historical coverage from Black newspapers like the *Chicago Defender* as well as reports available through the NAACP made it clear that Black news media accounts of violence against Black people were significantly different from those of white newspapers, which all too often became the prevailing narrative.

During this era, my grandparents would have been toddlers on their mothers' laps and then elementary students being educated by a state that brought an old law out of hiding so white people could once again legally enforce racial terror. When the 1920 rape law came into effect, the state executed nine men—eight of whom were Black—for rape. Of those executions, four were public hangings of Black men, although in most instances the crowd was small. The only one that seems to have been comparable to the Bethea hanging was that of Sam Jennings in Hardinsburg, Breckinridge County, in 1932. Jennings had been falsely accused and unjustly convicted of raping a white woman, Mabel Downs. Six thousand people viewed the hanging, and in a prelude to Owensboro's brutal picnic, there was barbecue and (concealed) bourbon and soft drinks; people came from miles around to view Jennings's murder.[18] The *Chicago Defender* and the *Pittsburgh Courier* each published an article on the execution. Both pieces argued the innocence of Jennings. A Black newspaper reported on the scene: "The hanging of the colored man attracted such a throng of men, women and children as might have caused P.T. Barnum of circus fame to hide his face in shame. It took Jennings seventeen minutes to die, to the delight of the crowd, who enjoyed every second of the event."[19]

Kentucky also holds the record for the most judicially authorized executions in a single day: on July 13, 1928, seven men were sequentially electrocuted by "Old Sparky," the nickname given to the electric chair in Eddyville. The men were disproportionately Black.[20] George C. Wright says, "The conviction that Afro-Americans should be severely punished for their real and perceived transgressions was, of course, nothing new but in the period from 1900-1940, white Kentuckians seem to have been more determined than ever that blacks accused of rape or murder be executed."[21]

One way to make racist laws ordinary is by ensuring the election of white supremacists. Kentucky had long been a racist state, run in this era (1929–1942) by Governor "Happy" Chandler, who became a senator in 1939 and, buoyed by the conservative Democrats, voted against an antilynching bill soon after being elected. The bill levied fines against local governments and government officials in counties in which illegal lynching had occurred. The bill passed in the House of Representatives in 1922 but was stopped by the Senate in a filibuster led by southern Democrats. Two more antilynching bills made it through the House, only to be blocked again in the Senate. Seven presidents petitioned the Congress to pass an antilynching bill. Not one succeeded, though most states had long since closed executions to the public and had started using the electric chair, which was grim in the kind of painful death it dealt prisoners but not open to mobs of onlookers.

Jim Crow continued in Kentucky well into the 1930s. Included among many anti-Black laws was the segregation of libraries and schools, separate textbooks for white and Black students, separate neighborhoods and nursing homes, separate railroads and other transportation, separate bathrooms for Black and white employees, separate recreation facilities, prohibiting Black people from apartments and places where white people dwelled, and prohibiting Black doctors and nurses from taking postgrad courses in public hospitals and in the city of Louisville.[22] This was the world of western Kentucky—one more punishing to people of color—that Bethea entered after he left his first prison term.

In 2019, I began to work with antiracism educator Elle Glenise Pike. In 2020, Pike heard an early version of this story and spoke with me about the power of defining the concept of lynch culture.[23] We had begun to meet a year before the murder of Breonna Taylor on March 13, 2020, and the murder of George Floyd on May 25, 2020. The catalyst for this work had been an essay I'd been trying to write about my grandmother's comments on the Bethea hanging and of my questioning of the use of the word *public execution* instead of *murder.* I'd shared an early draft of my work the summer prior, at the Tin House Summer Workshop, where the activist and author of *The Reckonings: Essays on Justice for the Twenty-First Century,* Dr. Lacy M. Johnson, and a cohort of writers had challenged me to think more deeply and clearly about the culture in which I'd been raised.

Elle Glenise's goals were to educate on antiracism's terms and concepts, as well as to provide a practical blueprint for becoming antiracist. Pike taught a simple definition of antiracism as acts that oppose racism in all forms. The tough work came in identifying the root causes of racism and putting an end to them in our own lives. Her program included identifying bypassing behaviors, which include common racial triggers and behavior that allow people to identify with racist tools of defense like wanting to help Black people, wanting to be a good white person, and identifying with a savior role. I read her book, *Becoming Antiracist,* and signed up for the online workshop. Her work was primarily in converting the racist tools of defense that perpetuated white supremacy to tools of accountability.[24]

I'd been awakening to the whiteness that surrounded my history, but I wasn't aware of how my obsequiousness toward educated white men played into upholding lynch culture. For over a decade, I'd been sidetracked in this essential work through believing other's views instead of fully researching Kentucky's and my family's connection to racial violence. Too much time was spent in ignorance and refusal of the racism that was so evident in my family, my community, my countries, and myself. I wanted to contribute to a more complicated understanding about the consequences when history is portrayed with key information missing, and to bring awareness to the lynch culture that doesn't just reside in the past but is everywhere in our family and communal lives. I'd shown up in Pike's class because of the silencing effect of my shame whenever I talked or wrote about this story. Pike coached me to see that my deference to white male historian accounts was a form of forgetting my power, which includes the power to work on behalf of others. Until that conversation, I wasn't fully aware of the ways I ongoingly denied myself the authority to speak about what I was growing to know—that the state was complicit in suppressing legal and other lynchings, a silencing that led to white supremacist laws and policies that kept legal systems in the hands of a controlling few. Some would say that lynching ended but the state killings would go on and on. During that year of doing this work with Pike and paying attention to what was happening, there were 189 days when police killed Black people in the US.[25]

State-sanctioned violence and the systemic nature of lynch culture were the forces through which Rainey Bethea's life had been controlled since the moment he entered Owensboro, Kentucky. How would I understand the forces that continued to maintain that death was just? I didn't think I'd be able to answer that question until I returned to Kentucky to visit with my extended family and interview them about their lives and to begin conversations with historians and scholars about how they viewed the hanging.

Writing this story meant that I was only being drawn closer to my bloodline, and in both national and familial lore, the bloodline could not be revoked. In much of my adulthood, I'd tried to stay as far as I could from this Kentucky home, meaning the physical ancestral land but also the felt place. In my family, I'd experienced cruelty, scarcity, distrust, indifference, violence, joy, and love. Early in my research, several colleagues had suggested that the primary place for me to focus my work would be with family and ancestors. I knew that I wanted to go back to Owensboro to talk with my family, to see how they saw their life on the farm and learn what they knew about our paternal grandparents' involvement in the Bethea hanging. In the summer of 2019, nearly every aunt, uncle, and cousin I asked agreed to sit with me to explain how they saw their lives on the farm and what they knew about the last public execution.

On that trip, I visited archivists, researchers, and librarians in Owensboro at the Daviess County Library; in Louisville at the Filson Historical Society; and in Frankfort, the state capital, at the Kentucky Department for Libraries and Archives as well as the Martin F. Schmidt Research Library. My husband drove me around the hills of the Bluegrass state, and we stopped to eat at barbecue joints serving sweet tea and cornbread.

I learned that my family's connection to the state's murder of Rainey Bethea ran deeper than I imagined. I knew my paternal side as the farm folk and my maternal grandparents as the townsfolk, though both sides of my family had come from farmers. We stopped in Lewisport to visit my mother's brother, my uncle Carl, whom I hadn't seen in years. We sat on the porch catching up all afternoon, and he told me family tales he'd been passed, some of which he considered suspect. His mother, whom I called Mimoo, was a strong presence in the lives of us children. In my childhood, both of my grandmothers were afraid for me to be in relationship with Black people, romantic and otherwise. On one summer visit to Mimoo's home in Owensboro, her obviously racist friend argued with me about whether I ought to be friends with people who, he said, pointing to the stove, were "as black as that skillet." Carl and I had spoken of Mimoo's racism as well as the way Mimoo's life had been characterized by losing her mother to strep throat when my grandmother was twelve years old. Soon after, Mimoo had become an orphan when her father died from falling into a grease pit at an auto service shop after having drunk himself into oblivion. Mimoo told stories of that horrible time and how she'd been sent to the homes of aunts to provide free labor and how she'd had to drop out of school. Her love for her mother was powerful, and it connected her deeply to my husband, who had also lost his mother too early.

I was back home from that trip when I opened the folder with the court records I'd requested from the archives, and something caught my eye in those legal papers—*Birkhead*. I heard the syllables in the voice of Mimoo, speaking her family name, reminding me of home. I opened the website Ancestry.com, to see the surname. Birkhead had been my great-grandmother's maiden name, Jessica Birkhead, the same name as the attorney for the commonwealth. The skin along my arms chilled.

Could I be related to Herman Birkhead, the one I now saw as responsible for Bethea's death? This Birkhead had asked for a trial when none was necessary, since Bethea could have been sentenced by the attending judge. Birkhead had been the prosecutor accountable for dropping the murder charge but upholding the rape charge, ensuring that if found guilty, Bethea would be hanged. Birkhead not only managed the unjust trial but also attended the habeas corpus hearing to ensure that Bethea met his death in the white town square. He was the most dominant influence in a culture led by race, class, and gender division. To me, Birkhead represented the state that perpetuated violence against Black Kentuckians.

In a few months, I had hired a researcher, given them much of our savings, and received my answer—Herman Birkhead and my great-grandmother were first cousins. Now both sides of my family were tied to this legal lynching.

My mind kept returning to the return to the land on which I'd been born. On that last visit, I'd driven out to the Kentucky farm where I'd spent some of my childhood and walked on the land, and everything shifted. I listened to the sway of the corn leaves, almost as tall as me, while my husband stayed in the car and let me remember. The barn, the dust road, the walk to the pond, the crickets, the horizon from which lightning could be seen miles away—these are what I could locate that felt both vast and close. I stood in the tall grass and turned around and around until the memories came closer. Granddad placing me on the quilt on top of the old crank ice cream machine, to help hold the ice chips and salt down so the steel tub stayed frosty while the dasher turned. Grandmaw carrying bowls of potato salad twice as big as her body. The smell of hickory smoke at a family barbecue. The crunch of the gravel as the last guest left and the lightning bugs cast their gold-green shine in the humid night.

Back then my grandparents lived in what we used to call a modest country home. When I returned to revisit the now vacant house while I was writing this book, I was shocked at the smallness of the rooms. Could this have been the house that slept ten people—and sometimes more, when the cousins arrived—in three little bedrooms? How on earth had the aunts, uncles, and their children—nearly forty of us—swept into the twelve-by-eighteen living room with a Christmas tree and presents? No one expected there to be more space, at least not us children.

Granddad liked to tease his wife, seemingly to loosen her rigid authority over the entire clan. When she wasn't looking, he would shower an entire buffet with a liberal dusting of his favorite pepper over every dish; when she discovered his sabotage, Grandmaw would yell, *Sherrel!* and he would chuckle like a boy. Granddad let me light his cigarettes with his silver Zippo lighter, a role I prized. I stood guard between the old coal stove, and his chair at the head of the table, waiting to set his Marlboro or Doral glowing, and sometimes he let me sit on his lap in the rocker and told me stories. He died too young, and his last meal was a blackberry cobbler Grandmaw made for him. That memory would grow so durable that I was compelled to make the same dish for my father decades later, when he was in his last days, suffering from a brain tumor and a stroke. I fed the thick berry sauce to Dad, even as his damaged reflexes caused him to spit it out over his chin. We never talked about our love, but we knew to do these things for each other. In my family, we assumed we belonged. But still, there seemed to be requirements for that belonging, ones that I learned as I grew into a young woman. We had to take our punishments, go to church, remain virgins (only for the girls), and keep the secret of the violence we encountered at the hands of our father at home. We were not encouraged to express emotions or to disagree with our parents. In my childhood, I learned that there was little sovereignty or authority in our choices.

I touched the dry corn leaf and remembered leaving Kentucky. By the time I entered third grade, my father, a chemist, left home to make whiskey for a distillery in a small town in Canada. I was educated in Canada, married a Canadian, had my two children in the iconic mountain towns of Collingwood, Ontario, and Banff, Alberta. Living physically apart from Kentucky intensified what it meant to be from there. Every memory amplified. And, no matter where I was, I was an outsider. In Kentucky, I became a foreigner who didn't know their southern ways. In Ontario, I was a "Yank" who would never fit into Canadian life. The one at the margins has a distinct view of the community.

We were a middle-class family who had risen from the working class, mostly due to privilege, though my father would have said it was due to education and perseverance. In Kentucky, my father had been a student and a chemist and my mother a homemaker. In Canada, we lived among a shipbuilding community who were hardworking and hard drinking, and we learned to skate and play hockey at the rinks our friends' fathers made in their backyards. I was always conscious of the depiction of my home state in the press and in the minds of friends and teachers.

From kindergarten to second grade, I had attended a Catholic school in Owensboro that was all-white, and I didn't meet people of color until I went to public school, briefly in Chicago for grade one and then later in Canada. That northern country felt like an escape, a freedom. I didn't yet know that my family history would follow me and that I would become like other white people who tried to leave home, that I would keep trying to run from all that I didn't want to see.

From my visits to the South on twice-yearly vacations, I knew that the neighborhoods in my birth town—the fourth largest in the state—were still segregated, including a concrete wall white neighbors had constructed so they didn't have to see Black children swimming at a nearby pool. After the assassination of Bobby Kennedy, my father had become disillusioned with the potential of civil rights. In Owensboro, I'd been a scared eight-year-old girl, sitting on my daddy's lap as he sobbed in front of the television on that day. By the time we moved to Canada, Dad had become loyal to Richard Nixon, who would become the thirty-seventh president. White voters shrank from the Democrats' commitment to affirmative action, school desegregation, and opposition to the Vietnam War. Nixon's Southern Strategy appealed to white suburban southerners like Dad. Even though by the seventies he had moved north, he was already prone to the anxieties of the white community. He showed contempt for liberal "social engineering" and most academic people and proclaimed his belief in states' rights. Because we lived in small-town Ontario, he concealed some of his racism, but it oozed from him, just as it would leach onto me.

In high school, I had a history teacher who allowed us to do research about a current event. Around the time of Watergate, I wanted to know what the rest of my Kentucky family thought about the public forgiveness of President Nixon and the unpopular public pardon by President Ford. On the day of the presentation, I was proud to show my class the anonymous surveys I'd conducted with family members, how I'd decided on the methodology, designed the questions, and analyzed their responses. I wrote the findings up in a style of social research and presented my family's mostly similar statements. I'd discovered what I expected—that my family members were supporters of Nixon (as 72 percent of white voters were in the 1972 election, my father staunchly so [he never wanted to be unknown in his views]). My teacher was enraged and shared with me that he didn't know how people could be so biased. I felt the indignity I always did when American biases collided with Canadian preferences for neutral territory. John Ehrlichman would later explain Nixon's dog whistle politics by saying, "The subliminal appeal to the anti-black voter was always present in Nixon's statements and speeches." I felt the hot burn of embarrassment for exposing my family's prejudices.

That year, my father brought home a shiny new red Cordoba and called it a *coon* car in front of my friends. Later, my friend repeated those words to her mother and was slapped. This is a story I don't remember until I tell my childhood friend that I'm writing this story, and she reports that it was the only time in her life that she was hit by a parent.

My father also burned a cross into the yard of the (white) lawyer I babysat for. I can't trace the meaning of this act, only remembering that he and others joked about the infringement later. Still, the shame burned hot, incessant, for this was the family who had taken me to their parties and receptions and trusted me with their child, whom others saw as troublesome but I adored for his smarts and wildness. My father had taken our inviolate Canadian home and brought a symbol of the Ku Klux Klan into it, and now the townspeople would know that we were hateful rednecks.

Dad dressed up as a blackfaced butler one Halloween and my mother wore a French maid's costume. I remember standing in the bathroom watching him spread burnt cork over his face. A teenager then, I was nearly always humiliated by my father's actions and words, but something in me knew that he was using this shocking visual to appall his polite, Canadian friends. I'd seen celebrities in blackface—Joni Mitchell on the cover of her album, Gene Wilder in the movies, and Johnny Carson on TV.[26] And I'd grown up with my father hoping to influence me about the interpretation of southern history, with wanting to define the meaning of the American experience. I knew that I didn't want to see any of this so-called Halloween celebration, and his effect on his friends. I went downstairs and siphoned off his whiskey, then out to forget who I was, which nearly worked: twenty years of blackouts—a form of deliberate forgetting—until the All-Soul's Day that I became sober. Sobriety was a part of this reckoning too; that "rigorous honesty" the twelve steps was designed to evoke also influenced seeing what had been true inside my family.

There were signs that my father thought in the ways that conservative white men from the South tended to think. He carted our family around on vacations to Civil War sites. He took me and our children to the outdoor theater performances of *The Stephen Foster Story* in Bardstown, Kentucky, which were to him a historic entertainment with songs that imagined the plantation South with a sickly sentimentality. I heard in those lyrics from "My Old Kentucky Home"—which is a song of a white man describing an enslaved person's feelings of the natural beauty of the Kentucky landscape and of losing his home by being shipped to a sugar plantation—a mournful nostalgia for a racist South.[27] History taught me that Foster's music was sung throughout the Civil War and that he'd brought great recognition to the role of Kentucky as a site for inspiring soldiers. Emily Bingham, author of *My Old Kentucky Home: The Astonishing Life and Reckoning of an Iconic American Song*, says that "this music has a past informed by thousands of performances, enactments, critiques, and defenses that, over time, encapsulates the United States' contradictory and contorted relationship to slavery and white supremacy."[28]

When I was young, I didn't know that Foster's songs began in blackface minstrelsy. Rhae Lynn Barnes, assistant professor of American cultural history at Princeton University, says that "minstrel shows counteracted abolitionists by arguing in favor of slavery's supposed nurturing attributes, making slavery appear benevolent to the working-class men who flooded the Bowery district in New York City and who had little or no protection from the abuse and usurpations of factory labor."[29] My father's great-grandfather would have arrived in New York from Ireland around 1862, at exactly the right time to see these minstrel shows.

When I was seventeen, my father had given me a Confederate flag, the same southern cross he waved at Fort Bragg, when he was in boot camp, before I was born. He handed me that folded and faded flag, and it was worn, like him. I didn't take the flag from him, but when, in my freshman year of university, my family moved back to Kentucky, he surreptitiously packed the flag in my metal locker. I found the flag on the first day in my new dorm room. My family had left to live in the South a week ahead of when I would start school, and so I was the first to arrive, alone in the quiet building. I tacked the flag to the corkboard on the wall. I wanted to see what it looked like up there. I wanted to see my history with my father and what he'd meant by sending me to school with this flag. There he appears, as if in the fabric itself, as he always was in the photo albums, 1950s crew cut, legs wide, proud grin, waving the blood-red flag. I snickered at what I saw then as his rebelliousness. I wanted to continue the family tradition of being the rebel. If I knew that Unionists had called the Confederates "rebels" it didn't register with me on that day. I only saw the right to resistance. In my mind, I saw the face of the son who wanted to please his mother, the man who had the courage to leave his home state when every family member for five generations lived on the farm. I felt his violence and domination, which he never had a problem enacting.

A prefect a few years older than me knocked on the door and stuck her head in to ask how I was. When she saw the flag, her eyes widened. After she left, I took the tacks out of the corners of the cloth and placed the flag at the bottom of my locker. In under an hour, she came back with another prefect. Their eyes scanned the wall where I'd placed a music poster.

"Is everything okay?" they asked.

"I'm fine," I said.

It was the late 1970s. This was a town in southern Ontario. I didn't know much about what the Confederate flag meant in history, but I knew that not knowing was something to be ashamed of. This moment became so shameful that—almost forty years later—when I first begin writing this essay, I still couldn't admit my teenage ignorance of the meaning of this flag to the women with whom I'd workshopped this story.

The flag's meaning has evolved, from one of several symbols flown by the Confederate army during the Civil War, to a revisionist symbol of nostalgia for an antebellum South, to a Lost Cause that denied the terror of slavery and lynchings, to a symbol of defiance of the federal government's Civil Rights Act that outlawed segregation in the 1960s. The greatest boom in its use may have been in 1948, when South Carolina politician Strom Thurmond ran for president under the newly founded States Rights Democratic Party, also known as the Dixiecrats. The party's purpose was to continue the segregation of the races. After *Brown v. Board of Education*, Confederate flags became popular across a variety of groups. The Confederate flag has since been used by various white supremacists and white nationalists, whether in the garb of rural rednecks, rebel bike bands, or the Republican Party taken over by MAGA insurrectionists storming the Capitol.

The Confederate flag that I was given by my father stayed in that chest until decades later when we moved to the Pacific Northwest. By that time, I'd become more aware of its racist roots. Was this symbol of racism to connect my father to his family? To align with his friends, his military unit? To sidestep the hatred of white supremacists (in his era) for Catholics? I believe that my father saw the Confederate flag as part of his American identity that harkened to the family myth of self-sufficiency, white settler ownership, and political outspokenness. My family story insisted on refuting our power, and seeing ourselves as outsiders, though we were privileged, and that's a significant part of how whiteness operates.

Two decades after that incident at university, and before the recent weaponization of the flag by far-right activists, I uprooted my father's flag from its hiding place and made a ritual to destroy it. I enlisted the help of my friend Judith, a witch and minister, and we created a ceremony to bury the flag deep into the ashes of a fire pit in my yard. I told the story that I knew then of racism in my family line, and she witnessed my words. We sang incantations into the forest that ringed our property, down to the protected stream below us, where the salmon had come to spawn.

At the time of that visit to the old Kentucky land I was fifty-nine, and I was at once a child, a mother, a lover, an elder. As I stared up at my grandparents' home on the farm, Richard watched my face, then opened the car door and came out to let me lean on his large body. I'd met my white Canadian husband at seventeen. His family played Motown on the turntable, and their ongoing party included people of color, LGBTQ folks, misfits, and bohemians. I was in love with him and the kind of freedom he'd grown up with. He was the child of a single mom who encouraged independent choices and self-expression. I imagined this all might have come from a kind of effortless cool. Then one day I learned in a whispered story he told me about how his mother, June, had traveled to Bermuda at eighteen, how she had fallen in love with a Black man. When June was a teenager, her very British upper-class mother stopped paying her bills, and June returned home to Ontario. Shortly afterward, her mother institutionalized her. June was given both LSD and electroshock treatments, inhumane methods used by mental hospitals in that era to control difficult patients, maintain order on wards, and diminish women's power.[30] By the time Richard was in high school, his mother had returned to Bermuda, where she lived as she wished, including being part of a community who welcomed her.

In our adulthood, Richard and I wanted to be with our ancestral stories without turning away from them. Our elders had injured and been injured, just as we had. Our shared humanity didn't arrive as a revelation. We still had a long, ongoing process to undertake, to learn to be with our families, just as they were.

Our "whiteness does not exempt people from exploitation, it reconciles them to it."[31] Noel Ignatiev, author of *How the Irish Became White*, said this, and when I first heard this statement, I was reminded of the ways that whiteness attempts to align poor southern people with the master class, proclaiming worth and inserting a hierarchy even though the rich rarely give a shit about poor white people. Grandmaw's story of our Irish ancestry hid our family's privilege under the myth of scrappy determination as well as a belief in being religious, deserving of benefit. I came from farmers and workers, as I knew them, people nearly always trying to secure an advantage as a family. Though our Ralph family had been marginalized in that rural community because we were Catholic, there's no doubt that we were benefited by whiteness. We absented certain historical and personal truths and never had to be called racists for doing so. We didn't concern ourselves with equality for all. When this happens en masse, bias becomes entrenched in institutions and creates systemic racism.

In a conversation the following year after my visit, my sisters and I talked about the strangest mystery in Grandmaw's interview—the moment when she seems to recall the jewelry stolen from Edward's home and paints herself as the one who tipped off the police to the missing rings and brooch:

Where this man lived was right upstairs on that alley where we went in and out my grandmother said, describing the boardinghouse she lived in during the time she worked in town, at the General Electric plant. *He had worked for that woman for twenty-seven years*, she said to the interviewer, aging Bethea to a fortysomething-year-old man. *He mowed the grass, just done everything for her, raised a small garden, cleaned her house, cooked, everything. All of a sudden, he just raped her and stole everything she had. . . . They tracked him to the river and couldn't find him. Us girls told them there's something up there in that shed. We told the old maids* [the proprietors of their boardinghouse] *where we were living, and they called the police. We stood out there and watched the police when the police came. They went up in there and found him and handed down all her jewelry.*

The trial transcripts indicated that the police already knew where the jewelry was to be found, based on a supposed confession from Bethea himself. (My grandmother's oral history interviewer simply footnoted that Mrs. Ralph's recollection was different from the newspaper stories.) My grandmother tells of a Black man's enormous servitude in an elder white woman's life. Grandmaw's storytelling often obscured facts in favor of drama, but I have found myself wondering if a white person did find those stolen objects and if the legal authorities lied about that confession as one of the five statements that they said Bethea had made.

For years, I read my grandmother's words over and over. What was becoming clear to me was that she insisted here that her acts be seen as necessary, heroic even. What was the function of inserting herself into the story, to be known as tipping off the police? This was not a tall tale, but a deliberate declaration of owning the narrative, of being identified as the defender of law, order, and whiteness. She wanted to be witnessed and remembered as "calling the cops." Her story does the work of overstating potential harm and influence so as to enhance both her vulnerability and the state's power. This ownership of white space, of assertion into the story, defines supremacy. She's telling us who her people are (and aren't). She's also showing us that when we enact the monstrosity of lynch culture, we become monstrous ourselves. This relationship to womanhood was easily recognizable to me; this was how I'd been taught. I'd been raised by my father and mother to know that one of the defining qualities of my southern womanhood—especially my white womanhood—was that I needed protection. The stories I'd been told about white womanhood included a kind of enabled victimhood and denial of harm to others.

My mother had been a favored daughter whose era-sanctioned blond, blue-eyed beauty and wisecracking personality led her to become a prom queen and the center of small-town social affairs. After her divorce from my father (and before her remarriage to him decades later), my mother went back to college to become a respiratory therapist, but before then, her gifts were not seen or utilized. Her Catholicism and orientation to diet culture meant she enforced strict rules for me as the eldest child, including restricting my appearance, activities, words, and sexuality. My parents warned me away from becoming friends with and dating men of color. We lived in what was then a very white town in Canada, though I had friends who were Black and South Asian. My mother's message was that my body and voice weren't my own, and that those seen as "other" would be harmful to me. In my conversations with Mom and Dad about the possibility of dating people of color, their insistence was that society would judge me harshly and that my relationship and potential children would suffer the consequences of social punishment.

My father used physical violence against my sister and me while he was a hero for his leadership and generosity in my small Ontario town. Both of these sides of him were true, but only one of these made my sister and me withdraw from him, restricting our time and refusing his influence. As a child, I'd been sexually assaulted by my maternal grandfather, advances he silenced by giving me Kennedy silver dollars, taking me on his restaurant deliveries, and sitting me on his lap at family gatherings. As a twelve-year-old, I'd been with this grandfather when he kissed a woman who wasn't my grandmother, and then he leaned over me and threatened to kill me if I told anyone. As a young woman, I'd been sexually assaulted by someone I knew, someone from a white working-class family. I never told any of these secrets until I got sober in my thirties. My white privilege didn't prevent me from being abused, and it was those white individuals I loved who were most often harmful. I'd been trained into stories that identified where I could be prey for Black men who wanted to sexualize my body, but it was the white fathers of my line who were the most dangerous. To identify as a victim was easy. I only closed my eyes and saw the hands of my father and grandfather on my body. Because of their need to have authority over my choices, I learned to go silent, to hide my actions, to avoid confrontation. I only quietly rebelled. I pushed back on their religious and other beliefs and learned about history and geography so I could debate my father at the supper table. When I left home at eighteen, I was smart, artistic, and painfully naive about how much my genetics and conditioning had already defined me.

I was challenged in parsing the ways in which I held white privilege because I'd also been a victim of gender violence and child abuse. I could see myself as perpetrated against, but it was trickier to find the ways that I perpetrated against others. When I stopped drinking, or suppressing my own power through reliance on substances, I could acknowledge the ways in which my class and race afforded me benefits. My grandmothers, who were survivors of a depression, who were factory workers and farmers, who were wives and mothers, who were responsible for all of the household duties and childcare, and who rarely saw land far from the places they'd been born, had less privilege than I.[32] The poverty of their young lives and the binaries imposed on sociocultural roles in their era made their white privilege much more impacted by class and gender than my own. I am a writer and teacher whose work is read, who has time to think, who declares their nonbinary identity in communities, whose middle-class salary and retirement fund keep our family in groceries and a yearly vacation. Perhaps an awareness of a relative white privilege can help us hold our ancestors accountable to their histories while remaining clear on the ways we, even in bodies damaged by gender violence, hold vastly more allowances than most.

I would witness biases against people of color in my ancestral line, but the power of these maneuvers came from a pattern beyond the individual. Our whiteness is derived from the collective, whose work is also to reinforce the messages of familial and communal patterns. For example, white women today are the coarchitects of the QAnon ideology and sustain white nationalist groups and movements. Seyward Darby, author of *Sisters in Hate: American Women on the Front Lines of White Nationalism*, says that white women are actually more likely than white men to hold "exclusionary views about what it means to be American, preferring boundaries around the nation's identity that maintain it in their image."[33] It's not such a big step from "clean" living, diet culture, and the weaponizing of wellness to racist beliefs like keeping one's family "pure." "Messages about avoiding genetically modified foods, for example, can slide into messages about keeping non-white children out of schools,"[34] reports *Vox*. Traditional culture overlaps with the racist right. White nationalists have more recently aimed their reaction to the "great replacement"—a racist theory that says white people are being replaced by immigration and low birth rates—toward white women. These racists and misogynist institutions and organizations encourage stances that are antiabortion and antifeminist. Backed by conservative billionaire Peter Thiel, a new "femtech" company launched a magazine and app that espouses COVID-19 denialism, transphobia, and the dangers of hormonal birth control for women as well as collecting their menstrual data.[35] Moving white women to traditional gender roles like mothers, caregivers, and homemakers, the "tradwife" movement aims to educate white women on natural birth control and the benefits of outsourcing one's authority. I recognized their methods. At twenty-two, the Catholic church/hippie holdovers convinced me to try timing-based birth control when I was first married, an experiment that ended up in my becoming pregnant.

The January 6 insurrectionists were supported by white women, who continue to play significant roles in attempting to overturn the election, including Representative Marjorie Taylor Greene and Supreme Court adjacent Ginni Thomas, wife of Justice Clarence Thomas. A report from the Program on Extremism at George Washington University said that female January 6 defendants were more likely to have evidence against them pulled from their social media profiles, where their culpability was denied through emphasizing their roles as mothers, daughters, and caregivers. The white women were less likely to get jail time than male defendants also convicted of misdemeanors. NBC reports that "the researchers also dived into the role gender has played in sentencing, as attorneys for female January 6 defendants have 'articulated narratives emphasizing their clients' naivety, vulnerability, and traditionally feminine roles.'"

Members of my extended family sympathized with those purporting the Big Lie, boasting on Facebook that they were ready to join the domestic terrorists at the Capitol. I do not know if anyone decided to travel to DC.

Throughout my adulthood, in my family's faith traditions, and increasingly in my country of origin, religion and politics conflated. In the version of Catholicism that I grew up around, priests and religious policies exerted influence over women's bodies and determined families' fates, including who was favored in the community and who survived the tyranny of limiting birth control. Just as before the civil rights movement, today white nationalism merges American and Christian identities. Political figures might decline overt expressions of racism and instead hide their biases using the language and symbols of the Christian religion, whose purpose can be to create an ideology as a cover for white supremacy. In this way, belonging isn't one's birthright but instead something that has a ticket price of a white forefather or a connection to native-born white people. Hard-right politics suggest that Christianity should be the basis for our laws and that a white-dominated, patriarchal society is the correct vehicle to "make America great again"—a reference to a place where people must adhere to strict gender roles, men act from a position of perceived dominance, and whiteness preserves power. Historically, in both religious organizations and the right, white men were considered the interpreters of laws, including those groups who identify as members of white supremacist, Christian nationalist, and militia, patriot, or constitutionalist movements. Their goal is to uphold male supremacy, a faction that scholar of right-wing movements Chelsea Ebin describes as "a complex system that serves to assert, support, and promote the supposed superiority of men" and subjugate women, trans, nonbinary and gender-nonconforming people.[36] It's not only biased individuals who desire to force women into subservient roles but also extremist movements, conservative politicians, influential billionaires, and powerful institutions who would prefer heteronormative systems that vilify LGBTQ+ people. MAGA's role in the Republican Party has been to trade fiscal conservatism for a new social order, one that would enforce racial and gender hierarchies, the social and cultural supremacy of both white people and men.

There was another story, inside me, that I was different from my southern relatives for being raised outside their racist expressions. I'm not. I lived in my biased conditioning before I became curious about antiracism and abolition. While my parents preferred me to withdraw from Black people with the racist fear that I'd been conditioned to maintain, my culture had me enthralled with Black southern cooking, Black dancing, Black fashion, and Black music. Sometimes they didn't even call these traditions *Black*. This didn't seem random but was a fantasy that I shared with a country (countries, if I include Canada) whose ancestral customs, conversation, stories, language, and gifts had been replaced with access to privilege and status inside a dominator culture, one that affirms that our identity is defined by the will to dominate and control others.[37]

My received familial culture was located partly in a disconnection from my ancestors. We had left behind relatives in our homeland in Ireland that in one story, prayed at every teatime for our stowaway ancestor, Tommy Moran of Ballintober, County Mayo, to return. These narratives prioritized the grief of the ones we left behind but never our own for having left. Likewise, we never grieved for those whom we had displaced, enslaved, harmed. Alan Taylor, author of *Colonial America: A Very Short Introduction*, said, "A cascade of interacting changes make up 'colonization' as the Europeans introduced new diseases, plants, animals, ideas, and peoples—which compelled dramatic, and often traumatic, adjustments by native peoples seeking to restore order to their disrupted worlds." We hardened ourselves to those possibilities. We erased them in our collective memory. We were not taught accountability to our history, our earth, our kin.

We were taught that we were better than the ones who came before. My father emphasized this teaching by insisting that it was first his education, then ours, that would allow us to rise above the farmers in our line. This belief happened alongside the myth that every generation's task was to "improve" on the fate of the previous generation in terms that didn't align us with shared resources but with consuming. We were to become successful, to become good capitalists. Built inside this notion of generational wealth and wisdom then was the requirement that we surpass all those ancient ways (and ones) that might keep us constricted. This was also the societal process of denying all those narratives and mythologies other than white that were in the past and are today used to refuse the existence of Indigenous peoples everywhere. To enact violence so as to take what was "ours," we had to also separate ourselves from our ancestral acts, to deny those genocidal histories that often remained untold in our narratives. We had to refuse the wisdom of elders. We were encouraged to dismiss forms of knowledge other than science or Catholicism. There wasn't just one, but many family stories that allowed me to discount my privilege, to instead see my ancestral inheritance as having come from poverty and resilience, when the larger story included that we had been advantaged with land and whiteness from the beginning. My grandfather had handed me that arrowhead like a talisman to ensure that I would know my place in history, right next to the white man. The movement toward truth began with my return to my Kentucky family, that specific land, and with the acknowledgment of the gift of ancestral life force that made me possible.

My paternal grandmother was not the hangman, not the lady sheriff, not the prison warden, not the priest who gave the last rites. But she was acting nonetheless as a perpetrator, a woman aligned with—and sometimes directing—the power of white men, enforcing a collective supremacy. Eula Biss, in writing of her reaction to the Charleston church massacre of 2015, said, "Hearing the term 'white supremacist' in the wake of that shooting had given me another occasion to wonder whether white supremacists are any more dangerous than regular white people, who tend to enjoy supremacy without believing in it."[38]

Likewise, there's little agreement on the definition of the term *lynching*, which continues to be fragmented based on its meaning as everything from racial violence and killings to a colloquial term for cancel culture. Historian Christopher Waldrep says, "There is no consensus today on the meaning of this important word that describes such a vital subject. It is clear that community support has long been a touchstone. When reformers call a particular killing a *lynching*, they do so as a way of criticizing some larger entity, the neighborhood, the community, the society. To call a killing a lynching asks: *How can you—all of you—tolerate such violence? What will you do about it?*"

Regular white people was people like me and my family, immersed in seeing ourselves as being ordinary folk, not recognizing that we are part of lynch culture. How often had I not recognized my whiteness or refused to see its fabricated social position? We were part of the same people everywhere whose complicity perpetuates stereotypes, who enact racial harm, who can't see that our bias is sometimes used by political and justice leaders toward systemic ends.

Racial oppression is maintained not only by racists but by those designing the systems of power. We are responsible for our actions. And individuals are not as responsible as the law enforcement and carceral structures that insist on the mass incarceration of Black people. Southern senators pass along lies that become the basis of how white people think and then refuse to acknowledge their responsibility in fostering the growth of white nationalists. For example, during the COVID-19 pandemic, Senator Tom Cotton (R-AR) reacted to a story about rising crime rates during the pandemic by tweeting that "we have a major under-incarceration problem in America," arguing for more jail time although the US already imprisons at a rate more than five times higher than that of the rest of the world. Cotton failed to mention that 40 percent of those imprisoned were Black people, though they account for 13 percent of the population,[39] and in this false sense of equality, he is complicit, both as a citizen and as a legislator designing the system of power.

The legacy of legal lynching in America is visible in who we have become in our families, towns, and nations, for whiteness is embedded in the systems we allow to be built without provocation. Whiteness is built into the ways we uphold certain myths, authenticate some histories, keep the artifacts of some peoples, and overlook the experiences of Black people. As I reckoned with my grandmother's words, my second cousin's murderous "justice," and the impact of a racist upbringing, this investigation of the last public execution in America opened a way to see the abolitionists who had been living in Kentucky and leading civil rights.[40]

Without a plan to abolish white privilege in ourselves, our communities, and our country, we can't mourn for what we have enacted. We can't hear the stories of the many uncelebrated marginalized and oppressed people. We can't offer reconciliation to those we have harmed.

3

On Lynch Culture

The 1936 hanging of Rainey Bethea was said to have been the last public execution in North America, but extralegal and legal lynching has never really stopped in the United States and Canada. Lynch culture was—and still is—created to legitimize violence toward people of color. We tend to think of lynch culture as that which arises out of the brutality and murder of organizations like the Ku Klux Klan and the Proud Boys. Often, we imagine lynch culture as being located in the past. But lynch culture is any act that upholds a system to make it easier to punish Indigenous, Black, and people of color (IBPOC) and other marginalized groups rather than to create and sustain a culture of justice. This extension of whiteness emerges from institutions and structures that uphold white supremacy. In lynch culture, victims are blamed, murderers are turned into heroes, violence is normalized, crimes are trivialized, and hate speech—including among leaders—is made routine.[1]

In 1947, Willie Earle, a twenty-four-year-old African American man, was being held in the Pickens County Jail in South Carolina on charges of assaulting a white taxicab driver. A mob of white men seized Mr. Earle from the jail, took him to a deserted country road near Greenville, brutally beat him with guns and knives, and then shot him to death. After they were arrested, twenty-six of the thirty-one defendants admitted participation in Mr. Earle's death. Judge J. Robert Martin warned that he would "not allow racial issues to be injected in this case."[2] The defense did not present any witnesses or evidence to rebut the confessions and instead blamed "northern interference" for bringing the case to trial at all. The all-white jury acquitted the defendants of all charges.[3] This is lynch culture.

In 2020, twenty-five-year-old Ahmaud Arbery was hunted and executed by white supremacists while jogging in his neighborhood in Georgia. The perpetrators included Gregory McMichael, a retired police officer who had worked for the district attorney's office and had once investigated Arbery. Following Arbery's murder, three district attorneys refused to make arrests for seventy-four days before the case exploded on social media and forced a grand jury and the Georgia Bureau of Investigation to take on the case.[4] This is lynch culture.

In 2016, in Canada, Colten Boushie was a twenty-two-year-old Indigenous man from Cree Red Pheasant First Nation who was shot in the back of his head at point-blank range by Gerald Stanley, who was acquitted after an investigation and trial that included several violations, including a flawed police inquiry, the lack of a forensic analysis, racist police communications, biased media commentary, and an all-white jury. The RCMP, Canada's national police, were also admonished for making the death notification to Boushie's family by approaching the home with long guns drawn and using tactical lights. Following the acquittal, there were protests across Canada, statements by politicians, and headlines like "Our reaction to injustice for Colten Boushie is a reflection of our soul as individuals and Canadians."[5] Because potential Indigenous jurors were rejected without reason, the federal government passed Bill C-75—later approved as constitutional by the Supreme Court—that eliminated peremptory challenges during jury selection. But the injustice was already built into the system. This is lynch culture.

In 2022, the dismissal of charges against Kyle Rittenhouse for shooting two Black Lives Matter protesters—following Jacob Blake being shot by police officer Rusten Sheskey—is an example of how a white supremacist delusion props up the use of violence for lynch culture's aims. The narrative of Rittenhouse's right to bear arms under the pretense of protecting property (or white bodies) lies at the root of laws that protect gun use as well as an extremist gun culture that embraces vigilantism. No longer just a legal tangle, gun laws have become an extension for militia groups to manipulate the blurred line between law enforcement and civilians to advance normalizing street violence. And as the Rittenhouse decision and other self-defense cases have proven, the American judicial system does not treat all self-defense equally. In the wake of the George Floyd murder—a police spectacle lynching by Officer Derek Chauvin—white persons like Rittenhouse used a new kind of hybrid authority granted by the legal system to enact street terror, shaped by violence masquerading as political identity.[6] White militants shelter and lionize those enacting vigilante violence, and that belief system is further politicized by people in power seeking to enlist mostly white men as a force against experiences perceived as "other," or nonwhite lives.[7] This is lynch culture.

To live inside lynch culture is to find lynch culture hidden from view. Some of us breathe its polluted air without knowing the damage to our individual and collective bodies. Some misunderstand the benefits received, the harm that marginalized people suffer. These invisible bonds obscure and conceal injustice as a strategy for maintaining comfort, status, and power. White people tend to think of lynch culture as something that happens *out there*, not in our communities, families, schools, churches, businesses, government, and nations.

Lynch culture has shown up in nearly all countries, including those where social media has become a powerful tool for the perpetuation of hatred of the other. Lynch culture can be seen in President Donald Trump's incendiary rhetoric. Trump fanned the flames of hate during his first four years in office, when he urged violent white nationalists to "stand back and stand by" when their appearance at Black Lives Matter protests was questioned.[8]

Likewise, urging a purge of Muslims from India, the founder-president of Bajrang Dal, the youth wing of the Hindu nationalist organization, Vishna Hindu Parishad (VHP), and speaking on the Alwar lynching of 2018, blamed the victims: "People from the Muslim community should abstain from touching cows and provoking aggressive Hindus."

The most common forms of lynch culture arise not in murderers or leaders whom we can point to and find hatred writ large. They're at our family dinner table, in our meeting rooms, and around the grill at the neighborhood cookout. Acts of terror toward Black people continue to happen because of a legacy of violence that our nation is unwilling to confront. In present-day America, that legacy shows up as learned whiteness, a society that positions everyone by their race, and a process of racialization that can present as regard or marginalization, and sometimes as what Noel Ignatiev calls *race traitors*, those white people who disrupt white conformity. Our inheritance is composed of the way race operates in the social institutions and structures that have influenced our lives.[9]

Lynch is a term for punishment without trial and goes back to the American Revolution, when Charles Lynch imprisoned loyalists to the Crown without having the legal jurisdiction to do so and then asked his friends in the early Congress to cover him for his indiscretions. For generations, white people have gathered to witness lynchings. Most lynchings, about 70 percent, are of Black people. Some white people were lynched for helping Black people or for being antilynching. Immigrants from Mexico, China, Australia, and other countries were also lynched.[10] Even in 1936, at the time of the so-called last public execution in America, the segregation of the races in neighborhoods, businesses, schools, marriage, and finance was not enough separation for white society. The ultimate form of power became the drama whereby white folks needed to play the role of spectator to the punishment of Black people.

The first African people intended for enslavement landed in the Chesapeake in 1619, and soon after, punishments and executions became part of Slave Codes, those regulatory statutes conducted under colonial and then state authority. Virginia was the first mainland colony to adopt Slave Codes. Kentucky formed the far-western frontier of Virginia and inherited its long history of slavery.[11]

Philosopher George Yancy says that the "Black body has been confiscated to serve the needs of whiteness. . . . Black bodies must be *stopped*, frisked, imprisoned, suffocated, shot dead in the streets and left to rot in the hot sun, or lynched and left swinging like some strange fruit. For the assumption is that they are always already about to do something wrong."[12] Enforcement onto the bodies of Black people came from a long tradition in Kentucky. The caste that dominated central and western Kentucky in its early history was formed from a southern aristocracy of enslavers who, following a decrease in tobacco production, sold enslaved Africans to the Deep South, making profits through the agricultural labor needed for cotton and receiving rewards for enslaved people who were executed or harmed.[13] In this period, fifty-one slaves were executed in Kentucky.[14]

Executions conducted by enslavers on those bodies they considered property were designated as private and are mostly silent in the research record.[15] In the antebellum period, Kentucky executed the third-highest number of enslaved people living in the Upper South region. Lynchings in Kentucky were more likely to occur following this period, in counties with heavy concentrations of Black residents, and this pattern is consistent with trends that prevailed historically throughout most southern states.[16] White enslavers punished Black men who raped Black women, but there were no punishments for white men who raped Black women, "as there was simply no legal apparatus in place to criminally charge the offender with a crime."[17]

The first public hanging in Kentucky was ordered by law in 1854, for Curtis Richardson, an Indigenous man who was convicted of murdering William Lanifer in Owensboro, Kentucky. Richardson was transported from the county jail to the scaffold in the back of a wagon, where he sat on his own coffin. Though extralegal mob murder remained the primary form of lynching in Kentucky, "the entire legal system upheld white violence by refusing to apprehend, charge, and convict white offenders of blacks."[18] There has been a long tradition of authorities enacting social codes to reinforce the white power to kill without recourse.

By 1908, fourteen lynchings happened in Kentucky, including four at Russellville, Kentucky, and seven in Birmingham, Kentucky. These racial killings involved the Night Riders, a group of tobacco farmers who initially formed to resist agricultural monopolies, but then turned into anti-Black armed vigilantes.

Rufus Browder was a tenant farmer who acted in self-defense when he killed a white Night Rider in a shoot-out. Browder was sent to prison to die, and four other men who were lynched—John Boyer, Joe Riley, and brothers Virgil Jones and John Jones—were members of the True Reformers lodge, a mutual aid society for Black people, who were organizing to pay for a lawyer for Browder. A note was posted to one of their bodies—"Let this be a warning to you n——s to leave white people alone or you will go the same way. Your lodges and halls better shut up and quit."[19] The point was access to power and wealth, and white vigilantes would find their brutal methods often supported by the courts.

In Birmingham, Kentucky, 150 Night Riders raided Black homes in the town, shooting 7, whipping 5, and "warning all the other negroes to leave under penalty of death," the *Louisville Courier-Journal* reported the next day. Four months later the *Courier-Journal* wrote: "White men anxious to get an opportunity to buy the property of negroes at low prices promoted the raids to drive negroes out of the State." Most did leave. By 1937, the town was flooded to create the recreational haven Kentucky Lake, where today 98 percent of the residents are white.[20]

Black activists and abolitionists had not only opposed slavery but also confronted the savagery of legal and extralegal lynchings. Since the late nineteenth century, Black educators including Ida B. Wells, Frederick Douglass, and John Mitchell were active in collecting data to determine that alleged violations of white women by Black men were baseless. It was Ida B. Wells in 1892 who, as a journalist, went to the sites of lynchings and offered statistics to demonstrate that this terrorized violence was happening not due to Black men raping white women but because of other societal factors, like consensual relationships between them. White women didn't need their femininity protected. Lynching was about the perceived threat to white men of social and economic gains of Black people.

There were other movements, interracial in their membership, who wanted race reform. Organizing since 1919, the Commission on Interracial Cooperation (CIC) was a significant reform organization in the South. The CIC was not fundamentally a Black civil rights organization but had the participation of white ministers, academics, and business people. The organization worked to oppose lynching, mob violence, and peonage and to educate white southerners about racism.

One of its outgrowths, the Association of Southern Women for the Prevention of Lynching (ASWPL), was formed in 1930—when lynchings were at an all-time high—by Jessie Daniel Ames, an advocate for racial justice and feminism. The Christian organization included some eight hundred local, interracial committees that worked to oppose lynching, mob violence, and peonage and to educate white southerners concerning the worst aspects of racial abuse. Ames asked women to sign antilynching pledges, committing themselves to not only eradicating this socially acceptable tool of terror but also subversively influencing the violent white men in their families and communities.[21] Southern churchwomen like Ames recognized "unless this idea of chivalry could be destroyed, lynchers would continue to use the name of women as an excuse for their crimes."[22]

The ASWPL discovered that lynchings tended to happen when Black entrepreneurs or communities were said to be too powerful, leading white people to organize mob violence against Black businesses, farmers, and community organizations. During and after Reconstruction, lynching was said to occur because of "the presumed norms of a white-male dominated racial-gender hierarchy that claimed to protect and defend the sexual purity of white womanhood." But it was economic competition from successful Black businessmen that was "the catalyst to hyper-anxiety surrounding interracial sex between white women and black men."[23]

As early as 1916, the National Association for the Advancement of Colored People (NAACP) had organized through the principle that American racism was national and not able to be corrected merely through altering the community at the local level. Moreover, they understood that racial terror was supported at the highest levels, and even legislators had to be educated away from the mob violence and injustice they had supported.[24] The NAACP wanted to collect and present data on lynching as well as help create the political will to pass an antilynching bill in the House, which it achieved by 1922; however, the bill was not passed into law because of multiple filibusters by white supremacist southern Democrats in the Senate, from 1922 through 1950, thwarting any federal legislation.

From the NAACP's earliest days, *The Crisis*, a news magazine edited by Black scholar and activist W. E. B. Du Bois, became the most influential race publication in the country's history. By the 1930s, and largely due to NAACP efforts, media coverage and public opinion were against lynching, even in the southern regions. Racial terror was seen as damaging to the South's economic prospects. When national lynching rates declined markedly in the 1930s, NAACP executive secretary Walter White attributed the trend to these shifts in the public discourse and to antilynching activism as well as to the Great Migration.[25]

Although Eleanor Roosevelt was a strong supporter of antilynching legislation, President Franklin D. Roosevelt feared alienating southern voters and never considered supporting the bills. It was not until December 2018 that the Senate passed a federal antilynching bill, after at least 240 failed attempts. Of the import of the civil rights movement, Robert Zangrando says, "Lynching became the wedge by which the NAACP insinuated itself into the public conscience among philanthropists . . . and opened lines of communication with other liberal-reformist groups that eventually joined it in a mid-century, civil rights coalition of unprecedented proportions."[26]

Partly due to interest from sociologists and psychologists, lynching began to be studied more in the twentieth century, bringing attention and scientific information to what had been concealed by the South's traditions and beliefs. Professor of history at the University of North Carolina at Chapel Hill, W. Fitzhugh Brundage conducted a careful analysis of the theories behind lynch culture in *Under Sentence of Death: Lynching in the South.* From Robert Park's theory of collective behavior, which "encouraged scholars to view participants in collective violence as disproportionally deviant and isolated . . . [and] poorly integrated into the larger society," to southern sociologists who asserted that lynch violence went along with "a rural culture corrupted by drunkenness, irreligion, illiteracy, poverty, and excessive license" (think J. D. Vance's theories of poor white folks in *Hillbilly Elegy*) to Freudian theories of white people projecting their forbidden fantasies onto Black people, mob-motivated violence has been well studied but little reckoned with by white Americans.[27]

But the mob isn't required if the state can be mobilized to enact racial terror through its laws, customs, and procedures. By the 1920s, when northern states and most southern states moved to private executions, killing by electric shock was considered to be both professional and modern. Several southern states moved to lethal injection, lethal gas, and firing squad, ruling that the use of the electric chair violated their state constitutional prohibitions against cruel and unusual punishment.[28] Death by execution was, and still is, thought of by many states as humane. Sixty percent of Americans are in favor of the death penalty, and execution is still legal in twenty-five states.[29]

In 2021, almost 2,500 people were on death row, waiting to be injected, electrocuted, hanged, gassed, or shot.[30] Those awaiting their deaths are no different from those condemned to die in the past: they're mostly poor, over half are racialized people, and the overwhelming majority were sentenced to death for crimes against white victims. Forty-one percent of those are Black, although Black people represent just 13.7 percent of the population according to the US Census of 2024.[31] While lynching declined in the twentieth century because of changes to segregation and disfranchisement policies (as well as the shaming of white supremacists by national and international press) lynch culture remained. State executioners replaced lynch mobs in carrying out the will of the white people in power.[32]

Stephen B. Bright, president and senior counsel of Southern Center for Human Rights, says, "The death penalty is a direct descendant of lynching and other forms of racial violence and racial oppression in

America. . . . The process of 'legal lynching' was so successful that in the 1930s, two-thirds of those executed were black."[33] By the time anti-lynching legislation was introduced in 1935, to maintain their claims to supremacy, white southerners had to disavow lynching, but legal lynching and other forms of racist capital punishment took its place. Bryan Stevenson of the Equal Justice Initiative (EJI) calls the death penalty the "stepchild of lynching."[34]

In the *British Journal of Political Science,* James W. Clarke says that the twentieth century marked a time when "there was no longer any need for lynching, Southern leaders insisted; almost the same degree of control and intimidation could still be exerted over Blacks with capital punishment. After swift and superficial trials before white judges and juries, the outcomes would never be in doubt."[35] The federal government never bothered to count the thousands of lynchings that terrorized Black communities across the country; there was no regard for keeping track of legal executions until 1930. What the state called "public executions" had the same ritual behavior and justifications as the white lynchings of Black people.

The Rainey Bethea case was a link to the South's racist past as well as its future. Historians made apparent the decline of lynching in southern states, partly based on the increased use of capital punishment imposed by court order following (often accelerated) trials. The death penalty's origins are of course found in the legacy of lynching, for public executions to mollify the mob continued after the practice was legally banned.[36] The EJI's *Report on Lynching* says, "Extrajudicial mob violence operated hand-in-hand with legal execution as a means of exercising lethal social control over the Black population. Neither lynching nor 'legal executions' required reliable findings of guilt, and complicit law enforcement officers handed over prisoners to the lynch mob."[37]

Few white people reporting on Bethea's hanging, then or now, called it a "legal lynching." The story of Rainey Bethea as a criminal who was rightly convicted and suffered a just punishment has been wrapped up in the American belief in due process protections. Within this race-neutral narrative of the death penalty, many white people remain convinced that courts are impartial to people of color. The Pew Research Center reports that "white Democrats and white Republicans have vastly different views of how black people are treated by police and the wider justice system.

Overwhelming majorities of white Democrats say black people are treated less fairly than whites by the police (88%) and the criminal justice system (86%), according to the 2019 poll. About four-in-ten white Republicans agree (43% and 39%, respectively)."[38]

Throughout our nation's history, we have continued to be certain that there's a distinction between the extralegal violence of lynching and the legal violence of capital punishment. The idea and the act of lynching is not so far from many of today's forms of capital punishment that—when focused on Black men—become a lynching under the pretense of the law. According to Bright, "The death penalty is a direct descendant of lynching and other forms of racial violence and racial oppression in America."[39] Slave patrols, Black Codes, bounty hunters, militia groups, and the convict lease system were precursors to a racist criminal justice system and its biases of racial profiling, excessive police force, and lawmakers being complicit in attacks by white mobs on Black lives and property.[40]

Bethea's death surely could have occurred at the hands of a lynch mob. But in this turn to capital punishment, the Commonwealth of Kentucky took on the role of the mob, killing Bethea as part of the symbols, rituals, and beliefs of lynch culture—the building of the gallows, the necktie parties, the hatted officials, the sense of righteousness. Lischia Edwards was a victim of rape, and Rainey Bethea was a victim of state violence. But he was also a victim of lynch culture that defined his body as a terror that might weaken the power of both whiteness and patriarchal rule.

Kentucky had long been engaged in a narrative of racial difference—the belief that Black people were inferior—to justify enslavement. That idea—and the systems and policies that enshrined those notions for generations—survived the formal abolition of slavery and Jim Crow while evolving to include the idea that Black people are dangerous criminals. Even today, Black men are six times more likely to be incarcerated as white men.

Breonna Taylor was a Black woman who was perceived as dangerous. Taylor was a twenty-six-year-old EMT in Louisville, Kentucky, who worked on the front lines during the early days of the COVID-19 epidemic and was attacked and murdered by those inside the criminal justice system. Just after midnight on March 13, 2020, plainclothes Louisville Metro Police Department officers Myles Cosgrove, Brett

Hankison, and Sergeant Jonathan Mattingly used a battering ram to force open her apartment door. Police say they were then met with a gunshot that injured Mattingly in the thigh. The three officers blindly returned fire with more than twenty bullets. Bullets entered other apartments, including a home with a five-year-old child. Five bullets fatally struck Breonna Taylor's body. Officers called an ambulance back to the scene and gave aid to their colleague, while Taylor, who was still alive, was not given any medical attention.[41] Taylor's boyfriend, Kenneth Walker, a licensed gun owner with no criminal record, called 911 to tearfully plead for help.

"Somebody kicked in the door, shot my girlfriend," Walker said to the dispatcher.

Tamika Palmer, Taylor's mother, said, "Kenny calls me in the middle of the night and says, *Somebody kicked in the door and shot Breonna.*"

Palmer went to Breonna Taylor's apartment that night, where the police questioned her, asking her whether she knew someone who wanted to hurt her daughter. Months later, Palmer said of the officers, "But you did it. Why couldn't you have just told me that the police did this? You asked me if somebody wanted to hurt *them.*"[42]

The day of Taylor's murder, the *Louisville Courier-Journal* ran the headline, "LMPD Officer Shot, Woman Killed during Drug Investigation off St. Andrews Church Road." There was little else to indicate that this death was unlike any other in a city where 65 percent of the killings were unsolved and there remained long-standing problems with the police. The year of Breonna Taylor's murder, Louisville's homicide record nearly doubled.

By the end of May, hundreds of protesters were on the streets in Louisville.[43] That month, prompted by the wave of protests against police brutality in the wake of the deaths of George Floyd and Breonna Taylor, a group of sixty-six United Nations human rights monitors issued a devastating critique of modern-day "racial terror" lynchings in the US, calling out state-sponsored police violence against Black Americans and making a link between police killings of unarmed Black men with the spate of thousands of racial lynchings that terrorized Black communities in the era of segregation.[44]

The *New York Times*, after an investigation of the video and other evidence at the scene, found that "the only support for a grand jury's conclusion that the officers had announced themselves before bursting into Ms. Taylor's apartment—beyond the assertions of the officers themselves—was the account of a single witness who had given inconsistent statements."[45] Throughout the summer, Taylor's family and protesters continued to show up in public to demand that Attorney General Cameron release the transcripts from the grand jury proceedings.[46]

In 2021, following the Breonna Taylor protests, the Kentucky Senate proposed a bill to make insulting a police officer a crime, its language sounding like an extension of the Black Codes: For anyone who "accosts, insults, taunts, or challenges a law enforcement officer using abusive, indecent, profane, or vulgar language used as instruments of assault and that serves no legitimate purpose, or by gestures or other physical contact, all of which would have a direct tendency to provoke a violent response from the perspective of a reasonable and prudent law enforcement officer." The bill outlaws people setting up camp on government property. Resisting arrest is proposed as a Class A misdemeanor "unless committed during the course of a riot, in which case it is a Class D felony."[47] The bill was aimed at the peaceful community protesters in the wake of Taylor's murder and originally included an element aimed at refusing to *defund the police*—a slogan and philosophy upheld by the Black Visions Collective, the Black Lives Matter movement, and many other Black-led organizations.

Over two years later, the Justice Department charged four police officers with federal civil rights violations, including lying to obtain a search warrant for Taylor's apartment. Justice Department investigators filed "a damning report" on the Louisville Metro Police, which "detailed a pattern of serious abuses, including excessive force; searches based on no-knock warrants; car stops, detentions and harassment of people during street sweeps; and broad patterns of discrimination against Black people and people with behavioral health problems."[48]

To understand possibilities beyond this long and very American history of white people implementing laws to punish Black people, one need only look to Black scholarship through every era. *Black Reconstruction in America* was first published the year before Bethea's arrest. In this work, W. E. B. DuBois wrote about "abolition-democracy," which advocated for the removal of institutions that were rooted in repressive practices, including prisons, convict leasing, and white police forces. Today, the EJI is foremost in developing scholarship and education in recognizing how historically, racial disparities lead to presumption of guilt. The EJI says that during "the decades of racial terror lynchings that followed enslavement, white people defended the torture and murder of Black people as necessary to protect their property, families, and way of life from Black 'criminals.'"

In a 2004 study, "Seeing Black: Race, Crime and Visual Processing," researchers learned that the "paradigmatic understanding of the automatic stereotyping process . . . is that the mere presence of a person can lead one to think about the concepts with which that person's social group has become associated. The mere presence of a Black man, for instance, can trigger thoughts that he is violent and criminal."[49] This has always been the intention of lynch culture, and it works just as successfully today as it did at the time of the legal lynching of Rainey Bethea.

Merely thinking about Black people can lead white people and others to evaluate ambiguous behavior as aggressive and to miscategorize harmless objects as weapons, triggering thoughts of crime. The image that the Owensboro and other newspapers placed on Rainey Bethea went far further and reinforced in headlines and images a vision of dangerous Black male criminality.[50] Still, lynch culture exists not just because of individual thinking and behavior but also because of the structural systems that support the punishment of Black people.

In the legal lynchings of the twentieth century, justice was always impossible when the threat of the lynch mob hung over court proceedings. The state emphasized the terror by making the hanging of Bethea *legal*, its narrative aligned with the same dynamics that represented the horrors of Reconstruction. Throughout the South, it was the specter of violated white women that set off horrific lynching spectacles. At the center of the Bethea execution, there were two figures—a white woman victim whose honor and purity were amplified through her widowhood and a white woman sheriff (also a widow) who would be compelled to uphold justice by pulling the lever. This case drew national media coverage also because of its gender politics—overseeing the execution was the forty-four-year-old sheriff of Daviess County, Florence Thompson. Many in America were vocal about whether a woman should be assigned such a gruesome task. Gender politics may have played a larger part in drawing attention to the Bethea hanging. Historically, not only did white women play essential roles as accusers and witnesses, but also their authority was limited to being used in well-defined capacities. Historian Carrie Pitzulo says, "The murders of black men were deliberately public in order to send a message not only to the African American community, but also to southern whites—male and female—as well. White men used white women's sexuality as a pawn of racial oppression in order to terrorize black communities for the imagined sexual crimes of black men. As a result, mob violence served both white supremacy and patriarchy."[51]

Institutional leaders molding modern lynch culture have remained condescending to women, in an attempt to limit their authority. In Kentucky's history, no woman has been elected to represent Kentucky in the United States Senate. Women of color have yet to be elected to Congress in Kentucky.[52]

While Ida B. Wells was first in naming lynching's gendered dynamics, it wasn't until the civil rights movement that Black activists, and later psychologists and sociologists, began to widely speak of the institutions that maintained white power through patriarchal means. White Southerners maintained the economic exploitation and political dominance they had during slavery, and white men refused to relinquish their freedom to violate Black women with impunity, according to the EJI's "Sexual Violence Targeting Black Women."

Historian Amy Louise Hood says, "The figure of the black rapist struck at the heart of the matter—that black autonomy not only diminished white men's authority over African Americans but threatened their dominion over their own households and women. Lynching was thus more than a white prerogative; it was a patriarchal duty through which white men restored their masculine dominance."[53] Meanwhile, throughout American history, Black women victims have rarely had their rapists tried and convicted in court. Even today, Black women, Black girls, and nonbinary people are seldom seen as victims.[54]

The white woman (then and now) is encouraged to play the victim (and sometimes a rescuer), innocent of her history. This is to say not that violent trauma doesn't affect white women but that white women identify with the role of the victim and are encouraged by white culture to do so. The more that we dig into this role, rallying supporters who pity or champion us, the weaker we become, for dramatizing under a pretense of innocence does not lead to empowerment. The white woman is also a perpetrator, and this is rarely acknowledged in lynch culture so that the aggressive aspects of our selves might never be seen and so that white women remain "pure." In the heteronormative, white supremacist patriarchy, purity is considered a religious as well as a bodily virtue. White women were drawn as the "fairer sex," forever tied to domesticity and sexual purity. To uphold the strange notion of a white race, they seemingly required well-defined gender roles, codes of conduct, and protection for their reproductive responsibilities. White men might utilize their power, as they did with Rainey Bethea, under the guise of being chivalrous toward the white woman's virtue (in this case, both the victim of the crime and the sheriff as the upholder of justice were necessary objects of their "loyalty"). White women learned to weaponize this racial anxiety, relying on white men and the institutions they controlled to inflict damage upon people of color. In lynch culture, this is played out in many violent ways, some obvious, and others more subtle.

The United Daughters of the Confederacy (UDC) are one example of a white woman–led systemic force that taught generations of southern children to uphold the Lost Cause as the only acceptable version of history. Through their official historians like Mildred Lewis Rutherford, the UDC created textbooks informed by southern authors who wrote state's histories that referred to the "War Between the States" rather than the American Civil War, and as Donald Yacavone, author of *Teaching White Supremacy: America's Democratic Ideal and the Forging of Our National Identity*, says, they "relentlessly demeaned African Americans and refused to include real images of them, preferring imaginary ones. By establishing a common national understanding of the characters of African Americans, textbooks created an illusory version of the past that served the separate and mutual interests of Northern and Southern whites alike."[55] White women were central in having white supremacist ideals inserted into textbooks to reject notions of sociocultural and political equality for Black Americans. Future generations of children would perceive the tenets of white supremacy as a governing principle of America.

Today's white women show up in yoga culture, in the white healing industry, on white nonprofit boards, as white social justice activists, and as white social media influencers, and these roles invest heavily in the denial of the power of collective perpetration. One small but widely experienced example lies in the white loathing of body fat and obsession with thin ideals, where it's culturally acceptable for white women to remain in willful denial of the harm they inflict on women of color. According to author and historian Sabrina Strings, "two critical historical developments contributed to a fetish for svelteness and a phobia about fatness: the rise of the transatlantic slave trade and the spread of Protestantism. Racial scientific rhetoric about slavery linked fatness to 'greedy' Africans. And religious discourse suggested that overeating was ungodly."[56] Fatness was stigmatized by the medical establishment only after class and race ideologies had been established, and "the phobia about fatness and the preference for thinness have not principally or historically, been about health. Instead, they have been one way the body has been used to craft and legitimate race, sex, and class hierarchies. . . . The fear of the imagined 'fat black woman' was created by racial and religious ideologies that have been used to both degrade black women *and* discipline white women."[57]

Today, this denigration of Black women continues in the systemic bias of the medical and healing industries. Elites use diet culture, including the denial of food, to prove their superiority and stance at the top of the hierarchy. The medical system and its technologies reinforce that bias through punishment and maltreatment of those bodies they consider "other," resulting in myriad deaths from poor practices and neglect. Bodily control, whether emphasized through the cultures of food, health, or ascetic practices, is seen by white women as separate from the potential for harm. But there's tremendous power that resides in regulating bodies of individuals, as well as those codes that mandate control over women's, trans, and Black bodies embedded in institutions, such as those related to reproductive health, equality, and inclusion.[58] Social media has only amplified the spaces where fatness is viewed as a coarse and greedy impulse tied to the lower classes. In this way, a body of size can be seen as a physical state arising from poor choices, not as white fear tied to the desire to regulate other bodies.

To be human is to be an offender. But there are excesses that people with privilege allow themselves based on habituated and leveraged responses. Built inside a dominator culture that values hierarchy and control over love and relationship is investment in identifying solely as a victim or rescuer, protective responses that offer either pity or valor, a taking or a giving of grace. The function of protection here is to limit authentic response. White women limit awareness of responsibility for harm and also limit the ways it's possible to respond, a disempowered position. Lynch culture is supported by mechanisms that create permission to perpetrate harm, cruelty, and terror, and a body reaction or a cultural permission can determine that violence against Black bodies is acceptable.[59]

In the retelling of the Bethea story, the criminality of Black men remains the central focus, a history rarely questioned by white-dominant media and gatekeepers. In 2011, at the time of the seventy-fifth anniversary of the Bethea hanging, as well as in the weeks prior to the 2001 Timothy McVeigh execution—witnessed by journalists, lawyers, government officials, survivors, and victims' relatives—media stories were written that identified the horrors of the 1936 public hanging in Owensboro, but there was little questioning of the crime or the societal system that created this punishment for Bethea. When there was examination, as in Ryan's book on the Bethea trial, the conclusion remained that the trial had been fair and that justice had been served.

Black legal experts, historians, and educators told a different story. Black Americans were able to identify that the Depression, and whites' economic frustration, was a factor in the escalation of lynchings in the South and that these lynchings happened when the white individuals under attack had more power. Likewise, lack of access to power played a significant part in those accused, including severe punishment for those who were former criminals, wanted on other charges, and without status or kinship networks in the community.[60] Rainey Bethea was an orphan with one sister in South Carolina, and limited relationships. He was, as author Edward Ayers writes of those lynched in *Vengeance and Justice*, one of the "blacks with no white to vouch for them, blacks with no reputation in the neighborhood, blacks without even other blacks to aid them."[61] Bethea had been made into a criminal by a white society that, even prior to the charges for the crimes against Edwards, refused him grace for his limited circumstances and his rehabilitation. Not only the alleged crime, but also an unjust trial, a complicit community, and Bethea's lack of resources to understand his situation made this legal lynching possible.

Most white institutions—including the media, academia, educational system, legal system, and government—were morally if not legally wrong in relationship to Bethea. Perry Ryan, the assistant attorney general for Kentucky from 1988 to 2022, is often referenced by national news media as a definitive source for the history of the hanging of Bethea.

Ryan has insisted he was the bearer of "a fair and accurate picture of the facts." Indeed, he has made a careful study of the newspaper reports, court documents, and private letters of this last public execution in America. But this version of Bethea's story sees this Kentucky as an ordered place, without the vigilante justice or bigotry that would treat a Black man differently from a white one. Interviewed as an expert by national media like NPR, the History Channel, and the *New York Times*, Ryan asserted that Bethea's crime was ably proven and that the young man was fairly treated by the law.

But he isn't the only one insisting that lynch culture wasn't a factor. In the eight decades since Bethea's hanging, through most of the stories about the last public execution in America, white historians and journalists didn't talk about Rainey Bethea as a real person. He was a criminal, an indigent defendant, a phantom of a Black man. Everything reported on him was in relationship to upholding the innocence of whiteness—stories of the brutal rape of a beloved white woman, stories of a good, white woman sheriff defending the rights of the white woman victim, stories of white police officers taking truthful confession after confession from a sometimes-drunk man, stories of the calm, white mob who witnessed the trial. In the trial of Bethea, white people, and mostly those in positions of legal authority, reported on the confessions that Bethea made. But some of these stretch the limits of credulity.

At the trial, Birkhead questioned Rollie Bristow, a police officer with just over a year on the force. Birkhead brought attention to the bloodstains on Bethea, reportedly noticed by Bristow, who took Bethea's first confession and his underwear from him, but not the pants that he wore.

"Did he make any statement about where he got the blood?" Birkhead asked.

"He said he got the blood when he assaulted Mrs. Edwards," Bristow answered, using legal language rather than reporting Bethea's words. When asked why Bristow didn't also take the pants that Bethea wore on the day of the arrest—pants that apparently also had bloodstains on them—the officer said that he "didn't have any other trousers." Bethea wore these same pants to the trial. No journalist or lawyer or witness in the room reports seeing the "bloodstained" clothing on Bethea in the courtroom.

This is how Ryan reports the assault of Lischia Edwards, using the narrative techniques of imaginative details and fictionalized sequencing of events and providing an altered point of view to represent Bethea's emotions and intentions in an attempt to dramatically tie together several pieces of evidence:

> To enter the house, he removed a loose screen from the window, and stepped on the top of a sewing machine draped with a cloth cover and left a dirty footprint on the cover. Mrs. Edwards was asleep in a bed only a few feet from the window. At some point, Mrs. Edwards awakened, but before she could cry for help, Bethea grabbed her throat and strangled her mercilessly, leaving bruises around her throat. Pervertedly [*sic*] enjoying the violent control over his victim, he raised her gown above her waist and brutally raped the widow, causing lacerations within her body. Blood flowed onto her bed and covered his own sexual organs.

These words are being written sixty years after the sexual assault and murder, and they act to concretize the impression of Rainey Bethea, to write him into history as a violent, psychopathic killer. To imagine him merciless—even after he has taken his punishment, even after his last rites—seems part of the fear in lynch culture that white society must control the symbolic interpretation of historical events and that by holding fast to these old racist forms, white people can shape events to make sense of the present and retain dominance. In other words, if this is a *public execution* and not a *legal lynching*, then white people were only responsible for enacting a proper punishment, and there is no ancestral or structural racism that they must remedy.

Ryan interviewed two dozen white people who were at the hanging and says, "I was aware that my book would have been 'sexier' if I had portrayed the 1936 hanging crowd to have been unruly and disrespectful" but that "none of them could remember any disrespectful acts."[62]

A portrayal of *respectful* white people doesn't include Ryan's interview with Bethea's lawyer Warren Wilson, who, decades later, when asked about Bethea's motivation for the rape, reportedly told Ryan, "Maybe Bethea was just horny"[63]—a statement denigrating women in its dismissal of the crime of violence as well as assigning a predatory sexuality to Black men, a bias for which Black people have been historically killed by white people.

A *respectful* Owensboro portrayal certainly doesn't cover Father Lammers, who visited Bethea for weeks and then baptized and offered communion and death rites to the orphan. Lammers would go on to become the director of Catholic Charities from 1939 to 1976 as well as a resident chaplain of St. Thomas–St. Vincent Home, an orphanage near Louisville, where he was accused in thirty-two lawsuits for child sexual abuse. Most of the victims lived as children at the orphanage he managed.

Though some might now ask for verifications of Bethea's innocence, we can't rely on the evidence in the Bethea case to find this certainty. The police records of the search, confessions, and crime scene images and objects were likely damaged in the old Owensboro jail. The Great Flood of the Ohio River in 1937, occurring just six months after Bethea's arrest and cresting at sixty feet near Owensboro, may have destroyed the evidence.[64] Sources about the crime and the hanging come from descriptions in white newspapers as well as some oral interviews with Owensboro townspeople. After Bethea had been sentenced to hang, there were Black voices to add to the narrative. The *Chicago Defender*, the NAACP, and others covered various aspects of the trial, the habeas corpus hearing, and the hanging. But what played out during this coverage, and indeed from descendants of those at the hanging, was a series of claims by white people who fictionally or in fact placed themselves and their views at the center of the story.

From the habeas corpus trial and the appeal, we know that Bethea and his lawyers said that officers intimidated him. Bethea confessed and later recanted. He'd been traumatized by the early deaths of his parents and was a man alone in a mostly white town. Bethea had on many occasions been found drunk, and his exchanges with the law portray the kind of confusion that comes with lack of sobriety. When he'd been in prison in his early twenties, he followed through on parole requests and other actions that suggested he was organized. Until he was accused of the crimes against Edwards, Bethea received work and places to stay from his white employers. Rather than recognize the influence of a mob threatening a horrific murder, police, prosecutors, and ultimately a white jury believed that Bethea's confessions reflected his character. Confirmation bias—the tendency to interpret new evidence as confirmation of one's existing beliefs or theories—encouraged white investigators to focus on what they already knew about Rainey Bethea.[65] They wanted a Black criminal, one with ties to Edwards and a prison record. And in what made the case particularly cruel, they wanted a trial. When the court accepts a guilty plea, the trial judge can determine the sentence. There was no reason to hold a full trial. It was Herman Birkhead, the attorney for the commonwealth, who, along with Judge Wilson, created this opportunity. If murder had been charged, and Bethea found guilty, he would have been electrocuted at Eddyville Prison. Birkhead wanted an indictment against Bethea only for the crime of rape, and with this maneuver, private punishment never occurred.

Bethea never had a chance to be exonerated.[66] At the trial, there was no defense. There was only the death penalty waiting four and a half minutes after the attorney for the commonwealth made his final statement.

Ryan, who, as of this writing, still works for Kentucky's Office of the Attorney General, says,

> As a prosecutor in 2021, I think the evidence against Bethea was compelling. The ring and fingerprinting evidence weren't as important as one of the interviews he did with the police where he told them where the [Edwards's] jewels were . . . and the police went there and found them. In modern times we would call that *guilty knowledge.* He had information about the case that he shouldn't have had, but for the fact that he participated. The other thing that's compelling is that he had blood in his underwear, that apparently had been acquired during the rape. The body was examined by an Owensboro physician . . . and the doctor stated that this woman was seventy, she had not been sexually active, and her private area was injured. So, the fact that they found blood on Bethea is compelling.

There is so much injustice in the trial of Rainey Bethea that I imagine that prejudice could have extended to building *guilty knowledge* too, that the police could have planted the bloodstains, as well as lied about Bethea being the one who identified the location of the jewels. And this is the problem with a system saturated in injustice—what's happened in a racist-skewed case can't be known as fact. Without a just trial, there can't be conclusions of criminality. Every truth bends with the harm that whiteness creates.

This public execution was about more than simply punishing a violator of the law. Even if Bethea committed these crimes, a hanging in the public square is far beyond what was required for punishment. The system conspired to ensure that a Black man was lynched by the very legal system that purported to protect him. Rainey Bethea's death was brought about through unjust acts of the state, and so what we think of as a sentence was instead a murder.

Sociologist Charlotte Wolf remarks on the still-present circumstance of fractured racial interactions in the Tennessee community she studied ninety years after a lynching: "Social distance has limited discussions of the lynchings between racial groups and has insured that rival constructions of reality seldom penetrate either community. This has made it easier for blacks and whites to live together."[67] But has it, really?

The lack of meaningful dialogue and even the refusal to admit the harm of lynching, both legal and extralegal, results in the upholding of a lynch culture that is tied to the persistence of whiteness. Swift, severe violence continues to be enacted upon Black people by the white community, ostensibly for the same reasons as in the past—to curtail what white people deem as "unacceptable" social behavior and to demonstrate its cost, often in horrific forms of torture, including those by officers of the law. In 1930, Arthur Raper estimated in his study of one hundred lynchings that "at least one-half of the lynchings are carried out with police officers participating, and that in nine-tenths of the others the officers either condone or wink at the mob action."[68] Today, more Black people are killed by police officers every five years than ever were lynched in America.[69]

Lynch culture remains entrenched in America because of America's carceral society, its state agents, and those who insist on punishment and who continue to weaponize books, courtrooms, schools, technology, and so on. Using systemic structures that have been built to align with white power, lynch culture's purpose is to punish Black people, Indigenous people, and people of color. The method is to orient minds toward accepting racial violence and to make white people believe that harm is found in the responsibility of a few bad actors.[70]

The *bad actors* can be anyone. They can even be Barbecue Becky or Central Park Karen, who call the cops out of ordinary discomfort and as an extension of white power and casual racism, a kind of upholding of lynch culture that white women in public places (and white men online) have been entrained to believe is their right.[71] White people have responsibility for their actions, and minimally, we ought to be looking beyond individuals to the legal-judicial, educational, medical, governmental, technological, financial, or publishing systems for where these personal acts find systemic support.

Dr. Apryl Williams, a professor at the University of Michigan and fellow at the Berkman Klein Center for Internet and Society at Harvard, says that "when anyone does anything that steps out of what is perceived by white people as normative, then they're breaking the social contract. . . . The idea that the white majority has to always be comfortable is a white supremacist idea because it really implies that white comfort is a superior need for society than anything else."[72] North America supports white normative views by police and others in the judicial system. The white person's fear of having their relative authority subsumed promotes violence in all its forms. The individual may act, but the social contract emerges from the rules and laws of the system as a whole.

For example, Black people in the South have long been inadequately defended and sentenced by all-white juries in trials as rushed as the few minutes it took to convict Rainey Bethea and order him hanged. And this injustice exists across time, in America's founding, history, and in the present moment. White society determines who is more likely to be sentenced to death, and it isn't white people. And representation in the courts is just as poor. In most communities in America, people of color are still significantly underrepresented in the jury pools from which jurors are selected.[73]

Even today, people of color have had their constitutional rights eroded in measures like the trial penalty. According to the Innocence Project, there's now a prevalence of people who, on their lawyer's recommendations and because of the promise of lesser sentences, instead of going to trial, plead guilty to crimes they did not commit.[74] John Oliver reminded us in a *Last Week Tonight* show that judges and juries are no longer deciding the fate of a defendant—prosecutors are. "Nearly 95 percent of the cases that prosecutors decide to prosecute end up with the defendant pleading guilty," explains Oliver. "No 'innocence until proven guilty'—just a prosecutor striking a deal behind closed doors." Even in the 5 percent of cases in which a defendant does decide to go to trial, there are many ways in which prosecutors can influence the trial's outcome, such as withholding evidence or manipulating jury selection—both of which can increase the probability of sending innocent people to prison for crimes they didn't commit. As Oliver points out, the National Registry of Exonerations approximates that 25 percent of wrongful conviction cases involved prosecutors hiding exculpatory evidence. Remember, this reporting is from the current era, not in 1936, when the negative attitudes toward Black people were even more likely to remain unnoticed or seem natural to white people, who were the owners of the justice system.

Likewise, people of color are more likely to be prosecuted for capital murder, sentenced to death, and executed, especially if the victim in the case is white.[75] White Kentuckians have a history of using the laws around the death penalty to oppress Black people through mob-influenced actions, including pressure for quick trials, displays of the accused and dying Black body, violence against the Black community during and following trials, and the necessity for holding racist systems like whites-only juries in place even after Supreme Court decisions have reversed them.[76]

One possibility is that white people historically maintained a belief in the legality of their system because those views held in place a structure whereby their own desire for vengeance could be directed while their power remained intact. If we believe the apprehension is just, the trial is fair, and the punishment is apt, we don't have to deal with our societal or ancestral participation in these debasing killings.[77] In the societal practice of whiteness, resentment is routinely transferred to Black people to fulfill a symbolic functioning that includes a sense of returning the society toward unity and order. "Law and order" candidates like Calvin Coolidge, Barry Goldwater, Richard Nixon (and his Southern Strategy), and Donald Trump showed that unity is based in whiteness and that order is based on a regulating uniformity that makes others pay the price for upholding a legitimate nonwhite realness.[78] The result is a lynch culture that devises a prison pipeline for Black bodies.

In a finding by the Bureau of Justice Statistics, Kentucky is notable in that only 58 percent of the 21,239 new prison admissions were because of a new conviction in court. The rest were due to probation or parole violations.[79] The state uses Black people for labor, penalizing those with criminal offenses, including those without secure lives and livelihoods. This keeps the prison pipeline open for longer sentences and free labor.

Corrections Corporation of America, one of the largest private prison companies in the country, still operates in Kentucky—even after reports of sexual abuse of women prisoners by its guards—and with the money their prisons make, this abuse comes very close to modern-day slavery.

Kentucky has long been an outlier on voting rights restoration, disenfranchising its citizens with past criminal convictions. This was even the case if Kentuckians were out of incarceration, living and working in their communities, and even if decades had passed since that conviction. It was only in 2019 that Kentucky's Governor Andy Beshear restored voting rights to some 100,000 of those with convictions in their past. Despite this gubernatorial order, Kentucky still denies the right to vote to those violent offenders who have served their time, more people with a felony conviction than thirty-nine other states.

Though rights restoration has had bipartisan support in Kentucky, racist politicians have, since Reconstruction, made criminal disenfranchisement laws part of the effort to maintain white control over access to the polls. The Voting Rights Act, signed in 1965, helped reverse the tide, but many felony disenfranchisement laws remain on the books, a relic of the past. With an interest in permanent criminalization, imprisonment, and reduced rights, Kentucky upholds a system that makes it easier to punish Black people.

Lynch culture operates well outside the justice system to legitimize violence toward Indigenous, Black, and other people of color. Even in Canada, where there has been only one documented lynching—by American vigilantes who crossed the British Columbia border in 1884, seized a fourteen- or fifteen-year-old Indigenous boy, Louie Sam, and hanged him—there's confusion about the pervasiveness of lynch culture. A lynch mob of one hundred from the border community of Nooksack accused the Stó:lō boy who was already in police custody, charged for killing shopkeeper James Bell.[80] Records indicate an American settler from then Washington Territory committed the crime and tried to place the blame on Sam. The real murderers were thought to be two white Americans who were leaders of the lynch mob—William Osterman, the Nooksack telegraph operator who took over Bell's business, and David Harkness, who at the time of Bell's murder was living with Bell's estranged wife. Neither man was ever prosecuted. But the setup was starkly familiar to anyone who knew how these mockeries of the law operated.

An American teenager had passed Sam on the Whatcom Trail and proclaimed him a criminal based on one supposedly murderous gaze—"The look on the Indian's face as he approached me, struck me with terror. I moved to the far side of the road in passing him."[81] On the basis of little evidence more than Sam's being in the same location as the crime, a local sheriff went out to call for Sam's arrest and extradition from a provincial justice of the peace. The Canadians would charge Louie Sam and keep him for a Canadian trial. But one hundred homesteaders and settlers chose instead to outfit themselves in their wives' skirts, blackening their faces and painting red lines across their eyes. The members of the Nooksack Vigilance Committee were disguising themselves, but also, they were attempting to take on the identity of the northern aboriginal people they hated. The vigilantes crossed the border on a dark night, stormed the home of the BC deputy who housed the suspect, and then they took the child and lynched him. The Stó:lō met in conference to determine what restitutions might be necessary. The Canadian government convinced the First Nations community to allow a federal investigation in the hopes of averting a cross-border Indian war, but little action was ever taken.[82]

In February 2020, over a pipeline dispute, thirty rail blockades by Indigenous people and environmentalists swept the country, halting freight, and passenger traffic. The RCMP arrested and assaulted Indigenous people to quickly address the interruptions to commerce. By that June, Alberta's conservative government had established the Critical Infrastructure Defense Act to increase jail terms and fines for those protesting pipelines on traditional Indigenous territory. But, when one hundred, mostly white, truckers protesting vaccine mandates closed the border to the US at Coutts, Alberta, for several weeks, there were few arrests or interventions by the provincial or federal government, causing the Athabasca Chipewyan First Nation to call the lack of response racist.[83]

Canada may believe it had only one lynching, but the government forced more than 150,000 Indigenous children to attend institutions run by various churches, most notably the Roman Catholic Church. The conditions of these "schools" whereby violence was legitimized to be used against children—including murder, systemic torture, starvation, rape, and sexual assault—arise directly from lynch culture where thousands of Indigenous children were murdered without notice. The absence of meaningful dialogue in Canada prior to its Truth and Reconciliation Commission (and many Indigenous peoples would say since then too)[84] was a part of the Canadian culture of complacency and a societal code that insists that politeness refutes white supremacy. And it lies too in the legacy of colonial heritage where gender-based violence against Indigenous women means that they're four times more likely to go missing or be murdered than other Canadian women.[85] Canada's belief in its kindness and the refusal of its institutions to radicalize out of racist structures keep Indigenous peoples at a distance. Anishinaabe journalist and author Tanya Talaga speaks to this white negation of Indigenous history: "More people are asking questions, more people want to know the truth. But it was just two years ago that people were denying there was a genocide happening in this country."[86]

Denial of harm was also rampant in the development of social media and various technologies through the late twentieth century and allowed white supremacist organizations to foment. Throughout North America, with the rise of the internet, there was hope that civil rights would be built into the expansion of technology, and indeed, brands interested in new audiences tied themselves to the promise of equitable structures. For the most part, technology has been late to creating racial equity and justice systems, and instead, its creators only began to consider their responsibility in the design and functioning of racist systems following the murder of George Floyd. Lynch culture can be seen today embedded in digital platforms that strengthen authoritarian tendencies and suppress conversations based in truth and fairness, sometimes resulting in threats as well as physical and emotional violence against people of color. A Tech Transparency study found that white supremacist groups recruit members, organize events, and spread their message on Facebook despite that corporation's insistence that hate groups aren't allowed on their platform.[87] Both the Unite the Right rally in Charlottesville, Virginia, which injured nineteen people and killed Heather Heyer, and the Capitol Riot, which ended in the injuries of hundreds of police officers, staff, representatives, and senators as well as the suicides of four officers, were organized on Facebook. Many of these injuries were to people of color. After Dylann Roof was educated by a white nationalist lynch culture on Facebook, he opened fire at a historically Black church in South Carolina, killing nine Black people.[88] On social media, any country's dominator culture can be magnified through disinformation while trying to appear democratic and diverse.

The film *BlackkKlansman* by Spike Lee, from a memoir by Ron Stallworth, shows us how the police force can infiltrate the KKK when there's support for antiracist actions. When the government is invested, the Klan is easy to suppress, as America has proved through ending that organization, over and over. But the organization of the new militias and white nationalists comes via the internet, where people are easily anonymous and tricky to discover. Inside the House and Senate there are those who deny the existence of systemic racism. Senators like Lindsey Graham deny the government's part in creating institutional racism, stating, "Our systems are not racist. America's not a racist country. . . . Within every society you have bad actors."[89] But it is governments that, along with demonstrating lack of understanding about the dangerous uses of technology, allow far-right extremist and hate groups to use social media, file storage channels, live streams, and encrypted message platforms to coordinate racist violence. While Facebook, X (Twitter), Instagram, and YouTube look the other way, violent rhetoric and conspiracy theories mount, unchecked by our institutions, and are even espoused by conservative leaders who have their own alliances with the far right. Susan Corke, director of the Southern Poverty Law Center's Intelligence Project, says, "Without immediate action to moderate these technologies and hold technology companies accountable while respecting free speech, there's no telling the violence these extremists could unleash next."[90]

And there are more signs of systemic racism being ignored. Increasingly, the push among conservatives to honor states' rights shrouds racist policies of every name and makes some places so dangerous for Black people to be that the NAACP has taken to issuing travel bans. In a move as old as early lynch culture power grabs, Missouri passed a law that raises the legal burden needed to sue businesses for discrimination based on race, religion, or gender.[91] What remained unaddressed by the state were Black people being held in jail without cause, threats of violence on campus, and potential violence in a lynch culture where Black people were 91 percent more likely to be stopped by police than white people. The NAACP travel warning, a first for the organization, told Black people that their civil rights could be violated if they entered the state.

Lynch culture remained across the States when Black and queer people were murdered in purposeful acts of violence, connected to America's early acts of lynching.[92] "As long as the White man lives, our land will never be theirs and they will never be safe from us," the alleged white supremacist mass shooter who targeted a Black community in Buffalo, New York, wrote in a manifesto.

Kentucky has proposed House Bill 487, which would make it illegal to instruct students about institutional racism and would require schools to teach about American "victories" over "international socialism and communism." Sponsored by two Republican state lawmakers of House Bill 18—which includes a ban against teaching critical race theory as well as a prohibition against teaching that a student should feel guilty about what members of their race or gender did in the past—this new bill goes even farther. Bill 487 explicitly forbids teachers from teaching "the theory that racism is not merely the product of individual prejudice but is embedded in American society for the purpose of upholding white supremacy," and calls those ideas "revisionist history." Instead of school-led educational design, the state would create a mandatory curriculum.[93]

Through tactics such as book bans, parents, activists, school board officials, and lawmakers around the country are challenging ideas about race, gender, and sexuality at a pace not seen in decades. Conservatives, inflamed by social media, are sending their objections to statehouses, law enforcement, and political races. Young adult author Laurie Halse Anderson says, "By attacking these books, by attacking the authors, by attacking the subject matter, what they are doing is removing the possibility for conversation. You are laying the groundwork for increasing bullying, disrespect, violence and attacks."[94]

In 2022, thirty-six states had introduced or passed laws that restrict schools from giving students information about racism and systemic discrimination. Teachers endured legal—and personal—reprisals and, in Virginia, death threats. In Kentucky, the state's largest school board restricted parent comments to emails after their public meetings descended into chaos. Indeed, Attorney General Merrick Garland asked the FBI to work with US attorneys and federal, state, local, territorial, and tribal authorities in each school district to develop strategies against the threats. The intention with proposals and threatened violence is considered a victory, for weaponizing ideas makes them dangerous for teachers and librarians to support. Laws don't even have to be enacted for books and ideas to be suppressed. If we retract around the hard truths, it's so much easier to uphold white supremacist standards, especially in children. Lynch culture operates to make violence seem necessary to uphold societal standards, and the movement from negating human experience to punishing humans for their experiences is not as vast as we would like to imagine.[95] The history we teach comes from the lynch culture we create, not necessarily the actual history we made.

In *On the Courthouse Lawn*, historian and NAACP president Sherrilyn A. Ifill writes extensively about the lynching of Isaiah Fountain in Talbot County, Maryland, where the pattern among white people was to deny their own history, much like Owensboro, Kentucky's response after the legal lynching of Rainey Bethea. Ifill speaks of the case of Fountain, and the ways that lynching is told by white people, including denials of a white mob appearance outside the courthouse, of the white refusal to admit that there had been danger. "Earlier editions of the paper conceded that there had been a mob, but a 'foreign mob,' which had come from outside the borders of the county."[96] In Kentucky, Maryland, and everywhere lynch culture exists, there's a seeking to diminish the accountability for the community's own actions, and instead there's a need to foist the whole affair onto a few evildoers or out-of-towners. There's a complicity following these violent acts, of white people who want to rewrite their memories to favor the images and stories of the polite, stoic faces of those who witnessed and not lay claim to the horror that a public execution is. In their refusals to intervene or even to acknowledge the power of their role, perpetrators become a strange, depraved community. Brundage says of lynchings that "some spectators may have been shocked and disgusted by the violence they witnessed . . . it was their visible, explicit, public act of participation and not their ambiguous, private sentiment that bound the lynchers both socially and morally."[97]

We ought to consider this principle in every act of lynch culture that we support, whether that's in promoting disinformation on social media, or refusing to call out our government representatives for the systemic racism our institutions uphold. In a blatant example, designed to call to white supremacists in advance of a presidential run, in May

2023, Florida governor Ron DeSantis signed a bill that defunds any state college or university with a diversity, equity, and inclusion program and that bans courses that "distort significant historical events or include a curriculum that teaches identity politics," a reference to courses that acknowledge racism or sexism. There are, as of this writing, only three states that do not restrict education on racism, bias, and the contributions of specific racial or ethnic groups to US history.[98] There's a tide that's now reaching back toward an era before civil rights became a part of our nation's laws, to return America to a mythical place, back when America was "great," but only for those invested in Christian nationalist notions of hierarchies of race and gender. Lynch culture has always utilized perpetrators on behalf of the state to embed violence into our laws, governance, education systems, and any place where there's a perceived danger of Black or marginalized peoples. What results is organized hate and extremist groups, ones who are more and more aligned with governments.

In 2022, the Southern Poverty Law Center documented 523 hate and 702 antigovernment extremist groups, totaling 1,225 active groups. And extremism is increasingly embedded into political parties in North America. Republican politicians in the US now socialize openly with members of the organized white nationalist movement and exercise their hateful rhetoric as freely as during America's Civil War. And in Canada—a country where a majority government can be won with 35 percent of the vote—Conservative Party leader Pierre Poilievre is transforming traditional conservatism into an authoritarian populist movement clearly through his associations with far-right influencers and extremist groups.

The most popular white supremacist slogan in the world insists on centering descendants in these fourteen words: "We must secure the existence of our people and a future for white children." These concerns for the continuation of whiteness through speeches, bills, and the many forms of structural racism are an argument for the next generation to acquire the privileges of the past. This is the coded teaching in "make American great again." But our inheritance is not neutral, and we can't continue to speak of it as if we don't know that power passes unjustly to the white community.

We cannot continue to imagine that lynch culture only existed back then, over there. Bethea may or may not have been a criminal, but he certainly was a victim of the white supremacist society that defined Owensboro, Kentucky. Our obligation as carriers of this violence is to tell the truth about our history, our ancestors, our homes. Reconciliation is not possible until we have seen into who we are, reckoned what we have constructed in the name of our power, and begun to dismantle all that's remained unchecked through the false idea of whiteness.

4

How Could This Happen Here?

You can't demand truth and reconciliation. You have to demand truth—people have to hear it, and then they have to want to reconcile themselves to that truth.

—BRYAN STEVENSON

I walked along the Ohio River where my ancestors hanged the body of Rainey Bethea. Bright red, white, and blue bunting had been draped along the dark rails of the new Riverfront Center. A wide sidewalk led from Smothers Park, named for the town's first colonizer, to the Daviess County Courthouse, where a seven-foot-tall bronze sculpture of a Confederate soldier sat atop a nine-foot pedestal memorializing the Civil War and the Confederacy, its prominent placement intended to make the views of white Southerners dominant. That Confederate monument was erected not at the end of the war, but in 1900, with four thousand spectators attending, one-third of the town. Markers near the sculpture commemorate the Confederate fallen, though they do not mention the Confederates who treasonously burned the courthouse to the ground during the Civil War because Black troops had been quartered in the building. The grassroots efforts to remove the statue had recently been tied up in legal issues.[1]

Here in the town in which I was born, there is no memorial to the last public execution in America or to the communal shame that caused the state to change its rape law. The only naming of Rainey Bethea in Owensboro is in a ghost tour that stops at the place where he was hanged, now a delivery entrance to a Convention Center. Then and now, there's not public awareness that Kentucky's lynch laws had been codified and adapted into the legal system so that the idea of a savage and morally depraved Black criminality might be maintained. After all, these narratives of Black blame and white innocence were learned at lynchings, and their history has rarely been questioned, even by the state's politicians and leaders. If we are to confront these stories, we must begin in the place where we learned lynch culture. My place was my hometown.

It would take fifteen years from the day I first read Grandmaw's words to want to know the truth about my history and the hanging of Rainey Bethea. When I returned home from her funeral, I unpacked my bags, set up my desk, prepared to research. If I was to know anything about this legal lynching, I was going to have to understand how Owensboro, Kentucky, was a place where this could happen and how my family had come to be involved.

I didn't have to read books to know the racist history that I carried. Even without researching the news coverage and trial transcripts around the last public execution in America, I knew who got to own the facts. History too often belonged to whiteness, whose job it is to uphold ownership of the story. I was soon to learn about the violence and trauma of whiteness, how it was reinforced through a painful disconnection from ancestry. But in 2002, when I first began to read about this historical event in my hometown, I simply asked myself the question rising to the surface after a lifetime of familial and communal suppression—what institutional, political, and personal forces were responsible for Rainey Bethea's death?

> *The head must bow and the back will have to bend.*
> —Stephen Foster, "My Old Kentucky Home"

Racism embedded in institutions emboldens people and nations to enact racial discrimination in everything from housing to education to employment. How do we inherit these biases? What is inherited and continues to grow in white families and communities that causes them to see others' identities as a threat?

From the South's earliest days, enslaved people were brought in by white colonizers to clear land and to build forts to defend against the Indians. Before 1792, Kentucky was the far-western frontier of Virginia, which had a long history of slavery and indentured servitude.

Antebellum agrarian Kentucky relied on enslaved humans for its lucrative and labor-intensive tobacco and hemp crops, and before the election of Lincoln, enslaved people constituted one-third of Owensboro's population. Enslaved people were employed as household servants, laborers, farmhands, firemen, cooks, waiters, stevedores, and steamboat deckhands. Known then as a "slave-breeding state," Kentucky landowners increased their wealth through forcing the reproduction of enslaved people. Treated as chattel assets, enslaved people were made to have sex. Black women had their reproductive lives controlled through these violences on their bodies. After the end of the Atlantic slave trade in 1808, to end labor shortages, states in the South systematically imposed these methods to increase the number of people they enslaved without incurring the cost of purchase. Those who sold more enslaved people were also more likely to be breeders,[2] and Kentucky sold and exported nearly one-quarter of its Black, adult male population.[3] Slave owners rarely verified whether captured Black Kentuckians were free or enslaved before transporting them, and for the enslaved people of Kentucky, the threat of being sold meant harsh punishment or death. "Sold down the river" is a saying first coined in the state. Author and history professor at Kentucky Wesleyan College Lee Dew—passing along the white myth of the contented enslaved person—says, "What is surprising about the history of slavery in Daviess County is not that there were runaways, but that there were so few. . . . Perhaps . . . many slaves were more comfortable with the paternalism of slavery and lacked confidence in themselves and their ability to survive 'on their own'"[4]

Slavery had come to Daviess County when the first settlers brought enslaved people with them, and growers soon needed vast amounts of labor to produce tobacco. Farmers, whose land was relatively small compared to the plantation owners of the lower states, still used enslaved people for tobacco and hemp harvests, and enacted severe forms of labor practices, referenced in Kentucky's state song, "My Old Kentucky Home," composed by Stephen Foster: "The head must bow and the back will have to bend." Many white owners, from small farmers to urban businessmen, hired out the enslaved on contract. Slavery lay at the foundation of every aspect of the economy and culture of the state. Kentucky had conflicts due to its interest in northern economic relations and westward expansion while supporting slavery, slave owners, and southern-style plantations. Still, there was little sentiment here for the abolitionism growing in the North, and some talk of seceding from the Union to protect their slave economy.

In 2024, under a conservative party with a white supremacist agenda, the practices of antiracism have become "racist." To understand this turnabout, we can look back over two hundred years to the roots of abolitionist movements and the reactionary politics that sought to erase ties to antislavery causes. But in the southern states, our histories have also included both white and Black abolitionists who have worked diligently to oppose racism, at great risk to their lives and livelihoods.

Baptist ministers David Barrow and Carter Tarrant formed the Kentucky Abolition Society in 1808 and published one of America's first antislavery periodicals. After two unsuccessful antislavery lobbies in Kentucky constitution conventions, slavery led to the third convention in 1849. Convened by antislavery advocates who hoped to amend the constitution to prohibit slavery, they greatly misjudged proslavery support. Instead, the convention was packed with proslavery delegates, who drafted what historians consider the most proslavery constitution in US history. Cassius Marcellus Clay was a Southern planter, a founding member of the Republican Party in Kentucky, and an emancipationist, though his antislavery crusades made violent opponents. He published *True American*, in Lexington, Kentucky, and soon after sharing his views, suffered death threats, leading him to move the business to Ohio. He left a tremendous legacy in the donation of the land to build Berea College in eastern Kentucky, open to all races, and one of a network of abolitionist schools. Berea's slavery objectors, including the college's founders, John Fee and Cassius M. Clay, were driven from the state by a mob in 1859, in the wake of abolitionist John Brown's raid on Harpers Ferry.[5]

There would be other abolitionists and civil rights cases in Kentucky, including, directly after the Civil War, two notable defenders in Owensboro. Edward Claybrook and others successfully sued the city to prevent a segregated method of using taxes to pay for mostly white children in public education. Claybrook led a committee who filed a suit challenging the "colored school" law on the grounds that it denied their children equal protection as guaranteed by the Fourteenth Amendment. In 1883, the federal district court agreed and declared the Kentucky law unconstitutional.[6] A segregated coach bill passed in Kentucky in 1852, preventing Black people from occupying whites-only train cars. Thirty years later, Civil War veteran Reverend William Hardin Anderson and his wife, Sarah J. Steward Anderson, tested the law by refusing to move from a whites-only car. They were put off the train and later filed a $15,000 lawsuit against L&N Railroad. A US district court ruled the law unconstitutional, and the Andersons won their lawsuit.[7] Still, until the mid-twentieth century, Louisville was the stop for trains coming from the North and where Black passengers had to move to the "colored cars" before continuing their southward journey.[8] Well beyond Reconstruction and past the Great Migration, Kentucky citizens remained to fight segregation and bigotry.

All the sacred rights of humanity are violated by insisting on blind obedience.
—Mary Wollstonecraft

The South turned toward investing in paternalism, a hierarchical form of restricting freedom led by white men who thought of themselves as stately patriarchs but who brutalized enslaved people in demonstrations of dominance and characterized white women as pure, requiring protection, and subordinate to white men. Northern states continued to worry about new slave states after the annexing of Texas in 1836, and the possibility that slavery would become national. But the South wanted to control the Union, and to protect its alliance with slavery. Those who got in the way of the slaveholders' vision of themselves as naturally dominant and blessed by prosperity were sure to be punished. Historian Heather Cox Richardson says of the South in this time, "Distributing anti-slavery literature brought whipping, imprisonment, or death. Vigilante committees formed and worked alongside slave patrols to intimidate poor whites who talked about land reform or workers' rights, appeared to be insufficiently supportive of the slave system, or seemed too friendly with their black neighbors. Such men were accused of being closet abolitionists and were whipped out of town or lynched as an example to others."[9]

Since the 1820s, Owensboro had been Whig territory, a party formed by the followers of Henry Clay, who was a slave owner, and "a 'favorite son' of the Bluegrass state."[10] Clay had struck the Missouri Compromise aimed at maintaining the territorial balance between slave and free states, which temporarily quieted the voices of secession. Although Kentucky's economy was steeped in the institution of slavery, a Unionist appeal resounded throughout the state. To head off trouble in Kentucky, Clay assured voters he would employ military might if necessary to execute the Fugitive Slave Law, called the "bloodhound law" for the dogs who chased Black people, often to their deaths. Clay pronounced that he would "cease to be a Whig" rather than embrace an organization that advocated abolition. The Whig Party's decline eventually came with nativist sentiment that had mounted for decades in Kentucky, fueled by anti-Catholic hatred. German and Irish immigrants continued to move into the state, while Clay refused to address the naturalization issue for fear of alienating ethnic voters.[11] By 1854, in the face of intense controversy over whether Kansas and Nebraska would enter the Union as free or slave states, the Whig Party, which had been divided on the issue, collapsed.

Lexington, Kentucky, was an early metropolis, and around this era, the town moved into the interstate slave trade. The slave trade was profitable not just to slaveholders, but to the slave patrol, who captured enslaved people who had run away and those reenslaved free African Americans who had the misfortune of crossing their paths. Jailers were often used as the market middlemen for those awaiting transport. Several jails in Lexington were the city's most profitable businesses. In 1840, Robert Wickliffe, the largest slave owner in Fayette County, boasted to the Kentucky legislature that as many as six thousand enslaved people per year were being sold to southern states from Kentucky. By 1849, Kentucky newspapers garnered a significant share of the slave trade economy through an increased number of paid advertisements and handbills for the sale of enslaved people, for the services of slave trade firms and brokers, and for the recapture of runaway and kidnapped enslaved people.

By 1855, the Democratic Party had been taken over by slaveholders, and in Kentucky this came with slaveholder justice systems. That year, Owensboro was feeling so optimistic about its future that it built a county courthouse, one that would be burned by the end of the Civil War. In this same year, Margaret Garner escaped across the frozen Ohio River for the promise of freedom and ended the life of her child rather than allow US marshals to take her into slavery, a story that Toni Morrison's *Beloved* later made known to the world.

A divided state in the Civil War, a place of Union troop occupation and guerrilla Confederates, Kentucky was torn geographically, ideologically, economically, politically, and militarily between North and South.

An embodiment of the Civil War's "brother against brother" conflict, Kentucky's families supplied 100,000 Union soldiers and 40,000 to the Confederacy, while white Kentuckians made widespread racial terror for Black families.

Even after the conclusion of the Civil War and fall of the Confederacy, slaveholders in Kentucky continued to trade Black people for eleven more months, through 1865. Slavery may have ended that year, but the Thirteenth Amendment was not ratified in Kentucky until 1976.[12] Lynching remained a strategy of racial terror here into the next century, with acts as violent as those in the Deep South. That's partly because former Confederate politicians allowed violent groups like the Ku Klux Klan (KKK) and the Night Riders to operate, creating a culture of fear that helped politicians squash opposition and regain power.[13] Indeed, the Gallatin race riot of 1866 came out of the congressional Civil Rights Act of 1866, which gave Black people the right to testify against white people; however, it was ignored in state courts across Kentucky, and as a result, white vigilantes went unpunished. Government soldiers prevented mass violence in Louisville, but sixty-five miles north in Gallatin County, where the Black population was relatively small, a band of five hundred white individuals, including members of the newly formed KKK, whipped Black residents, stole their property, and forced hundreds of them to flee across the Ohio River.[14]

> *The native land of the American negro is America. His bones, his muscles, his sinews, are all America.*
>
> —Frederick Douglass

A century ago, Kentucky was part of a campaign to distort Civil War history, creating a Lost Cause myth that permeated textbooks and popular culture and went largely unchallenged for decades. Today, the latest front of the right's culture war is against Black Americans, LGBTQ Americans, and other marginalized people and continues in history books, school curricula, government policy, and Supreme Court interventions. Though Kentuckians were divided in the way they fought the Civil War, by the 1870s and the decades thereafter, "with amazing accord, white Kentuckians elected five governors who had sympathized with or fought for the Confederacy. . . . They built Confederate monuments, published sectional periodicals, participated in veterans' organizations and historical societies, and produced literature that portrayed Kentucky as Confederate, while seemingly leaving the Union cause and the feats of its soldiers largely uncelebrated."[15] While Confederate memory dominated the state after the war, causing white Kentuckians to welcome Democratic politics, racial violence, and Jim Crow laws associated with former Confederate states, white Unionists and Kentucky's African Americans "drew on the Union victory and their part in winning it to lay claim to the fruits of freedom and citizenship."[16]

By 1892, almost three decades after the war, throughout the South, there was a lynching every thirty-six hours. George C. Wright, in *Racial Violence in Kentucky, 1865–1940: Lynchings, Mob Rule, and "Legal Lynchings,"* reports that from Reconstruction to the mid-twentieth century, Kentuckians lynched 353 people, and 80 percent of those put to death for rape were African American. Wright says, "Given the white racist belief that rape was a 'Negro crime,' it is a wonder that only 80 percent . . . of men put to death for rape were African American. No one—black or white—died for raping a black woman. Furthermore, only a few of the 130 blacks who died on the gallows or in the electric chair were convicted of killing African Americans. Since no blacks served on juries during these years, all of the blacks put to death were convicted and sentenced by all-white juries."[17]

Lynching in Kentucky employed a consistent pattern of legally sanctioned and extralegal violence to ensure that Black people remained oppressed, even after World War I. In the South that Rainey Bethea had been born into, alleged rapes by African American men aroused the fury of white communities and received significant coverage by newspapers. Although the Black population declined from 1870 onward, representing less than 9 percent of the state by the 1930s, Kentucky remained one of the top-ten states in number of lynchings. White people lynched Black individuals as a warning to other Black people not to topple the status quo, though white people had such power and population that this threat to white supremacy could hardly have been actual. Thousands of KKK members met here, the focus of their parades, fireworks, and cross-burning ceremonies not only white nationalism but also terrorism toward Catholics and Jews.

In 1915, Kentuckian-born son of a Confederate colonel D. W. Griffith cemented the perceptions of Southern slavery as benevolent, Black people as violent (especially to white women), and the KKK as a band of heroes restoring the rightful order when he made *The Clansmen*, later retitled *The Birth of a Nation*, which would become the first film shown in the White House, under President Woodrow Wilson. The film was a recruiting tool for the KKK, causing lynchings to rise fivefold after its distribution, and even eighty-five years later, by 2000, those places that showed the film had substantially more active "klaverns" (Klan chapters).[18] One of the largest klaverns in the US is in Dawson Springs, Kentucky, which hosts a compound and a festival of racist music and attracts an array of white supremacist groups and their families, including skinheads, neo-Nazis, and other KKK groups. Kentucky remains one of the least diverse states in the nation, and its small towns are increasingly white.[19]

Kentucky was nearly always a poor state, but the Depression battered its industry and workers.[20] In that era's onset, due to Prohibition, two hundred distilleries had dried up. Likewise, coal mining had fallen on hard times due to the shift to electricity and oil. By 1933, with funds frozen by bank failures, half of Kentucky's businesses had closed. That winter, the highest number of Americans ever were without jobs, children were underweight, and even farming incomes fell. Thousands of farmers, struggling from recent droughts and unable to sustain their losses, were selling their land, often in forced sales. Prior to the stock market crash, and well into 1933, highways all around Owensboro were being constructed, a bridge connecting the town to Indiana was being built across the river, and passenger rail lines and steamboats moved through the city.

Franklin Roosevelt was inaugurated in March 1933, with hopes that he would bring the region into a new economic era. Kentucky had to rely on the New Deal; thus, it would need to learn to bend to the federal regulatory powers that forced the state to undergo labor reforms. Entire counties went on federal relief, often for years. The Works Project Administration (WPA) hired workers to improve the roads, cook for schools, grow gardens, and lead bands. In 1936, the WPA, via the Federal Writers' Project, would lead a significant project in the state to record slave narratives that are preserved by the Library of Congress.[21] Throughout the Depression, the director of the Urban League tried to convince industry to hire Black people, and while white managers reported that Black workers were unskilled, lazy, unreliable, and unable to be trained,[22] the unstated truth was that white workers would not work alongside them. Not everyone was happy to share a dwindling pool of resources. These were the strained economic and social conditions, especially for African Americans, that Rainey Bethea found himself in when he moved to Owensboro in the spring of 1933 to find work.

The Recurring Tendencies, Wounds, and Harms of the Family and Community

The summer of 1936 brought one of the worst heat waves in Kentucky. The South was still recovering from the Depression, and in a few months, Roosevelt would be reelected in a landslide. Most Black voters had abandoned their historic allegiance to the Republican Party and joined with labor unions, farmers, progressives, and ethnic minorities in ensuring FDR's win. A new coalition was shifting the balance of power in the Democratic Party, from its Southern bloc of white conservatives, toward this new alliance. White people were benefiting from the New Deal and the WPA, but widespread tenant and sharecropper evictions continued to make finding jobs difficult for Black people.[23] That summer, white people were agitated. And the agitation of white people mattered, because the entire legal system was set up to ensure Black people were at their mercy.

The facts of the Bethea case are in just a few documents that courts noted that summer. No evidence remains. The reconstruction of events through the white media should be suspect, since at play was a kind of information disorder, set up to cement compliance with white biases. After the legal lynching, the white media in Owensboro referred to the breaking of Bethea's neck in front of the white audience as him being "dropped into eternity" and mentioned hangman Hash the next day in the headline "Rainey Bethea Dies on Gallows; Trap Sprung by Ex-Louisville Cop." What they also meant is *the white lady couldn't do it.*

In this era of sensationalist press, journalists sometimes acted in collusion with authorities. Indeed, in the same newspapers where headlines on the Rainey Bethea case appeared, there were multicolumn portrayals of scandals, exaggerated headlines, pseudoscience, and reinforced gender and racialized roles. Reporter Keith Lawrence of the *Owensboro Messenger-Inquirer* knew the lead reporter for the Bethea case. Lawrence, a soft-spoken man who has covered Owensboro news for fifty years, started at the *Messenger-Inquirer* right out of college and had come across the last public execution through his research for his master's thesis on violence in the American news and entertainment industry. In an interview with me, Lawrence said, "Once I got to Owensboro, I started researching the Bethea case and talking to people who were there."

L. D. "Birdie" Gasser, once a candidate for mayor, covered the Bethea arrest, trial, and execution. Though Gasser had retired from journalism by 1972, Lawrence reports that he often dropped into their newspaper offices. Gasser would insist to Lawrence that much of the out-of-town and negative coverage of Owensboro after the Bethea hanging wasn't true. This perspective—that Owensboro wasn't as racist or violent as the outsiders made them sound—continues to be a common refrain among white residents of this region. Indeed, in documents from a 1936 court hearing, Gasser testified that he believed there had been no danger of mob violence in Owensboro and that Bethea would have been safe without the state police providing security during the trial. "The people had too much respect for law and order to resort to violence," Gasser said.[24]

So close was the white legal and carceral system with the white media that Gasser had escorted the suspect to the jail. Lawrence told me that "Birdie was close with the police department. He was telling me about one time he got to the murder scene before the cops got there . . . by the time he went up to the office and came back again, he saw that he'd left his hat at the [investigation] site." Lawrence chuckled, and the tale was, on one level, an amusing small-town anecdote. But the white Kentucky newspapers wrote early and often of Bethea's guilt, in some cases seeming to amplify the rage of the white community. This made it even more dangerous to be any Black person in the region.

Most often in Southern newspapers, Bethea is only called the "Negro." Unless, as in the Owensboro paper, he's called the "Slayer." It was common in the 1930s, in Southern newspapers in particular, to echo the language used by owners and the industry of slavery, including those newspapers in Kentucky that made fine profits from advertising to auction the enslaved. That legacy continued into the 1960s when Kentucky's *Lexington Herald-Leader* refused to cover the civil rights movement, for which it has since made an apology. But in these Kentucky cities, as in many places throughout the South, Black media coverage mostly existed to represent stories from police reports on arrests of Black people. Brent Staples, Pulitzer-winning *New York Times* editorial writer says, "The white press in the South dictated how anti-Black atrocities were viewed all over the country by portraying even the most grotesque exercises of violence as necessary to protect a besieged white community. White news organizations elsewhere rubber-stamped this lie. The editors of small, struggling Black publications often risked their lives to refute what they rightly saw as white supremacist propaganda masquerading as news."[25]

Few reports in Owensboro mused about Bethea's fear of white mob violence constantly shadowing him from the time before his arrest to his execution and whether that cultural pressure might have influenced Bethea's confessions or guilty plea in court. Black newspapers, Black scholarly research, and historians studying lynching spoke notably then, and still reflect today, how Black and white people experience different realities when it comes to legal and extralegal violence.

Lawrence reports that the Black community in Owensboro, who mostly lived in Baptist Town, would have been harassed and silenced by the preparations for the hanging. "Back then, they [Baptist Town] were terrified. From the Fourth Street district to where the hanging occurred is three blocks," said Lawrence. The community may have known that the anticipated crowd of ten thousand might impact their safety, as indeed white people "spilled out as far as Third Street, one block away."[26] But silence came also from the necessity of living alongside such terror as might happen in an environment where, for more than two decades, nearly all of those who had died on the gallows were Black men convicted by all-white juries. "The white death" was what author Richard Wright called the threat of lynching that "hung over every black male in the South," the effect of which was to create "a dread of white people . . . [that] came to live permanently in my imagination."

Indeed, Lawrence spoke of the anniversary stories the *Messenger-Inquirer* did in 1986—fifty years after the Bethea hanging—and the pressure he received even then from Black Owensboro residents who hoped he might avoid telling the Bethea story: "A lot of Blacks were upset by the publication of the story. They didn't see it as historical; some of the older people saw it as a way to keep Black people down," Lawrence added. There seemed to be a legacy left in the community, all that time later, a sense of white-centered history still being used to suppress the Black community.

Richard Brown, Kentucky State Human Rights Commission, and a leader in Owensboro's Black community, said that since he was a little boy, he's heard stories about Bethea's execution being racially motivated. "From my knowledge that I received from African Americans at the time, it was [racially motivated]," Brown said. A tale of "sitting on the porch during my early days, listening to these elderly black women who had their stories surrounding the hanging of Rainey Bethea."[27]

Author Sherilynn Ifill speaks of the Eastern Shore lynchings in Maryland as having deeply affected the white community, who "remain strangely caught up in a continued bond of complicity—pleading ignorance or faded memories to avoid at all cost talking about a shameful part of their history. White children, now elderly, who witnessed these lynchings experienced a unique trauma reinforced by years of silence within their families and communities."[28] Ifill's study indicates that the "macabre details had so entered the consciousness of the black community . . . that even fifty years later its image had the power to keep many blacks from attempting to register to vote."[29]

And there is another truth in the journalistic and imagistic storytelling about Kentucky. The Southern-based photos depict a moment in time that convinces more distant white Americans of the righteousness of their own lives. If they can point to the brutal carnival that happened at the last public execution in America, then they're safe from being known as the *worst* racists. Not just white Southerners but most white people and white authorities failed to act as Black people were terrorized and murdered in these six decades of lynching and legal lynching. While white Southerners used lynching to enforce a postslavery system of racial dominance, Northerners and federal officials watched and did little.[30]

Charlotte Wolf, in her essay "Constructions of a Lynching," interviewed members of the Black and white communities in Palmer, Tennessee, ninety years following a 1900 lynching in that town. Her conclusion: "It should be emphasized that for blacks it is in this process of defining, of naming, of shaping the symbolic value of *what happened* that the black community has taken possession of the event, has asserted a power over it that they did not have when it occurred; but as such, it still remains a deeply etched part of black identity."[31] White people tended to deny their ancestors' involvement in community lynching, and thus, their connection to an ancestral history of violence remains cut off from them.

The Home We Seek Is the Home We Already Are

What happens when we shift the camera view from that favored by white people, and indeed, by nearly every media outlet in mid-August

1936—of the Black man at the gallows—to one focused on the whiteness that created racialized violence? There, in the photographs and reportage of the day is the view that white people refused to reckon with.

All there was, as far as you could see, were white people in that town square.

Owensboro's Rachel Abbott was five years old when she woke in the dark and followed her older sister to the gallows, two blocks from her home. Eighty-one years later, she told a reporter what happened that day: "I seen what they were doing but I didn't realize what they were doing. . . . He [Bethea] wasn't crying, he wasn't fussing, nothing—I guess he just accepted it. But he looked over at the girl that came out of the crowd with him, and he told her 'I didn't do this.'"[32]

Nearest the gallows were sixteen white women—from grandmothers to infants—who had waited for hours for the execution. Later, many white newspapers would report with horror on the appearance of women and children at the scene, forgetting that white women and their descendants had always been a part of lynch culture.[33]

White women and their babies were featured in much of the coverage, the white journalists unable to grasp the history of white women as perpetrators of lynchings, legal and otherwise. One Texas newspaper clipping was sent to Thompson that read, "No more shocking spectacle has been seen in this nation in many a year. . . . Half of the crowd . . . assembled to witness the execution were women, young girls, and children. Mothers with babies in their arms and children clinging to their hands fought to get closer to the scaffold."

The photographs from August 14, 1936, depict a full range of human emotion on those white faces—fear, curiosity, solemnity, anger, mockery—but there was no denying that the scene in Owensboro had been a grotesque shindig. Reflecting the original meaning of a *shindig* as a shindy, or a ruckus, the event both *was* and *caused* a commotion that continues throughout history. The disturbing images the newspapers carried of the hanging-day crowd echoed the postcards of lynchings that had circulated for years. In those photographs at the Bethea hanging, there are our white ancestors, the grandmothers with their strong shoulders and gleams of crowlike hair; the men in uniform who prefer to be seen as heroic; the teenagers handing out cold bottles of Coca-Cola; the children who were carried in their parent's arms to witness a cruel death. These were white folks who knew themselves to be protected witnesses, in a communal ritual with all the signals full of white virtue, including feeling morally superior to the Black man they would punish. These white bodies had allowed the state to use them as an extension to enact unjust laws, policies, and systems and had been allowed to think themselves to be decent people in exchange.

Owensboro and the state of Kentucky, like many places in America, built its lynch culture through colonialism, genocide, and racial terror. The state's customs, policies, laws—the architecture of its story—are saturated in whiteness. But there also existed movements that were counterforces in enacting systemic change. Kentucky was a regular stop for the Reverend Dr. Martin Luther King Jr., whose brother served as a pastor in Louisville. In 1964, King, Jackie Robinson, Kentucky's civil rights leaders, and ten thousand Kentuckians marched on the state capitol, which, two years later, helped pass the Kentucky Civil Rights Act to make discrimination illegal. Sit-ins, pickets, and marches led to landmark victories, and though Louisville integrated its schools after the 1954 *Brown v. Board of Education* ruling, the 1970s brought clashes in the city and elsewhere over the busing of students. There would be generations of movement action before these places in the South registered systemic change. Many, like the multigenerational families on the streets in Louisville following the murder of Breonna Taylor by police, are still protesting to end the violence.

Before reconciliation, we must be willing to tell all the truths in our towns. As Bryan Stevenson has said, "You can't jump to reconciliation. You can't jump to reparation or restoration until you tell the truth. Until you know the nature of the injuries, you can't actually speak to the kind of remedies that are going to be necessary."[34] In naming our past we begin to repair the damage of structural oppression. To belong to a place, we must reckon with the history that many in our communities are, even today, still trying to deny.

5

Canada's Lynch Culture

After living in the US for thirty years, we returned to Canada in 2016, six months prior to the election to the highest office in the land someone whom academics, journalists, and the American people would soon consider to be a white supremacist.[1] This man had already refused to renounce Ku Klux Klan leader David Duke, telling CNN that he didn't know anything about white nationalists. This man had promoted the arrest of five innocent Black teenagers whom white people called the Central Park Five (now known as the Exonerated Five) and called for the return of the death penalty in New York and the expansion of police rule. What this man did in supporting violence against Black people and Black Lives Matter protesters was obvious—"Maybe [the protesters] should have been roughed up," he said to audiences in Alabama and Kentucky, seemingly without a need for the subtlety of a dog whistle because he was so aligned with the racist uses of authority.

I spent election night texting friends in Seattle, listening to them say, "You're so lucky that you got out when you did." But I didn't want to be out of America. It felt more essential than ever to show up for people who were being targeted because of their race—a Muslim ban, aggressive deportation, rolling back environmental regulations that would impact more communities of color. That first year we moved back to Canada, I left nearly every month to return to the Pacific Northwest. I walked in protests, listened to my friend's and colleagues' fears, and tried to know what useful acts of support might be while I lived across the border in a national park, a relative paradise.

When I returned to Banff National Park, where we had lived two decades prior, I went out every day to hike the trails that took me onto mountaintops, alongside rivers, over frozen lakes, overlooking glaciers. My husband and I were often nearly alone on ledges and staircases built by hand by Swiss and Italian guides in the last century. We mostly walked in silence over boulders and shale, through forests of pine, white spruce, aspen, balsam, larch, and Douglas fir. There was a deep peace on the trails. I could look out for miles and not observe another human. My legs became strong, and after a few months, I developed more stable footing. We moved in silence, with the sense of knowing how to pace ourselves at altitude, taking breaks for conversations about our dual identities—one foot in each country, we said, each nation struggling with its history of oppression. We watched giant ravens catch the wind on the mountain southeast of our home, Eyarhey Tatanga Woweyahgey Wakan, Sacred Buffalo Guardian Mountain, renamed by Indigenous leaders in the first year we arrived.[2] We were living in the way that St. Bernard of Clairvaux had spoken of when he said, "Stones and trees will teach you that which you cannot learn from the masters."

But also, there were human masters among us, Elders and educators from the Treaty 7 Nations who began to teach from our town square near the Bow River that flowed from Bow Glacier and then all the way east to Lake Winnipeg. The gatherings were part of our community's response to the 2015 Truth and Reconciliation Commission's report, which documented thousands of deaths of children at residential schools across Canada, the causes at the time of their deaths listed as unknown. We sat on blankets on the dewy grass, listening to the speakers, who told their stories of being removed from their families and of being tortured and raped; we heard of the multigenerational harm caused by the church and state. We learned of the Catholic Church's refusal to release records of the residential schools, and of their refusal (even in 2022) to make an apology for the hundreds of deaths their priests and nuns caused. Catholic Church lawyers had been resistant at the time of the signing of the legal agreement to pay almost one-third of what amounted to Canada's largest class action settlement. Years later, after the church boasted it had honored its $79 million agreement to compensate survivors and its bishops issued an apology, the Canadian Broadcasting Corporation (CBC) reported they'd barely paid 15 percent.[3]

The Elders of the Stoney Nation (Goodstoney, Bearspaw, and Chiniki bands) taught us that truth and reconciliation are sequential. We must address oppressive histories by honestly and soberly recognizing the pain of the past. We learned about the Truth and Reconciliation Commission's ninety-four Calls to Action and the ways that Canada had taken symbolic but not substantive action on them, leaving eighty-three actions incomplete, according to the Yellowhead Institute. We got up from those gatherings and drove out to swim in a deep, cold lake at the foot of Waskahigan Watchi, meaning House Mountain in the Mountain Cree language.[4] The mountain had been renamed Mount Rundle, for a Methodist minister who traversed large swaths of what was in 1840 called British North America to convert local Indigenous Nations to Christianity under the invitation of the Hudson's Bay Company. He wanted to remain sympathetic to the British government and limit the influence of Catholic missionaries who were backed by France.

More recent violences were found with evidence of 215 children's graves at Kamloops Indian Residential School. Chief Harvey McLeod of the Upper Nicola Band, who attended Kamloops, said that when schoolmates disappeared, they were simply never spoken of again. "I just remember that they were here one day, and they were gone the next," he said. The result was not just cultural genocide but met the United Nations' definition of genocide—killing members of the group, causing them serious bodily or mental harm, imposing living conditions intended to destroy the group, forcibly transferring children out of the group. At least 3,200 children died of abuse and neglect while a student at a residential school—one in every 50 students enrolled during the program's nearly 120-year existence. The chair of the Truth and Reconciliation Commission, Justice Murray Sinclair, has said the true number of deaths could be as high as 6,000.

Canada's lynch culture is located not only in history but also in a modern trend that seeks to legitimize violence toward Indigenous peoples and people of color. Lynch culture—a holdover from every era—is a legacy that damages marginalized people, and in Canada, both Black and Indigenous people have suffered. Lynch culture also costs white people. For all the ways white people receive privilege from lynch culture, we are also harmed by it. We are diminished in our capacity to love and disconnected from others. We have forgotten our ancestors' lives, rituals, and wisdom. To end the suffering of others and ourselves, we must become aware of the codes written into our families and communities. And then we must be willing to defy them. To defy them, we first must honor the truth of how we got here. I began with the land I called home.

The Lie That Made a National Park System

In 1885, the Canadian Pacific Railway (CPR) was completed by workers, including fifteen thousand temporary Chinese laborers who toiled in dangerous conditions to construct a coast-to-coast transportation system to "unite the nation." The planned route tracked through the Bow Valley in the Canadian Rocky Mountains. There, at railway siding 29, three white railway workers had recently stumbled on a series of natural hot springs near Sulphur Mountain and began vying for rights to develop the potentially lucrative site that they said they "discovered." This land had for thousands of years remained integral for medicines, hunting, and food gathering for Indigenous peoples, primarily the Stoney Nation. The Canadian government wanted its own authority over what it envisioned as a future recreational and sport hunting paradise and drew up laws against "sale, settlement, or squatting" in this territory, creating first the Rocky Mountains National Park, and then later allowing for the renaming of the place for the CPR president's birthplace. Thus, Canada's first national park became Banff.

Soon after, the government, which viewed the Stoney as "stragglers," lobbied for them to be confined to reserves, increased Parks land, and introduced provincial game laws. By 1915, the federal and provincial governments had barred the Stoney's historical ties to hunting, fishing, gathering, and traveling through the Rocky Mountains and its foothills. In his first annual report, Park Superintendent George Stewart wrote that "Indians" had to be excluded from Banff: "Their destruction of the game and depredations among the ornamental trees make their too frequent visits to the Park a matter of great concern."[5]

The Stoney had vital connections to the area that became Banff National Park. Banff was traditional Stoney territory. The Stoney people lived in Banff and traded with the Blackfoot Confederacy's Kainai (Blood), Piikani (Peigan), and Siksika as well as the Tsuut'ina (Sarcee), Ktunaxa (Kutenai), Secwépmc, and Cree people, who traveled through the area.[6] Ancestors of the Ktunaxa (Kutenai) hunted here before the smallpox epidemics, and Cree bands were familiar with the territory.[7] Treaty 7, signed a few years earlier, had been created out of a management philosophy whose aims included assimilating local Indigenous peoples into a more sedentary, agricultural way of life. Signatories rightly understood that the treaty would enable Nations to hunt, fish, and gather as they had before. The federal government also stipulated that the Nations' traditional ways were subject to government regulation and that tracts of land could later be exempted from these rights for any purpose. Ending thousands of years of relationship with the territory around Banff—lands central to their existence as storytellers, healers, and providers—Indigenous peoples were soon forbidden to hunt, gather medicines and food, and maintain alliances with neighboring relatives and communities within these new borders. The Canadian Department of Indian Affairs introduced a segregationist pass system to confine Indigenous people to reserves and repress resistance. The apartheid-like policy was in place from the 1850s to the 1950s, though no law was ever passed to instate it. Much like the Slave Codes in the US, the Canadian government used criminal code vagrancy laws, loitering provisions, and other aggressive acts by Northwest Mounted Police officers to detain Indigenous people who were off reserve without documentation.

The CPR had a vested interest in helping people believe that in Canada they could access a vast wilderness—one seen in the art deco posters the corporation commissioned—and take a journey that could fill their luxury hotels, ocean liners, and opulent trains. From its beginnings, Canada's national park system was designed to center commerce over Indigenous sovereignty, the nation impoverishing Indigenous peoples in its desire to preserve a lie (or two)—that the land was best known as an untouched wilderness and that white people had superior knowledge of land management and game conservation. But according to Nathan Cardinal, manager of resource conservation at Gulf Islands National Park Reserve, "All these landscapes were actively managed by First Nations for millennia."[8]

The creation of a national park at Banff, created just eighteen years after the country was born, would set a standard by which Parks Canada continued its removal of Indigenous peoples. In central Canada, members of the Keeseekoowenin Ojibwe band were expelled from Riding Mountain National Park. As the Ojibwe left, park wardens set fire to their homes. These policies were not unique to national parks—in the late nineteenth century, First Nations were also forced from Stanley Park in Vancouver in the west and Algonquin National Park in what's now known as Ontario. Indeed, the federal government did not begin to change its exclusionary parks policies until the 1970s. Writer Robert Jago, a member of the Kwantlen First Nation and Nooksack Indian Tribe, whose territory is along the present international boundary in the Nooksack river basin, says that "in the early twentieth century, as non-Native settlements such as Banff and Jasper grew, the livelihoods of Indigenous peoples were destroyed. . . . In 1895, Aubrey White, Ontario's assistant commissioner of Crown lands, wrote of the presence of Algonquin people in language that we now reserve for the Asian pine beetle: 'You know the predatory habits of these people, how they roam about, and how difficult it is to keep watch of their movements in the forest.'"[9] After the creation of its first national park, the government would soon refuse Indigenous title and recognition within park boundaries across Canada. Indigenous people were eventually forced out into distant reserves, where, even today, access to clean drinking water technologies and federal support to manage resources remains a problem, including on the Stoney Nation reserve near Banff, at Mînî Thnî (Morley), Alberta.

The values that forward wilderness as a state of pristine purity have historically supported keeping Indigenous peoples from their lands. Banff still tries to be a natural cathedral for its visitors. The tourism bureau shapes its image as one of grandeur, where people might worship the transcendent. People visit to find places of awe, and to capture a particular Canadian west—an imagined recollection of a simpler or nobler time, both uncorrupted and ephemeral.

In the American wilderness ideal, developed over the last century, one version of its past paints Indigenous peoples as never really inhabiting what would become the national parks. But a wilderness unaffected by humans is an illusion. Mark David Spence, historian and author of *Dispossessing the Wilderness*, speaks of the American Wilderness Act of 1964, where "humans are visitors who do not remain. Amazingly, if we follow this reasoning to the logical extreme, the park service has managed to protect the only areas on the North American continent that Indians did not use on a regular basis."[10]

But, in Canada, the reason behind the removal of Indigenous peoples was even more arrogant than assuming that the land hadn't been used for over a hundred generations. In the Canadian removal strategy, there was an insidious denial of the adept Indigenous stewardship of the land through strategic forest management as well as fishing, trapping, hunting, guiding, and conservation practices—all of which happened here well before the creation of the national parks.[11] Indigenous peoples did not insist on keeping land "unspoiled" but on being in relationship with it. Controlled wilderness parks were a concept created by governments, in cooperation with corporate interests that wished to reinvent nature. These governments were also influenced by white sportsmen's associations, white ethics, and white views of game conservation. When Indigenous hunting was suppressed, it led to a game increase in Banff National Park, which could create surplus game in adjacent territories specifically for white sport hunters. Likewise, the future use of the parks was intended to be preserved for white business models of tourism and recreation.

Historians Theodore Binnema and Melanie Niemi report that "sport hunters already had become influential, organized, and activist, and their opinions of aboriginal hunters were reflected in policy and legislation."[12] White hunters were condescending toward Indigenous ways, especially as Indigenous people hunted for sustenance while white sportsmen hunted for trophy heads. Just as in today's white-influenced diet culture, the sportsman wanted there to be no appearance of the necessity for food, the cachet being entirely located in being wealthy enough to do without. These trophy hunters appealed to the Department of Indian Affairs to enforce game laws on all the Indigenous people hunting in Banff. Policies called for Indigenous hunting to end when white Canadians began to be interested in tourist traffic and business owners became oriented to the revenues they would create. There were subversive ways that Indigenous peoples continued their hunting practices, including working for local entrepreneurs like Norman Luxton, who hired Stoney hunters to harvest bighorn sheep and elk heads and pelts for unlucky trophy hunters, who only used what they might display, thereby offering the Stoney access to food sources they'd been forbidden.

Creating national parks in Canada had the effect of centralizing control in relationship with industry, primarily the railroad companies, who restricted access to the mountains to "upper-and middle-income tourists willing to pay substantial sums for a sanitized view of the mountains."[13] Sportsmen spent huge sums to take home big game heads. At a time when residents were growing in Banff and Bankhead, and Banff lands were being expanded to over eleven thousand square kilometers,[14] laws dictated that Indigenous people must not only be restricted to reserve land but also that they could no longer hunt on land reserved for its first national park. Though the railway development and non-Indigenous hunters had likely caused much of the game depletion, the Stoney and other Indigenous peoples were blamed for the demise of elk and other animals. But Canada needed its tourism industry to grow, and hunters were already being replaced by visitors who wanted to photograph animals in the wild, to memorialize a kind of history that had never occurred. It wouldn't be until 1979, with new federal management strategies, that the ideals would change to preserving the park lands in an unimpaired state through "ecological integrity and restoration," moving away from development based heavily on profit.

Canada's parks were created in the same year that the last spike was driven in by CPR railway financier Donald Smith, the Métis leader Louis Riel was hanged for treason in what might be called a legal lynching, and oil and natural gas were being explored in Alberta, and a singular view of national parks—one that sought to epitomize Canada's grandeur—became a kind of identity transference for a sentimental notion of beauty.[15] These industry-centered values and white-focused imprint remain in Banff.

Romancing the Mountains

I inherited this "romantic" vision of Banff National Park when I moved there in 1983, after receiving a postcard that detailed an iconic scene of Banff Avenue with a backdrop of the giant Cascade Mountain, Mînî hrpa in the Nakoda language, for "the mountain where water falls." Fresh out of university, with a new husband and baby, I'd left Toronto to explore the promise of a place that seemed to offer the kind of spaciousness I'd seen only in the movies. We took jobs in house cleaning, ski resorts, bus companies, and hotel marketing and waited for a spot in the daycare to open so we could both work and possibly afford a used car, or even a meal at a restaurant.

We were there too because Banff National Park was a protected area where grizzly bears and wolves migrated, trails remained unspoiled, and the mountain air was relatively uncorrupted. Parks Canada had issued a new policy, colloquially known as The Beaver Book, which contained the first mention of "ecological integrity" in Canada. A few years later, the National Parks Act would be amended to center protection of natural resources and ecologically minded management practices. We believed we lived in a place that could become a model for the nation, and we wanted to belong here, to see ourselves as part of this vanguard.

Eventually I won a position at the Banff Springs Hotel, carting film crews and journalists to the Canadian Pacific Hotels in the west. I was selling media and their public on the dream that the postcard had promised me, even though I'd become aware of the cracks in the town's commercial model—it was run by mostly white males in management that made servants of working-class people, most of us under thirty. The European hotel manager whom I worked for was a master at enticing wealthy visitors to the mountains, inventing celebrity ski events and honeymoon rituals to fill the hotel during its then sparsely occupied winter season. One day he brought me into his office, closed the door using a mechanical and intimidating button under his desktop, and let me in on a special mission. He wanted me to approach the Stoney Nation to bring back Banff Indian Days, a three-day spectacle that had first been created in the 1890s to entertain tourists trapped in Banff by spring flooding and that had been so popular that it continued until 1978.

Banff Indian Days was a tourism boon that brought Indigenous people from the reserves back to the park and encouraged white people to photograph the Stoney people in their traditional attire as an "opportunity of a lifetime to capture and preserve an authentic Indian person in their natural surroundings."[16] The Stoney people invited Cree, Muskwacis (Hobema), the Ktunaxa (Kootenay), Tsuu T'ina (Sarcee), Siksika (Blackfoot), Piikani (Peigan), and Kainai (Blood) Nations. In Banff's early days, as part of the removal of local Indigenous peoples, the Sundance and other spiritual ceremonies of the Stoney Nation had been banned by the federal government. Tommy Snow of the Stoney Nation said that for generations they'd had to practice much of their culture in secret.[17] Though the festival was created to appeal to white tourists, Stoney Elders reported that this was the continuation of a tradition of gathering for trade, exchange, and socialization in the summer months.[18] There was a daily parade, as well as dancing, singing, and sporting competitions. The Stoney came because they wished to come.

They received tangible support—food rations, payment to bring their horses, reciprocity for photographs. They might also have a chance to visit distant relatives and participate in ceremony on those days when the camp was closed to the public. These were important connections during the Depression era, and in the hundred years when the pass system controlled Indigenous movements.[19]

"Talk to some people about bringing back Indian Days. We need to fill up the hotel in the shoulder season," the manager told me, dismissing me with his hand.

I had no understanding of the traditions of Banff Indian Days. I didn't want to be charged with undertaking a responsibility where I had no experience or connections. I felt this invitation was a setup. I pretended we'd never had the conversation. Then, I didn't know the traumatic history of Indigenous removal from Banff National Park lands, but it was already clear to me that the hotel corporation I worked for believed that any effort to represent Indigenous culture had to attract park visitors and hotel guests and prioritize the enjoyment of white people. I wasn't comfortable with this notion. A few months after my passive refusal to re-create Banff Indian Days, for reasons I would never know, I was laid off from the Banff Springs Hotel.

I would later go on to work at history museums and science centers, beginning at the Whyte Museum of the Canadian Rockies in Banff, which specialized in mountain art, culture, and history. Every museum reflects the biases of its leadership and conveys values about the objects it collects and exhibits. Throughout my career, I witnessed colonialist, racist, and patriarchal manipulation of content that resulted in missing information, poorly interpreted artifacts, a refusal to acknowledge a thriving contemporary culture of Indigenous peoples, and the portrayal of Europeans and settlers as superior and dominant. Throughout my adult life, in these institutions as well as the Canadian education system, I'd not heard an honest portrayal of the pass system,[20] one enacted by the Canadian government on Indigenous communities. And outside a few academic journals, there hadn't been public interpretation that Canada's first national park enshrined a dispossessed landscape, that it had been set up as a model not only for preservation but the disinheritance of Indigenous peoples from the lands that provided them sustenance. It would take me thirty years to learn that we hadn't been at the vanguard of ecological integrity at all; we'd been enacting the white supremacy we were trained to endorse.

Homeward

Indigenous land in the national parks needs to be returned, not just because much Indigenous wisdom has been lost—after generations of Indigenous nations being prohibited from Banff National Park—but because we live in a time when reassessment of our history can lead us to new awareness and action. In an article published by *The Walrus*, Jago denounced "a parks system that has robbed and impoverished Indigenous peoples." He suggested that Canadians need to change their concept of wilderness and said, "As Indigenous peoples rebuild, we are striving to reconnect with our lost territories. This means reclaiming parks whenever possible and asserting stewardship and economic rights when we can't get the land itself back."[21]

There are movements within Banff National Park to organize for Indigenous leadership. After being invited to sit on the diversity, equity, and inclusion committee for Banff's long-term tourism plan, I was pleasantly surprised that the group conversation turned toward land back initiatives. Young people, marginalized people, and modest income entrepreneurs are increasingly frozen out of investing in the small town, whose businesses are coalitions of wealthy, white owners with capital and power. For example, the Banff Hospitality Collective owns twelve of the town's restaurants, while family-owned restaurants dwindle, with few able to afford the cash outlay of renting inside the town's tourism corridor. In a recent presentation led by Indigenous artist Nahanni McKay, the diversity, equity, and inclusion group brought forward ideas for the plan like prioritizing Indigenous naming policies, indigenizing historical interpretation, increasing art projects and foodways,[22] and providing streamlined access and policy approval for Indigenous businesses. Now it will be up to the town and the tourism board to determine the direction of its program.

Truth and reconciliation may mean that local Indigenous people might once again act as witnesses on the land from which they were removed. In eighty guardian programs across Canada, Indigenous peoples have been placed in charge of looking after parks and other conservation areas on their traditional lands. These programs are funded by a $173-million commitment over five years in the federal government's 2021 budget. Guardians manage protected areas, monitor animals and plants, test water quality, and help develop land-use plans. America's Pew Charitable Trusts now want to form a cross-border partnership to help fund the Indigenous Guardians program in the Northwest Territories, a model that could be utilized across the country. Frank Brown, a Heiltsuk hereditary chief and professor in resource and environmental management at Simon Fraser University, along with Calvin Sandborn, legal director of the University of Victoria Environmental Law Centre, wrote of the role of Guardians, who "patrol their territorial lands and waters, enforce environmental laws by reporting violators and educating the public, and watch for issues such as overfishing, poaching, illegal logging, damage to cultural sites and pollution."[23] Environment and Climate Change Minister Steven Guilbeault said, "There's great interest in the federal government in continuing to support this program." And why not, when it's proven to be one of Canada's essential resources for good land conservation and management?

Eli Enns, a research fellow at the University of Victoria and member of the Nuu-chah-nulth First Nations, said his people's experience with the Pacific Rim National Park Reserve reveals a vision of the future. In 2004, Parliament passed legislation to return eighty-six hectares of land from the Pacific Rim and Riding Mountain parks to dispossessed Indigenous peoples. The Pacific Rim reserve for the Tla-o-qui-aht First Nations on the present Pacific coast of Vancouver Island, British Columbia, has become a residential community powered by geothermal energy.[24]

Hayden King, Anishinaabe from Beausoleil First Nation and executive director of the Yellowhead Institute, writes of the ongoing dispossession of Indigenous lands in Canada in a land back report by the First Nation–led research center and speaks to the questions of defining self-government and Aboriginal rights as "informed consent." "The argument that we're making, and the argument that has been made by others, is if you're going to go into Indigenous territories, whether it's a treaty or nontreaty area, let's just work to get the consent of the Indigenous people affected. And those communities can define what consent means to them," King says. Strategies for land back might include reoccupying the land, environmental assessment and monitoring, and what King calls "consent protocols or permitting protocols." As disputes over land and failures of negotiation are increasing, in pipeline land disputes and elsewhere, the call for new models of leadership and collaboration must be led by Indigenous thinking and ways of being.

Robert Sandford, Global Water Futures chair with the United Nations' Institute for Water, Climate & Health, spoke at a 2022 tourism conference in Victoria, British Columbia, regarding the shifts necessary for Canada and the impact on those who traveled here: "We are aiming to protect 30% of our landmass by 2030 and 50% by 2050 so that we prevent the collapse of the entire self-regulating, biodiversity-based planetary life support system. I can't see how we can hope to achieve these goals in Canada without full Indigenous engagement, and that cannot be possible without meaningful reconciliation. Who would not want to come to a country that after centuries of division and environmental disregard looked inward?"

This is only a beginning of what might happen if Canada oriented toward a model of a natural world that included kinship with its Indigenous peoples. Outside the linearity and excesses of capitalism and the dogmatic confines of a purity ethic for wilderness, our Indigenous peoples have held the historic knowledge of what it means to make a land home. What might that look like if a local movement for land back initiatives unites toward real reconciliation for Canada's forced losses? People whose identities are white and settler must be open to seeing historic and present definitions of wilderness that have been brutal, confining, and all too separate from every being who made this place home. Perhaps then we might remain truly awed by these national parks.

6

Truth, Grief, and Reconciliation

The antithesis of lynch culture is kinship—and *kin* is not just associated with lineage or biological markers or bloodlines but is a way of relating that asks us to go beyond extracting value. Kinship relations include our ancestors, and all the ways of connecting with our family dead, including those names, gifts, stories, and traits that have been passed to us. Kin can include people, plants, animals, waterways, weather, and celestial bodies. Indigenous cultures speak of the responsibility to the collective, including an awareness that we belong to, and are in relationship with the earth. Dr. Zoe Todd, Métis anthropologist and researcher-artist in Indigenous Governance and Freshwater Fish Futures at Simon Fraser University, along with geographer and sound artist AM Kanngieser, says that "relationships are connections and interactions between people, environments and beings through time and space that are lived through the body and the senses. We are relations. To be in relation is an agreement of, and a commitment to, care. It is an intention of reciprocity."[1]

Queer cultures have affirmed that it's necessary and generative to make kin beyond families. Kinship doesn't occur only from a heteronormative nuclear family model. Across cultures, intimate relationship extends outside the relationships defined by marriage and child making and parenting. The state supports a few family and relational forms and economic arrangements but tends to bestow status on white and patriarchal organizations of belonging.[2] Still, kinship goes beyond approaches defined by political, legal, and religious regulation.

My experience of kinship happened throughout my life in living close to the land, becoming sensitized to hearing the voices/beingness of the more-than-human, in practicing seasonal Celtic rituals with my family and community, in Pagan practices that were nonhierarchical and magical, in creating ceremony for ancestors, in moments of recognizing interconnected mutual belonging. The notion of kinship arrived in an embodied manner, most fervently in 2016, when the mountains of the Canadian Rockies invited me into reciprocal relationship, and then in the following months, when I was seriously ill in a room where I watched the light and the trees and the mountains outside my windows. When I was able, I could move into groups of women and nonbinary people, people I considered kin, people who spoke of what was happening to their bodies as they realigned with their families and their ecosystems. All along, these ways made kinship materially felt, lived, and in my sense and language, with an openness toward experiencing a reciprocity. Author and professor Joseph M. Pierce (Cherokee) says, "The land is not 'fictive' or 'chosen' kin. Our bodies are not symbolically made of stars. We are those cosmic elements, and in recognizing ourselves as cosmologically interrelated, in connecting cross-temporally as part of an emergent and ongoing epistemological project, we maintain the bonds of reciprocity and collaboration that are at the heart of our stories."[3]

I also live with a mind trained by colonial thoughts and normative ways. I'm young in my awareness of what it is to become responsible to kin. I'm reading Indigenous scholars and listening to my elders and arching toward land-based awarenesses of reciprocity. And this mind often experiences interconnection beyond what I have the capacity to think.

This is what I'm learning. We live in webs of mutuality—we influence our friends, we take care of more than descendants, we make family from more than nuclear groups and create partnership from more than dyadic romance, we have relationships with land and place, and we might live as more than a power exchange based on wealth and whiteness. Our governance models need not be imitative of the governments we live under.

The writer and social critic bell hooks has said that "one of the most vital ways we sustain ourselves is by building communities of resistance, places where we know we are not alone."[4] If lynch culture is created to legitimize violence toward marginalized people, then it is in making kin in community and its attendant coalitional work that it is possible to build democracy, end systemic racism, combat hate and extremism, and enhance bonds.

Structural racism informs lynching's apparatus. Lynch culture is part of a system that finds ways to exert violence on Indigenous, Black, and other marginalized people rather than live in a culture of justice. The motivation of modern lynch culture is toward punishment, using white supremacist beliefs as its fuel. Instead, in kinship systems, communities might rely on compassion, awareness, and the recognizing of the other as oneself. Though we are in human interdependent relations through the stewarding of life and being with death, kinship necessarily extends beyond the bloodline. Kinship involves the ability to see through the eyes of another, to believe others' experiences, to divest from fixed views, to recognize that we exist in a multiplicity. Kinship doesn't require political affiliation or alliance to certain beliefs or habits, but instead embraces the self and the self's interconnectedness with all. Kinship might extend to more-than-humans, a cosmology informed by Indigenous peoples worldwide whose stories are collective and relational. These kinways can be both enacted by individuals and built into systems.

In one example of this more-than-human kinship, Haudenosaunee and Anishinaabe scholar Vanessa Watts and Mohawk scholar Sandra Styres created new forms of study by speaking to Land and place as correlational. "Place refers to physical geographic space and Land (capital 'L') is more than a physical geographic space. It is a place where spirituality exists, and the living beings present on that Land are all connected."[5] Canadian scientist Suzanne Simard found that plants and trees behave in ways that engender forest diversity, community, health, productivity, adaptability, resilience, equanimity, and provide a recognition of kin that might be instructive to humans.[6]

Kinship includes not just ecological empathy but the awareness that our minds and bodies are not solo enterprises. Recent microbiological research tells us that humans are built from relational networks that connect us to every other being. We live as an interspecies gateway to bacteria, archaea, fungi, protists, and viruses who live in our skin, mammary glands, seminal fluid, uteruses, ovarian follicles, lungs, saliva, and gastrointestinal tracts.[7] There are more nonhuman cells than there are human cells living within our bodies. Regardless of whether the presence of microbes is beneficial or detrimental, our lives are inextricably linked to them, perhaps even changing the nature of what we might mean by "our" bodies. We have a coevolutionary history with these more-than-humans, leading to the question of who is sustaining whom. It's suggested in recent research that even blood—the liquid medium that carries and sustains the most basic, and most essential elements of life—has metabolically active bacteria that can be found not just in disease processes but in healthy humans.[8] Despite what white nationalists ascribe, purity will never be possible in the bloodline; we already have foreign cells in human blood, and we are healthy humans with their existence. These microorganisms are what we might call the *other* and yet they're making us their Land. We're forever being altered by a microbiome that is whole within itself, incapable of being split into subject and object. This blood is never contaminated with the *other*: we are it. Indeed, it's truer to infer that there are parts of us that exist without fear of contamination, without identification with stainlessness.

This literal reshaping in my body about who kin might be or become leads me to questions about my racist past. What if the ancestral wounding of lynch culture—instead of being a fixed history we can't change—had potential to become the gateway into another being's experience? What if the whiteness that's part of the ways that we think and imagine our lives—and even where whiteness continues to replicate in forms of modern racial violence—could be transmuted, a kind of portal to kin-making?

Kincentric ecology is informed by Indigenous worldviews, but it's problematic to suggest that the systems responsible for disowned relationality—slavery, colonialism, legal lynching, capitalism, imperialism, and environmental injustice—might truly reckon with a full awareness of Indigenous forms of relations. Kim TallBear, Sisseton Wahpeton Oyate professor at the University of Alberta, who specializes in racial politics in science, says that "making kin is to make people into familiars in order to relate. This seems fundamentally different from negotiating relations between those who are seen as different—between 'sovereigns' or 'nations'—especially when one of those nations is a militarized and white supremacist empire."[9] Colonial practices and capitalistic ways disadvantage settlers toward relating, both historically and in the modern era. Even though we are settlers living at the height of capitalistic excess and with the powerful influence of an untaxed multimillion/billionaire class, we might still consider the ways in which we can organize systems open to kinship. To become a familiar, to invite into familiarity, we must collectively disarm habitual ways of reacting and knowing, especially when those are based in holding dominant our beliefs, stories, and governing traditions.

Exclusion is a dominant belief and practice that's taken hold in this era and is opposed to kincentric movements and organization. As political journalist Ezra Klein and other data researchers have posited, it is our differences (particularly in the electoral politics and nation building of the last century) that have significantly defined our personal identities.[10] Our politics are increasingly polarized not necessarily because of who we find affinity with but because we share antipathy for an *other*. Historically, othering is how whiteness behaves—it creates an enemy, and we are placed in a position to bond or exclude. This behavior impacts our families and our kin. From our dinner tables to our national interests (and rivals) in this era, we create ever more divisiveness than belonging. TallBear and Kahnawake Mohawk political anthropologist and Indigenous feminist Audra Simpson have stated another alternative: "it does not only matter what we claim about who we are; it also matters who claims us as kin."[11]

Canadian philosopher Alexis Shotwell took up this question of who declared her as kin in her essay "Claiming Bad Kin" and noted, "White nationalists claim me, as a white person, as kin. Though they may not know me personally and though they would likely despair of my politics, they are working for a world in which I and white people like me hold citizenship, reproduce 'the white race,' and are safe and flourishing."[12] To claim rather than disavow our connections to people who have done wrong, to commit to address social relationships where racism exists but isn't acknowledged, to join as collaborationists to undergird the efforts of racial justice movements is a hefty challenge. We may already be in kinship with those we deem "bad," those who are active perpetrators of racism and misogyny, those who didn't vote as we did, and those who hoard wealth. In any case, we do not "cancel" those kin we find offensive in their behavior and ideas; instead, we take them on. We retrieve them. We oppose their acts while we belong to them.

Interrogating our settler inheritance is uncomfortable and humility-producing. But if we are to care for more than our white families, we can't keep sidestepping the past and refusing its effect on the present. I do not want to co-opt the work of Todd, TallBear, Simpson, Watts, and

Styres in regard to Indigenous theory and kinship practices but rather want to speak to their impact as well as the influence on my work and my life of Shotwell's ideas of relational thinking.

But first, I wanted to find models of those who were actively working within movements and communities to deal with harm, abuse, and amends processes. Author and activist adrienne marie brown points out the difference between serious abuses of power in relationships—ones where positional power affects subordinates—from those making missteps, or continuing a kind of flawed process of learning, and the tendency in cancel culture to treat all mistakes with the same removal from spaces. In *We Will Not Cancel Us*, she says, "We won't end the systemic patterns of harm by isolating and picking off individuals. . . . We need to flood the entire system with life-affirming principles and practices, to clear the channels between us of the toxicity of supremacy, to heal from the harms of a legacy of devaluing some lives and needs in order to indulge others."[13]

I wanted to release my binary thinking away from *good* and *bad*, especially in regard to my family and ancestors. This was a seemingly oppositional position, for legal lynching was state-sanctioned violence at the cruelest edge of what one human could inflict on another, and my family was directly implicated on my paternal side and on my maternal side, responsible for Bethea's murder. Still, there might be more radical (indeed, revolutionary) love if my practices could allow the noticing of supremacy where it existed and if I focused on working with others to collectively break those cycles of harm.

Tufts University professor and author Christina Sharpe's essay "Lose Your Kin" says that "whiteness is a political project, and it is also a logic, by which I mean it is a calculus, a way of sorting oneself and others into categories of those who must be protected and those who are, or soon will be, expendable."[14] Lynch culture operates by this same distorted logic, using whiteness to inflict violence while also protecting whoever is perceived as kin from consequences for that harm. This is how the white endorsers of Rainey Bethea's murder could report the atmosphere that day at the hanging was one of hushed witness and white historians could hide the horror in their desire to protect their white townsfolk. That's how these stories are passed in our families, if they're recognized at all. Our traditions aim toward the reinforcement of belonging, ignoring that our very presence at a state-sponsored lynching is in itself horrific.

There was no acknowledgment of reparations being needed in Owensboro or in my family because there had never been awareness that the punishment was unjust. The state operated as if Black people were considered disposable and wholly ungrievable. This belief is passed as policy and law through families, school systems, justice systems, and others complicit in this denial. America is composed entirely of limited kinship relations that operate in just this way.

I understand about the refusal to repair.

I've spent much of my adult life resisting connection to my extended Kentucky family and ancestors. Living in the Pacific Northwest and then in Western Canada, it seemed easier to remain at a distance. I couldn't reconcile these cultures that were so different from each other: one northern, progressive, cool, and passive-aggressive; the other, southern and traditional, with bless-your-heart, sometimes disparaging judgment.

When I first learned of my extended family's connection to this legal lynching, I wanted to end my connection to them. I wanted to exclude everyone except for my siblings, not just end what I saw as "their" racist behavior. But exclusion is problematic for not just the ousted. As the trees would tell us in their mycorrhizas, or "fungus roots," aliveness is a symbiotic act, one that transmits nourishment, regardless of the ability for the other roots to respond in return. In contrast, we live in a human society that values hierarchy, enforces the binary, insists on conformity to belong, and likes to associate with those who are not needy. Unlike trees, whiteness is known for being afraid to give beyond what's owed, and to those who are consistently stressed.

Today, I don't consider racist members of my family to be "bad" kin. From the vantage point of one who has been both a victim *and* a perpetrator, I consider myself to carry as many "bad" racist behaviors as any of my family who were also raised to center whiteness and perpetuate lynch culture. I can sense a possibility that we as kin can find our way toward a conversation about truth and that we might repair what has been fractured in the Bethea hanging and offer reconciliation for our family's and community's part. We are knit together, and love has the capacity to change perceptions. So does being willing to confront wrong. I didn't start out with an idea that any acknowledgment of harm would be possible.

Like many children in white families, I'd been raised by parents who wanted me to put family first, beyond our family's self-interest, but I hadn't much context for how to do so. We prioritized holidays, reunions, Sunday gatherings around the table, and the sharing of food, but strict rules had been set up to define conditions for belonging and that had prevented us from reconciliation with each other and those beyond our shared genetics and relational bonds. Belonging was also complicated by the secrets in our family, secrets that kept me and other family members fearful of violence that might be enacted against us.

My aunt told me that she'd been sexually assaulted by a neighbor at three, but when she told her sisters of the crime, they didn't believe her and threatened her with isolation for speaking about it. I recorded my aunt telling the story in an interview for an essay I was writing, and when my extended family found out, they accused her of lying. My aunt called me in tears that day, terrified of the loss of belonging to her family, and said that she felt she had to withdraw her consent for the story. (We later talked about a way she could go forward with restrictions on the content of the essay, and she changed her mind and chose to include some of the material.) This was common socialization on both sides of my family. We were taught not to admit what was happening in front of us, and we were controlled through the threat of banishment. When I was a child, I learned that there was a limit to what kinds of truths could be told. But when I became an adult, there were times that, to keep myself and my children safe, I had to choose constrained relationships with my extended family. To rejoin with my parents, I had to communicate boundaries. Usually, I talked with them once a week, but while I was learning about what had happened in our common traumatic past, and around the racism that had connected us, I didn't always have the skills I needed to be in conversation with my parents, cousins, aunts, and uncles.

And even now, when I write about the possibility of connection, I know that sometimes it can be damaging for people to stay in an active relationship with family. We can create a chosen family rather than be harmed by a living family who would seek to harm our bodies and restrict our lives. Those who are banished from their families need the support of the rest of us who have enough love and resources to share. Interconnected kin networks form out of this trauma and repair. We share everything—mutual aid, multigenerational homes, climate change, comradeship, and numerous social conditions, among others. "Tell me about your family," Sarah Sentilles, the author of *Stranger Care* says, "because I know belonging comes in all shapes and sizes, visible and invisible, hidden and made and chosen and found."[15]

But there's a defining stasis in disassembling lynch culture in that settlers exist on stolen land, owning the benefits of slavery and harm against Indigenous people, Black people, and people of color. We break this spell by, as Shotwell suggests, "recognizing the resources white people have to offer to resistance are not our own, even as we use them."[16] As white individuals living inside a lynch culture we created and wish to break, we live on both sides of the line—we must divest of whiteness while becoming ever aware of how it asks for our participation. And this whiteness shapes most everything we desire and acquire. As Noel Ignatiev has noted of whiteness, "Without the privileges attached to it, the white race would not exist, and the white skin would have no more social significance than big feet."

Before Breonna Taylor's murder happened in Kentucky, I didn't actively intervene in questioning the authority of the police. After we moved to Seattle in 2006, I remember walking past two police officers who had handcuffed a Black man in my Seattle neighborhood. I didn't stop to ask questions. I was suspicious of the police but unable to intervene.

Like some white people, I'd been focused elsewhere, including on diminishing the violence enacted on me, those moments when I had been demeaned, devalued, objectified, and sexualized. Those of us who have experienced violence in relationships might have become used to physical abuse but remain unaware of the wounding we enact on others. Some of us have chosen not to claim that we have been injurious because we have become accustomed to thinking that we have limited power and control. Some of us still identify as a victim, though our injuries are long gone. But to be fully in the human condition, white women must recognize that the white female body is leveraged—including by white women—for the purposes of racist, patriarchal systems.

The week that Breonna Taylor was murdered, my sisters and I talked, but not about Breonna because the story was then referred to in the media as "serving a search warrant" and didn't receive much notice.[17] Perhaps there wasn't news because it was the beginning of COVID-19 or because there wasn't any graphic video footage to bring attention to the case, but also, Black women's experiences of social injustice have nearly always been left out of mainstream media and political attention.

That week, following a difficult treatment for a blood disorder that compromised my immunity, I'd gone into quarantine, my first of the COVID-19 pandemic. My hair was falling out in handfuls from the steroids I'd been given. I'd resigned from my work teaching veterans because I was too sick to show up. I was to be treated with transfusions of plasma until the Canadian government approved another drug that might return me to health. In the weeks after Breonna's murder was reported in the news, I was confused and angered. Being immunocompromised, I wasn't able to cross the border to join protests, but I could send letters to government officials, file petitions, give money, and ask my friends and family to do the same.

During the summer and autumn of 2020, my sisters shared their impressions of what was happening in their city. They were concerned about the violence of the protests downtown. I talked through my experience with marches in Seattle, how I'd first stayed at arm's length from them, but because I was aligned with labor and antiwar causes, I had to shift my thinking around what interventions were necessary, including direct action. I shared my belief in the necessity for protest violence to gain attention when violence against Black people had always been accepted by white communities. We exchanged information on activist campaigns like those being organized for Breonna's birthday, Fight for Breonna, and the #SayHerName campaign, created by the African American Policy Forum headed by legal scholar Kimberlé Crenshaw. Had the place I'd known as home since my teenage years become ever more terrifying for its Black citizens? Or had the racial terror finally registered with me because of the rising awareness of the Black Lives Matter movement everywhere?

After I learned about the reckless endangerment and illegal actions of the Louisville Metro Police Department (LMPD), my husband and I wrote letters calling for the removal of Mayor Greg Fischer from the US Conference of Mayors presidency, and we also asked him to resign. Being part of a group that was able to take action was helpful when I felt geographically distant from all that was happening in my home state.

In those years, I became aware that intellectual ideas are helpful but not necessarily tied to understanding lynch culture. The work that I undertook in the process of writing these essays and letters to leaders and government officials demonstrated that this awareness comes also from being with feelings and sensations in the body, with undertaking an ongoing practice of recognizing lynch culture as it reveals itself, our daily disquiet. Even when it became clear how very favored my white body is, it took me longer to claim allegiance with my family and community because I didn't want to speak of the violence built into political parties, policies, and institutions. Until the moment that I chose to speak, nothing changed.

With two decades of sobriety, I had clarity about how shame functioned to suppress my power and creativity and how costly it is to make invisible human frailty. A movement toward family was necessary to begin unraveling what had really happened and what the work ahead might be. From 2015 to 2020, in addition to talking with my family, I continued in my antiracism education while also choosing a nonintellectual way to understand my racism. Body-oriented practices carried me through my research and writing work and provided a way to help me understand my family patterns in a fresh way.

While researching my ancestors, I made an altar for my parents and grandparents, and I found a sound bowl to create a ceremony. Every day for years I struck the sound bowl and offered gratitude to four generations of my maternal and paternal line, naming them, and thanking them for my life. Over time, I began to feel their presence and offered gratitude. I felt permission to write this book from them and that they were willing to be resources to assist its development. As Nick Cave has written of ghosts and ancestors and dream visitations, "these spirits are ideas essentially, but they are our stunned imaginations reawakening after the calamity. Like ideas, these spirits speak of possibility. . . . Create your spirits. Call to them. Will them alive. Speak to them. It is their impossible and ghostly hands that draw us back to the world from which we were jettisoned, better now, and unimaginably changed."[18]

When I thought about my ancestors, it seemed that Grandmaw Ralph wasn't only to be known as the perpetrator, though that was, at the time, the way that I'd been defining her. As I returned to her as a granddaughter, my love for her deepened. And I began to acknowledge the ways that I'd remained silent rather than confront racist institutions.

I researched my family tree, so I could understand the movements across land that my ancestors had made and know how our origin stories had come to be. I asked mentors like transpersonal psychologist and wilderness leader Sheila Belanger to help me learn ways to be with my ancestors, including my deceased parents, which would include ceremony and journeying. I considered these practices to be similar to what my Gaelic forebears might have ritualized. Belanger and I went out on the land together on Whidbey Island, Washington, and talked about the vision I was carrying to help me end these outworn patterns in myself and my family. I told her I wanted to be honest about my history. I wanted to stop being cowardly about my past, America's past, and I wanted some elders to show up to help me.

My mother and father were dead, I was the eldest grandchild, the next generation in my family aging toward death. I needed to know how it might be possible that the injustice done to Rainey Bethea would be taken up by me, as a descendant. Was it possible for the next generations in the family line to redress the wrongs done in the previous generation? The more I learned about the Bethea case, the more I saw injustice. But as I interrogated the patterns of white womanhood, I was learning to be cautious about identifying with the victim. My shared fate with my grandmother would have to be part of my life. We were knit together through a common force, related to each other and the hanging she and my grandfather had witnessed.

What was I willing to do to risk the loyalty of my kin? How might I see beyond family and notice those I refused to include? Would those I considered *my* people allow me to challenge them, or would I have to refuse to repair a relationship? Would I be challenged by them in the same way?

For generations my kin had only known the white version of the story of the last public execution in America—that Rainey Bethea undoubtedly committed the crime, that the punishment was just, that the crowd was somber, that Owensboro got a bad rap in the press coverage of that day. Among white Americans like us, there's been a rejection of the acts of perpetration by our ancestors, even as we benefit from racism in the present, even if we can't acknowledge this privilege, even if we don't want it. At the same time, there's been a reshaping of public history at places like the Whitney Plantation, the National Memorial for Peace and Justice, the Legacy Museum, and the Canadian Museum for Human Rights, near my former home in Western Canada.

Alongside narratives that include class, gender, race, and sexuality in their interpretations, there's been an outcry from white people who do not wish "their" histories to be rewritten to tell the stories of their kin as perpetrators. Reactions in the form of book banning, revisionist interpretations of civil rights, dismantling efforts to address systemic racism, lies about the influence of teaching children about racism, threatening loss of funding to schools and other institutions that teach about racism—these are the headlines of the present, not of the past. To see beyond victimhood, to know how our perpetrator-selves get built involves returning to our ancestors as well as hearing how our kin see their lives. It involves the confrontation with the empathic fallacies that convince white people that their racism doesn't exist, like the one several of my relatives told me when they said we couldn't be racist because we had Black people in our family, we had Black folks as friends.

I knew that these new practices didn't function as, or substitute for, my antiracism education and activism. But, in the beginning, I couldn't act until I brought myself close to my family and understood what it was like to reckon with all that had happened. I knew that I couldn't absorb ancestral information and work on an antiracism plan unless more of my family knew about what I was writing and what work might lie ahead of me. In 2019, years into the research for the book, I decided to take a trip to Kentucky.

That June, my Ralph family hosted a dinner for my husband and me at Moonlight Barbecue, where we reminisced and talked about our love of the barbecue tradition that had been in our family for generations and was likely influenced by African Americans and, before them, the Indigenous peoples of the Americas, another history that remained unacknowledged.[19] At that time, there was a rift between family members over a will of a favorite aunt, and there were hard feelings about how things had happened after her death. I met with some aunts who would speak with me, but there were others who were afraid I was going to use the research process to expose their views on the aunt's legacy to other members of the family. I began to interview the family members who were willing to speak, not just about their knowledge of this legal lynching that our ancestors had been a part of but also about their lives, what events had impacted them, and how they experienced our family. I met six aunts, uncles, and cousins in their homes, and in our hotel room, and in a diner that still served that southern staple of meat and three.[20] I also met with the closest tie to our Birkhead family, my mother's brother, and stayed with him and his wife in their home outside Owensboro. In the process, I learned about the myths that had been passed along to us, how we held common secrets, and most of all, how we rarely spoke of racism, ours or anyone else's. Very few knew about the details of the Bethea hanging, except that our grandparents had been present. No one was taught about the legal lynching in school, and no one imagined that the event was anything other than a public execution for a criminal.

I returned from Owensboro to see my sisters, who lived in Louisville near each other, and their children and grandchildren, and they took me out for dinner to share stories about the trip. I told them that one interview included a cousin's use of a racial slur and their sibling admonishing them for it. I'd heard the cousin excuse their statement by saying they used this name for all low-life people, Black or white. My sisters and their husbands reported that people in their workplaces and communities had done the same thing and noted how prevalent racist denigration was not just in rural counties but in the city of Louisville too.

After dinner, we stood near the porch, talking softly about the racist parts of our childhood. Our father had taken us for brunch at the Jefferson Club, an elite professional club that unlike the Pendennis Club in Louisville did not exclude Black people, Jews, and women from membership, though I'd rarely seen a Black member dining there. We talked about the lore in Louisville that after the street the Pendennis building was located on was renamed for the city's most famous native, Muhammad Ali, it had prompted the club to change its address for a time to a side street.[21] I was reminded that white people called these choices "traditions." I also remembered that I rarely refused my father's invitation to his club.

I told my sisters that I believed that most white people who participated in the last public execution in America were there to experience a communal sense of white supremacy, but after the headlines from across America berated them, they mostly turned away from acknowledging that they'd witnessed the event. Despite these denials, my grandmother, many white Americans, and white media preferred instead to claim that the Bethea hanging resulted from legal legitimacy and just punishment.

My ancestors had benefited from lynch culture in Kentucky; they'd taken jobs when Black people were limited in the work they might do and threatened if they overstepped their position. My ancestors were mostly European immigrants, and I benefited from immigration policies preferential to them. On my paternal side, William Thomas Ralph, my third great-grandfather, had come from Virginia to Kentucky around the turn of the nineteenth century, and our family's presence in the state had resulted in farmland being available to us as white tenants, and some of my relatives were direct inheritors of acreage and property. On my maternal side, Jesse Abraham Birkhead, my fifth great-grandfather, had come from Virginia around the turn of the nineteenth century and had been given 160 acres of land by the state of Kentucky. I lived because others died, and were enslaved, and had their lands stolen from them.

I returned home to Canada and reflected that I hadn't said anything when my cousin used a racial slur. I rationalized that it was because his sibling jumped in so fast that I didn't have a chance to call him out. But I think that I preferred to stay in the role of the journalist asking the questions, to remain an outsider, to refuse to become oppositional in case there were more disclosures coming that I could report on. I couldn't tell which of these behaviors I disliked more—refusing to take a stance or pretending that these folks weren't my own.

I thought about what bell hooks meant when she said, "For me, forgiveness and compassion are always linked: how do we hold people accountable for wrongdoing and yet at the same time remain in touch with their humanity enough to believe in their capacity to be transformed?"[22] Despite the stories I'd heard—of people canceling their families, of refusing holiday celebrations and family reunions, of ending any contact with racist relatives—it seemed that I didn't have to cut myself off to stay safe, but I wasn't yet willing to see myself fully in my southern family. I felt like I was neither here nor there, weighted with ambiguity and nostalgia, existing in a ghostland. This seemed a very colonial way of reacting to family.

My family had shared ancestral stories of strife and scarcity, and these were focused mostly on our Irish, English, and German family lines. We told stories of ancestors who had cut themselves off from their elders and their extended family to leave for America. There were few narratives that showed us how to live as a collective. There were tales of survival, of stories lost, of languages and dialects we no longer spoke. We told of where we were raised and wronged, praised and wounded, loved and hurt. There were not tales of other nonwhite humans as kin, of LGBTQ kin, of feminist kin, of mentally ill kin, of refugee kin, much less recognizing kinship in plants, animals, fungi, protists, archaea, and bacteria. I wanted to leave the centering of the desire for status, wealth, property, and land and instead experience what it would be to grow in empathy and solidarity. I wanted to be with a movement, community, or multigenerational group that acted with the kind of inclusive compassion that I longed for. The closest I'd come was in being with the community of mostly queer artists in Seattle, where we'd lived for two decades. I wanted a family story of authentic expression *and* belonging.

My grief intensified during this time. Rage and regret in waking up to the reality of legal lynching. Sorrow for Rainey Bethea and his family. The sadness in feeling apart from the family that raised me and (like myself) hadn't grappled with our connection to this injustice. I'd mourned too because I'd pushed away my family out of anger and refusal to believe in their capacity for change. I saw their need for membership in political parties, faith congregations, community boards. But I also knew this was not the same as belonging, the kind of belonging we can have when we are deeply loved and valued, when there aren't conditions for inclusion. Speaking about the violence of whiteness risks judgment in groups that center the power of membership over those considered *other.* In movements toward justice, there's often unsteady alliances, places where the status quo is difficult to contest, but holding our voices can become more painful than speaking. My sisters and I continued to talk about racism in our family, and my family and I had difficult discussions about the role of the police in Louisville and elsewhere. Still, as I discovered more about my family's participation in the legal lynching, there was a very old sense of being disloyal as a descendant, including a desire to keep the information a secret, and these sensations rose up through my body. In my confusion and shame, I didn't want to speak to friends and fellow writers about what I was learning about the racism of our Kentucky ancestors. For years, I kept my writing quiet.

Jonathan M. Metzl's *Dying of Whiteness* tells stories of white Americans who harm their own well-being out of racial resentment. Political movements in the South coalesce around exclusion of rights to shape state and political party agendas. These movements promised to "restore white privilege or quell threats to idealized notions of white authority represented by demographic or cultural shifts."[23] Policies extend to how we think about family, and how we raise our children, how we think about our elders. These policies have most impacted those Black and other marginalized people who would have harm inflicted on them by such actions, but they also affect white people.

Some of my family members used the language of racial resentment that Senator Mitch McConnell, Senator Rand Paul, Representative Thomas Massie, and other Kentuckians encourage. Others were aware of how politicians boosted racial antipathy or hatred. Returning to my extended kin seemed counterintuitive because I needed to be vulnerable with them, to share what I was learning and feeling, and sometimes I didn't want to open up to them. The way forward was to reconnect with my extended family, to enter into conversation when I heard racist ideas, to invite them to educate me on their perceptions, to share responsibility for what would no longer be tolerated. This path seemed contrary to protection through absenting myself, but I knew that I had to take it. I had to rejoin with them so we might begin to make another way. I wasn't sure that I could give like the trees, without concern for reciprocity.

In the past, I'd let myself off the hook for my responsibilities to ancestral deeds by blaming the racism of the era. Like most white people, I had tended to believe that there were some white folks with racist biases, rather than assign blame to the systems that created and perpetuated harm. Contemporary writers like Clint Smith, Ibram X. Kendi, Camonghne Felix, Roxane Gay, Ta-Nehisi Coates, Jesmyn Ward, adrienne marie brown, and Tanya Talaga address system-wide reform and the historic and ongoing harms of systemic racism, including the conflation of individual responsibility with systematic transformation. Many Americans continue to reconstruct the history of lynching to reflect their changing perspectives on moral behavior, denying their ancestors' involvement, obscuring their memories, and being asked by their kin to keep secrets. I wanted to know what it would take to invest in new models of safety and communal well-being. How might we return our broken institutions to those centering kinship?

As part of my studies with Sheila Belanger, I was introduced to Systemic Family Constellations, a form of witnessing to make connections with family and ancestors as the source of life. These practices happen within a ritual form with a facilitator, and usually they occur in person. Based in family systems therapy, existential phenomenology, and ancestral rituals, this is a practice to highlight patterns of family members across generations, as well as illuminating the hidden dynamics that affect the family, including the ways we think, feel, or behave. Whole-body approaches are known to rewire the brain, alter the character-self, and change behavior.[24] Theoretically, we might all feel effects of things that happened to each of the family members before us, not just because of our genetic inheritance or lifelong conditioning but because we also influence each other in unseen ways. Members of one's family can act as though they have a common conscience. We can align with people in the past who share a fate with us. I thought of Nietzsche and amor fati, the love of one's fate, and the kind of multigenerational orientation that can make everything, even suffering, instructive.

In this embodied work, there was the possibility to know the ways that whiteness "hid out" in an unacknowledged but powerful bind. I was murky about the effects of knowing some of my family stories, wishing for resolve, and far from understanding the deep roots of the work. But inside the form itself, I could see how rigid family systems unraveled in front of my eyes, whether that was in my constellation or someone else's. Constellation practices brought into visibility those secrets and other family patterns that had been hidden. In response to my constant searching for a solution, Lisa Iversen, a therapist and constellations facilitator, said, "This modality is not about fixing anything. The truth is not a problem." This phrase became a guide to noticing how I couldn't intellectualize my way out of a dilemma. In my family, as in many families, there had been physical violence, sexual abuse, emotional abuse, mental illness, addiction, war, immigration, child loss, and other generational traumas that complicated what we could acknowledge. Each of these personal and communal histories began to be seen.

For two years during my research of the history of lynchings, I met with a group of white women above a Re-use Center in Washington State, and we made ceremonies while below us, people in the community came looking for used toilet bowls and old wood trim. These were not conversations, though we did share questions and insights at the conclusion of each ritual. These were body-based practices that allowed us to experience and witness the traumas of our families. When the deepest traumas began to emerge, those frozen memory fields unfurled like familial clan flags. These women helped me to know that only if the perpetrators are included can the family find peace. Since both historical trauma and our generational histories are stored in our bodies, trauma might be perpetually enacted until it is seen, and resolved.

As white women, we were conditioned to see ourselves as victims and saviors but rarely as perpetrators. This is part of our history of being trained into a system that upholds what writer-educator bell hooks named the "imperialist white supremacist capitalist patriarchy."[25] Our small group was unused to knowing ourselves as enactors of white supremacy, and had experiences of violence with men, who we tended to see more often as perpetrators. While we could recognize that there's far greater harm to the lives of Black women and women of color than toward white women, awareness of how class, empire, capitalism, racism, and patriarchy worked together remained unsettling. The embodied practices slowly changed the ways we'd been conditioned by exposing the ways a racist culture lived unseen in our families and communities. We tended to be leaders in our communities, we were all mothers, and we often saw ourselves as the children of those who endured significant traumas. In dialogues with white women friends, I asked myself: If I am not identified as a victim, where do I stand?

At the bottom of my confusion was the way I both sought and rejected belonging. In the past, I thought I would be safer when I formed my identity as separate from my Kentucky family, especially far from Grandmaw, not realizing that there was another way to know who we were. In these years of reflection, another awareness emerged—that I lived in a world without separateness. I belonged everywhere; we all belonged.

And too, I saw that I had been a perpetrator, just like my grandmother. Like everyone living on stolen native land, like everyone who continues an anti-Black justice system, I benefit from a lynch culture that dispenses injury and death. My safety is made the highest priority by a government who refuses to protect Indigenous women in Canada and a government who charges, incarcerates, and turns away from police brutality and assault directed toward Black and marginalized people in America. Shotwell notes, "The ethical and political imperative to claim bad kin also falls solely on the people—white settlers—who benefit from white supremacist actions, policies, and inheritances."[26] I believe, as a benefactor of specific patrimonies and white privileges, that I have an obligation to become a traitor to the kind of power that's organized by white supremacy, that is, to resist the impulse to unite with white voters who align with leaders whose primary obligation is to accrue power and wealth for white community. I need to be with those who don't agree with my viewpoint, to call forward that relative using a racist slur, to speak about racism in our family lines, to change histories that ignore injustices in plain view. To do so, I'd have to refuse self-censorship when I act in political and communal solidarity, even when that could result in making mistakes. I want to resist the kind of solipsism that results in a degraded reciprocity. I want to see the truth of another.[27]

To make this change, we, as individuals and communities, have to be willing to embrace the rejected parts of ourselves. Scapegoating is intergenerational and systemic. We build societies that require scapegoats by refusing to see the humanity in the other. Individuals might enter into shadow work that excavates unseen parts of themselves but resist going beyond the personal. Justin Michael Williams and Shelly Tygielski of *How We Ended Racism* say that "what you haven't resolved in yourself gets projected onto the work you're doing for the collective. The opposite of this is also true. If you don't look at the *collective shadow,* then the shadow of the collective seeps into your personal growth and self-care practices, causing spiritual or emotional bypassing, limiting results on the healing journey, and a self-serving focus that keeps perpetuating the same cycles and patterns you're trying to end."[28] This had been true for me in over-empathizing with the victim, in being fearful of losing status and belonging, and in giving authority to those (usually white males) in power.

We turn toward our own histories to see that whiteness isn't equated with goodness or rightness. We envision the possibilities for intergenerational change. Truth and reconciliation is not simply about a time of internal reflection or strictly for the individual. We invite organizations, leaders, and elected representatives into a larger process, one that can reconcile communities, cities, regions, and nations. These are efforts oriented toward researching and revealing past wrongdoing by governments, religious institutions, and other nonstate actors, and they attempt to resolve conflict that happened in the past, which is often operational in the present.[29]

"Hierarchy and property may derive from notions of the sacred," say anthropologist David Graeber and archaeologist David Wengrow, "but the most brutal forms of exploitation have their origins in the most intimate of social relation: as perversions of nurture, love and caring."[30] Lynch culture is more interested in preserving capitalism and the status quo than it is in caring for those at the margins. The turn toward image, identity, or political affiliation as self-definition is what foments a sense of scarcity that drives white people toward defense, protection, and violence.

Everywhere in America, and certainly in the rise of this decade's mass shootings, there were young white boys and men who were recruited to white nationalism in a kind of perversion of caring that sometimes moved them away from their families and communities and toward violence and hatred. Indeed, the birth of the Ku Klux Klan came from the white, male sense that institutions were not upholding their interests and that it was necessary to organize vigilantes to maintain order when they saw Black people "rising up." Historically, politicians or media have encouraged white people to "do something," when "lawlessness" is rampant, as happened with president Trump and his followers prior to the Capitol Riot during Trump's former governance,[31] or when FOX's Tucker Carlson told his viewers after the Rittenhouse murders—"Those in charge, from the governor on down, refused to enforce the law. How shocked are we that seventeen-year-olds with rifles decided they had to maintain order when no one else would?" In the twenty-first century, white men continue to kill. They use cops who look the other way at them carrying AR-15s, use the cover of self-defense, use the bias of judges, use the power of the white heroic image. These uses are built into lynch culture. Today's right-wing military groups engage in domestic terrorism, and their function is to intimidate or ridicule, just as the Ku Klux Klan—and my father—did when they burned crosses on a lawn.

I think of what my life would have been like if my father would have wrestled with his toxic anger and dysregulation instead of acting out in violence toward our family and friends. How might his life, and ours, have been different if he'd dealt with his own reactions? What would it have been like if, when his friend had pissed him off, he'd delivered to him something he loved, like his homemade biscuits and gravy rather than that symbol of white supremacy, a flaming cross? I knew that my father was shaped by a harsh childhood, and I didn't believe him, or anyone, to be disposable; so it was important to me to both hold him accountable and see him in his humanity. Dad was a generous man, and he believed that he would have done anything to protect me, his child. But we never talked about the ways that he was trained into the white, heroic male role or how his anger had been weaponized by a culture in which punitive means were favored over respect and compassion and understanding. He was a good provider, a scientist, and an accomplished distiller, but we never discussed how conservative forces had engaged him in participating in wealth inequality by promising him a generous executive salary and access to one of America's wealthiest families in his employer, the Brown distilling family.[32]

We were dishonest about the ways that we extended kinship to some but not to others. This is how we are taught to hate in America. This perversion of care extends to all the ways our emotions can be hijacked by a culture. How can we build institutions oriented to care (and not supremacy) if we can't be present to others' trauma? How can we end systemic racism if we can't become responsible for the harm we enact? There were loving people in my community who held me when I was at my worst, who forgave me, and who had not policed my out-of-the-norm behaviors and ideas. Being present to these moments led me toward the first steps in extending my resources and building an understanding of transformative justice.

I think of my friend in a twelve-step group who, over twenty-five years ago, asked me to help her find donations, manage, and deliver meals to a dozen families in need on a Thanksgiving eve. We had been tipped off by a teacher that these were immigrant, refugee, and other marginalized people who each had a middle school child, and they fell outside the bounds of any organization who could offer help. On that dark, rainy Seattle evening, newly sober, I delivered turkey and all the fixings to homes of Black and Indigenous and Latinx and Asian and white settler people, some of whom invited me to stay. I was not considered just an addict, nor was I merely doing something for them; they brought me into a web of care. We were all connected through an educator who recognized need. None of us had to appeal to a charity's grace to get what we needed (them—food with dignity, me—a real hospitality). No one had to decide about who was deserving of aid, who needed a new beginning. No one was harmed by a racist, misogynist, ableist government while we longed for the state to be benevolent. We didn't have to wait for Bill Gates to research and approve a program; we marched into our communities and asked if they'd donate food. The families took what they needed; we gave what we could. We knew that we hadn't changed conditions for anyone; we knew we weren't addressing root causes of poverty. But we were meeting each other in that moment. These times when we can be present to another accumulate and orient us to the potential for care in kin groups.

It isn't enough to take antiracist actions on our own. We (and by *we*, I mean *me*, this I who is still practicing these things) can grow our circles, using our friendships as a starting place, moving our kin to action with us. We can support those grassroots organizers and movements that are already happening. We can organize where we are. We can find and support rapid response to hate crimes, cruel policies, prejudice and bigotry, and police violence—all those places where white supremacy lives. We know it's far less fatal for a white person to get between a land defender and the RCMP; we know we can stand up to a MAGA cousin and survive. You (and I) can be with these reclaimed kin, as well as the relations that include the people we'd rather not declare as rooted in the same whiteness, out of a desire to end the perversion of care that has been tearing us apart.

Journalist and author Tanya Talaga says that "the root of the word reconciliation means the coming together of two equal parts—but that is not the case in Indigenous-Canadian relations. The sides have never been equal." Talaga reports that Justice Marion Buller, the chair of the National Inquiry into Missing and Murdered Indigenous Women and Girls, prefers to use the term *rebuilding* instead of *reconciliation*. "*Rebuilding* signifies you understand the relationship is broken, needs to be fixed."[33]

Rebuilding relies on actions that might help white people see that we're not personally responsible for all of the conditions and relationships that came before us but that we can be accountable for what we do in response to those conditions. As we rebuild, we can see the ways that whiteness functions in our ancestral and family histories, as well as the ways we continue to uphold lynch culture.

Together, we can ask ourselves to make radical changes in the ways we relate to our families, communities, and organizations. We can open to another kind of belonging, a communal solidarity with the people doing this work across disenfranchised communities, including through mutual aid and in support of cross-cultural groups, and especially against those systems continuing to enact lynch culture.

Here's what I know—we can ask for the entirety of our communal histories to be told. I want my descendants to know all that happened in our bloodline. The author Maud Newton of *Ancestor Trouble: A Reckoning and a Reconciliation*, says, "There is no more intimate connection to history than through our individual families. And with the rise of laws forbidding discussions of racist histories, sharing our own ancestors' shameful wrongdoings has never been more urgent."[34] Reparations4Slavery makes a case for "reparative genealogy," where we might research our heritage, acknowledge connections to slavery, and "daylight the history of those our ancestors enslaved" to repatriate that history to help African Americans trace their heritage, often absent due to the lack of detailed recordkeeping during the slavery era.[35] White people might study ancestors who participated in atrocities to learn about those harms, be public about them, and commit to the reparative work that must follow. Acknowledgment, action, and advocacy are vital. The Reparations4Slavery website suggests many ways of engaging in repair beyond sharing your own family history, including committing time and money, being intentional around these histories, and working against their persistence as we move through the world. I am following their recommendations to design and enact a plan of repair.

I've joined the organization Coming to the Table, a community with working committees oriented to dialogue and reparative work between descendants of enslavers and descendants of people who were enslaved, between those who caused injustice, and those who were victims of it. I'm supporting Black farmers and Indigenous families in Kentucky and elsewhere, those potentially displaced by my family when we took what was never ours to take. I'm rebuilding by asking Owensboro to create a memorial to Rainey Bethea, and all that happened there, including the injustices of the trial, and the white supremacist actions of the white power at the legal lynching. There are other actions that I can't speak of yet because I'm tending to my ancestors and family and communal wilderness with the kind of care they need, beyond the family history of transactional reciprocity. There may still be truths unveiled, and more owed. The way is at times rigorous but not without the satisfaction that comes from honest interchange. In these ongoing practices, we can become aware of the patterns that underlie blind loyalty to an ancestor—bearing their fear or suffering out of our desire to protect or love them—witnessing a familial pattern is operating in ourselves or a descendant, each of us carrying something that isn't ours to carry. Living with the truth means that I can leave my ancestors to their own ordeals and resolve, and I can take responsibility for what is mine to acknowledge and repair. I bless them on their journey; they bless me to continue with my own life. Personal work is not an excuse for disavowing reparations work; rather, it's a process to remove the suffering that prevents us from real change at the personal, institutional, state, and other systemic levels.

In the wake of those historically and currently harmed by lynch culture, we can grieve. Judith Butler notes that "the practices of public mourning and political demonstration converge: when lives are considered ungrievable, to grieve them openly is protest."[36] We can assemble in the streets of our towns and cities, we can join with our communities in vigil, we can unite with others to oppose racist violence. There can't be reconciliation until grief is registered in our personal bodies and the body politic. State reparations for families of the enslaved is one form of acknowledging the history of slavery, segregation, and the costs of not being born white.

We can stay in opposition to the white supremacy that has formed us. We can stop dispossession of lands. We can go beyond extracting value. We can remove ourselves from the obedience and conformity and intolerance that has defined white identity. We can join with groups and movements who want to acknowledge and document lynch culture. We can direct resources toward organizations, communities, and people who are stopping violence against Black people, Indigenous nations, and all peoples of color and marginalized communities. We can ask our governments to make reparations to Black people for the unpaid labor of enslaved Africans and their descendants, and we can ask ourselves to address the legacy of slavery. We can experience solidarity with everyone here and now, as well as the generations before us who have been willing to fiercely, tenderly, extend care. We can honor our kin who have passed, can acknowledge our ancestors, and can find our way to new stories beyond those we have inherited. We can develop relationship with people, plants, animals, waterways, weather, and celestial bodies, supporting their right to flourish. Our atonement includes the awareness of the relationships broken by whiteness, of the antidemocratic and antihistory forces harmful to our communities and antithetical to the meaning of repair. Because we are not separate, we rebuild.

Acknowledgments

There are stories that find you through happenstance and yet seem like they've been waiting there all along for you to notice their existence. I'm grateful for every person who spoke to me about Rainey Bethea and America's so-called last public execution and especially those who also knew that lynch culture had never ended but simply changed forms.

This work began twenty-two years ago with an interview handed to me at my grandmother Ralph's funeral. As I researched the history of the people, places, and influences of this time, archivists, historians, and memoirists shed light on my way. The University Press of Kentucky provided professional aid through peer reviews, people whose insights and guidance have offered a fuller, more representative analysis. These writers and academic peers helped underscore that Bethea's story is significant toward noting a history of American racial violence that's often undertold within educational systems and media. I'm honored through a collaboration with the University Press of Kentucky for this work to become a part of the racial justice values of the seventeen colleges and universities that they represent. Thank you to Abby Freeland, who adeptly steered the book through its approval and editorial process. Ashley Runyon was enthusiastic about the book from the moment it crossed her desk. In these two women I felt I found people who understood about the importance of an institution in Kentucky beginning a truth and reconciliation process by considering a social justice lens for this story. I'd also like to extend my appreciation to Ila R. McEntire, Josephine Fabiola, and Gayathri Umashankaran for their editing support and to Jackie Wilson for a stellar publicity program. Julia Turner's fine copyediting helped me hone my ideas.

American Bloodlines could not have proceeded without the support of the Canada Council for the Arts and the Alberta Foundation for the Arts, which each offered me financial aid to travel, research, and write the book.

Dr. Lacy M. Johnson and the Tin House Summer Workshop broadened my understanding of how a historical event and a personal story might intersect. I'm grateful for Lacy's wise guidance and mentorship through the years that I was writing this book, including helping me envision an essay through the perspective of cultural criticism. The writers of personal narrative whom I met in Portland, Oregon, at Tin House helped me interrogate myself and my family's history, and for this and their literary companionship, I'm most grateful. Katie Quach was of particular help in defining the story.

My interviews with Keith Lawrence of the *Owensboro Messenger-Inquirer* were fundamental to understanding how the community lived and how Black people were threatened by the events in Owensboro, including the impact of anniversaries. Historian Carrie Pitzulo offered a wise analysis of the gendered implications of legal punishments as well as the term *lynch culture* in her seminal essay published by the Kentucky Historical Society. I owe a debt of gratitude to many librarians and archivists including the Kentucky Department of Libraries, The Filson Club, Daviess County Public Libraries, and the Martin F. Schmidt Research Library. Perry Ryan laid the groundwork for one of the first histories of the events leading up to and surrounding the execution, and my interviews with him provided context for my reportage and analysis.

Elle Glenise Pike was first an antiracism educator and then a mentor and a friend who gave me the confidence to explore the idea of lynch culture. Her work in educating on racist bypassing behavior is essential learning. Elle Glenise was generous in helping me see the truth of my and my family's history and how to expand the potential for readers to identify their own family histories as they overlap with the violence of our national identity.

An enormous debt of gratitude for the work of Anna Badkhen, Emily Bingham, Eula Biss, adrienne marie brown, Elizabeth Catte, Alexander Chee, Ta-Nehisi Coates, Claire Dederer, Camonghne Felix, Roxane Gay, bell hooks, Lewis Hyde, Sherrilyn A. Ifill, Lacy M. Johnson, Ibram X.

Kendi, Kiese Laymon, Audre Lorde, Imani Perry, Mab Segrest, Alexis Shotwell, Clint Smith, Sabrina Strings, Tanya Talaga, Kim TallBear, Zoe Todd, John Vaillant, Jesmyn Ward, Irvin Weathersby, Jr., Isabel Wilkerson, George C. Wright, and Lidia Yuknavitch. Their books, essays, scholarship, organizational innovation, and foundational experiences offer a way forward in this time of deep divisions and collective reckoning.

The community of those working in justice was enormously supportive, including the historical and present-day reporting of Bryan Stevenson and the staff of the Equal Justice Initiative and their "Lynching in America: Confronting the Legacy of Racial Terror" report. I'm grateful that a museum and monument exists in the Legacy Sites in Montgomery, Alabama, and for their leadership in making visible that "the power of history is in telling the truth." For fifty years, the Southern Poverty Law Center has been reporting on extremism, and its annual report and current papers on the intensifying hate and anti-government groups built on the oppression of Black people, women, immigrants, Jews, Muslims, Latinx, low-income groups, Indigenous people, and LGBTQ+ communities remains ever important. The Innocence Project works long, hard hours to restore the freedoms of those unjustly accused, and alongside policymakers, partners, and supporters, it transforms systems. The project's information on coerced pleas, false confessions, inadequate defense, and race in wrongful convictions and instances of the death penalty was enormously valuable.

The long gestation of this book brought me into the ringing truth of Audre Lorde's words *Without community, there is no liberation*, but I hadn't yet lived into the fullness of that idea. Thankfully, my people emerged to share their own experiences of their processes of rebuilding, grief, and reconciliation. I could do none of this without the counsel of writers and thinkers Kristi Coulter, Dagny Dubois, Warren Etheredge, Gina Frangello, Sebastian Hutchings, Judith Laxer, Priscilla Long, Suzanne Morrison, Devyani Saltzman, Robert Sandford, and Kim Schnuelle, all of whom read early versions of the manuscript and brought insightful feedback and, most importantly, their challenges, friendship, and love. The smart insights from fellow Kentuckian, writer, and editor Lisa Whipple grounded the book, and the work was improved by the questions she asked about guilt, innocence, fairness, justice, and the white desire for spectacle. Holly Whittaker came in at just the right time to offer her wisdom on what's required to release a vulnerable story to a readership and the public, and my life was made better for meeting her. I cherish every writer I worked with in classes, workshops, and retreats over these years. You taught me about commitment, honesty, and love. Thank you.

At a critical time in the writing, artists Carole Harmon and Gary Sill provided their home and the beauty of that space across the water, including an owl presence that felt divinely given. Thank you for the encouragement, dear ones.

For their work in guiding transformational experiences, I'd like to acknowledge a community of teachers. Transformational psychologist and mentor Sheila Belanger's coaching sessions and rituals in the forests of Whidbey Island brought me into right alliance with my ancestors. Lisa Iversen's work in Systemic Family Constellations was powerful and altering, particularly in relationship to transgenerational trauma and the transmitting of the fundamental awareness that American democracy is sourced in the violence of whiteness and that groups are the ones who must deauthorize whiteness. Thank you to the women of the Constellations cohort as well as the essayists from *Whiteness Is Not an Ancestor*, where my first writing in relationship to this material appeared alongside those of white women also questioning their familial inheritances.

Writer and mentor Lisa Cairns was an ally toward making peace with the changing circumstances of the past decade, and her bravery and honesty allowed me to see new possibilities for my life.

Thanks to my sweet, fierce friends Judith Laxer and Lisa McCrummen, who sat in a room with me each week to talk about the secrets and lies of our whiteness and to witness our rage, grief, fears, and activism.

Carol Mills and Bruce Railey had the foresight to do an interview with the elders in the small farm community near Owensboro, Kentucky, where my grandparents lived, and I appreciate that they placed the words of Frances Moran Ralph as she said them. It's these kinds of oral history projects happening in families and kin groups that might help us remember where we came from and who we are. Thank you for handing me what became a strong and complicated connection to my grandmother.

This book was a family journey too. I appreciate the members of my extended family who sat with me for interviews, including Carl Hardesty, Robyn Bandy Brown, and the Ralph aunts, uncles, and cousins. Thank you for welcoming me into your homes and hearts. My sisters, Christie and Shelley, have been generous with their time, and they have kept me accountable to my intention, sharing memories and filling me in on all that I missed when I left home.

My beloved partner Richard Bandy supported me and gave me the needed grounding to experience two decades of powerful learning, and it was his acknowledgment that I needed to write this story that helped us mobilize the resources to devote the time to the project. Over these years, our children grew to adults hearing the stories of Kentucky. This book belongs to their legacy as descendants and inheritors of what we could speak and what still needs mending.

For my ancestors, my grandparents, and my mother and father, thank you for your hand at my back as these words unfurled, and truly, thank you for life.

Notes

1. The Legal Lynching of Rainey Bethea

1. I went searching for the family of Rainey Bethea, since he had written to his sister Ora from prison just before his execution. The name and address on Bethea's letter was *Mrs. Ora Fladger, R.F.D. #3, Box 135, Nichols, S.C.* I believed Ora had been alive at the time of his execution. I searched at Ancestry.com, found names of those who may have been relatives of Rainey Bethea Sr. and Beulah Bethea, and then made the choice not to approach them, out of a desire not to inflict further harm. I didn't speak of this to this book's publisher until a peer reviewer asked if I had taken any action to contact the family. I wish to clarify my intention to bring this work to the descendants so that Rainey Bethea's legacy might also include the possibility of being wrongly charged, unjustly tried, and inhumanely treated.

2. Various census records indicate discrepancies in Bethea's birth date, name, and family members (Gerald L. Smith, Karen Cotton McDaniel, and John A. Hardin, eds., *The Kentucky African American Encyclopedia* [Lexington: University Press of Kentucky, 2015], 44).

3. Court Record, Daviess County, Owensboro, Kentucky, June 23, 1936.

4. Perry Ryan, *The Last Public Execution in America* (Alexandria Printing, 1992), https://web.archive.org/web/20091028105135/http://geocities.com/lastpublichang/Chapter4.htm.

5. Court record, Daviess County Court, Owensboro, Kentucky, 1936.

6. The Kentucky Innocence Project, among many other organizations, has made statements regarding fingerprints as junk science.

> The misapplication of forensic science contributed to 52% of wrongful convictions in Innocence Project cases. . . . Another example of errors—from an even more "well established" method, such as fingerprint comparison, has faced criticism. Many fingerprint analysts use standard procedures to mark different levels of detail in a suspect's

fingerprint in a "latent print" (meaning one left at a crime scene). But making a so-called "individualization"—a conclusion that the prints are from the same source—is where things can get fuzzy. After examiners look at enough prints known to be from the same source and from different sources, the examiner's brain starts to see patterns of similarity, and it is more likely that they will start finding points on the prints that match. ("Junk Science," Kentucky Innocence Project, accessed October 4, 2024, https://www.kentuckyinnocenceproject.org/junk-science)

7. "Alleged Slayer Caught," *Inquirer,* June 10, 1936, 1.

8. "Negro Admits Daviess Crime," *Louisville Courier-Journal,* June 11, 1936, 1.

9. Author's interview with Keith Lawrence, *Owensboro Messenger-Inquirer,* June 10, 2021.

10. "Bethea Tells Reporter He Is Willing to Die in Chair," *Messenger,* June 14, 1936, 1, 10.

11. Florence Thompson's descendants possess the letters she received as well as newspaper clippings and other ephemera. The collection is unprocessed and kept privately by her son, James, who shared access to them with Pitzulo and Perry Ryan. Pitzulo reviewed all of the approximately 250 letters in the collection ("The Skirted Sheriff: Florence Thompson and the Nation's Last Public Execution," *Register of the Kentucky Historical Society* 115, no. 3, [Summer 2017]: 380).

12. "Sheriff, Mother of Four Children, Prepares to Hang Negro in Slaying," *Atlanta Constitution,* August 14, 1936, 1.

13. Pitzulo, "Skirted Sheriff," 382.

14. Ryan, *Last Public Execution in America,* 13.

15. Ryan, *Last Public Execution in America,* 13.

16. Instruction to the Jury, Court Record, Daviess County Court, Owensboro, Kentucky, June 25, 1936.

17. "Negro to Pay," *Owensboro Messenger-Inquirer,* June 26, 1936, 1.

18. "Negro to Pay," 1.

19. "Youth Doomed to Death upon Thin Evidence" *Chicago Defender,* July 4, 1936, 1.

20. Ryan, *Last Public Execution in America,* 17.

21. "Killing the Black body is an act that functions to provide the white body with an 'omnipotent' consciousness, giving whites the illusion of absolute power to take a Black life, which according to racist ideology, is no more problematic than taking the life of a subhuman animal. In this way, although the Black body is negated qua killed, the dead Black body, the burned, castrated, and lynched Black body, is still needed in order to magnify white existence" (George Yancy, *Black Bodies, White Gazes: The Continuing Significance of Race in America,* 2nd ed. [Lanham, MD: Rowman & Littlefield, 2016], 113).

22. Ryan, *Last Public Execution in America,* 23.

23. Ryan, *Last Public Execution in America,* 20.

24. Ryan, *Last Public Execution in America,* 20.

25. "Kentucky Town in Holiday Mood for Hanging," *Chicago Defender,* July 18, 1936, 1.

26. "Denial of Writ Dooms Bethea," *Louisville Courier-Journal,* August 6, 1936, 3.

27. Ryan, *Last Public Execution in America,* 15.

28. Pitzulo, "Skirted Sheriff," 402.

29. "Crowd Awaits Dawn and Woman Hangman," *New York Times,* August 13, 1936, 4.

30. "The Last Hanging: There Was a Reason They Outlawed Public Executions," *New York Times,* May 6, 2001, 45.

31. Herbert Agar, "Hangman's Holiday," Time & Tide, *Louisville Courier-Journal,* August 19, 1936, 6.

32. "15,000 Witness Bethea Hanging," *Louisville Times,* August 14, 1936, 1.

33. "Execution of Bethea Is Set for Sunrise," *Louisville Courier-Journal,* August 14, 1936, 1.

34. "15,000 Witness Bethea Hanging," 1.

35. "Death Trap May Be Sprung by Woman Sheriff," *Owensboro Messenger-Inquirer,* August 14, 1936, 9.

36. "Crowd Tears Hood Seeking Souvenirs," *Louisville Times,* August 14, 1936, 1.

37. Ryan, *Last Public Execution in America,* 25.

38. "Woman Sheriff Has Aide Spring Gallows Trap," *Chicago Tribune,* August 15, 1936. The "long drop" hanging was designed in the nineteenth century to break the neck, a method created to shorten the amount of time from the drop until death, but it was also created to make the process less traumatic for the people who would no longer have to witness the struggle of the prisoner.

39. "Crime: Party," *Time,* August 24, 1936.

40. Author's correspondence with Perry Ryan, August 30, 2021.

41. "Panderers Galore," *Owensboro Messenger-Inquirer,* August 16, 1936, 4.

42. The editor's note says, "Mr. Fishenbaum, a graduate of an Alabama University is one of the most gifted correspondents in the Southland. He was secured by the Defender several weeks ago to 'cover' the legal lynching of Rainey Bethea as a member of the Race press could hardly have gotten within ten miles of the scene without placing his life in jeopardy. Mr. Fishenbaum tells a remarkable story of the 'carnival,' describing in detail the horrors of the affair, as well as the fiendish glee of the morbid-minded citizens who enjoyed the sport" (Abraham Fishenbaum, "20,000 Kentuckians Cheer as Bethea Hangs," *Chicago Defender,* August 22, 1936, 1).

43. "20,000 Kentuckians Cheer as Bethea Hangs," 1.

44. "Owensboro Must Denounce Its Detractors, (Editorial)," *Owensboro Messenger,* August 18, 1936, 1.

2. Regular White People

1. From the author's interview with Perry Ryan, August 18, 2021.

2. At least eight states saw their murder rates rise by 40 percent or more by 2020, with the largest percentage increases including Kentucky, at over 61 percent,

according to the CDC (John Gramlich, "What We Know about the Increase in U.S. Murders in 2020," Pew Research Center, October 27, 2021, https://www.pewresearch.org/short-reads/2021/10/27/what-we-know-about-the-increase-in-u-s-murders-in-2020/).

3. Carrie Pitzulo's work in "The Skirted Sherriff" was the first time I saw the words *lynch culture.*

4. W. Fitzhugh Brundage, ed., *Under Sentence of Death: Lynching in the South* (Chapel Hill: University of North Carolina Press, 1997), 252.

5. By the mid-1930s, "forward-looking white Southerners were compelled to adopt the position that lynching was barbaric and disgraceful, even as they continued to defend white supremacy or rail against Black criminality" (Amy Louise Wood, *Lynching and Spectacle: Witnessing Racial Violence in America, 1890–1940* [Chapel Hill: University of North Carolina Press, 2011], 263). But legal lynching converted to a carceral system such as that outlined by Stephen Bright, director of the Southern Center for Human Rights, when he stated, "The death penalty is a direct descendant of lynching and other forms of racial violence and racial oppression in America" ("Discrimination, Death and Denial: The Tolerance of Racial Discrimination in Infliction of the Death Penalty," *Santa Clara Law Review* 35, no. 2 [1995]: 439).

6. Interview with the author's grandmother, Frances Margaret Moran Ralph, received January 5, 2002, at her funeral.

7. The myth of an empty Kentucky—one perpetuated by land speculators in the late 1700s—has had a lasting effect on people's understandings and beliefs about the presence of Indigenous Americans in the state. Many different tribes once called Kentucky home, including the Cherokee, the Chickasaw, and the Shawnee. The Shawnee hunted and lived in the Bluegrass region. These clans were a part of the larger Shawnee tribe who lived in the Ohio Valley ("Indigenous Americans in Kentucky," February 4, 2022, https://www.visitlex.com/guides/post/indigenous-americans-in-kentucky/).

8. When Kentucky was declared the fifteenth state on June 1, 1792, more than twenty tribes, including the Cherokee, Chickasaw, Chippewa, Delaware, Eel River, Haudenosaunee, Kaskaskia, Kickapoo, Miami, Ottawa, Piankeshaw, Potawatomi, Shawnee, Wea, and Wyandot, held legal claims to the land (History.com Editors, "Kentucky: The First People in Kentucky," History.com, original November 9, 2009, updated December 13, 2022, https://www.history.com/topics/us-states/kentucky#the-first-people-in-kentucky).

9. Marianne Mithun, *Languages of Native North America* (Cambridge: Cambridge University Press, 1999), 312.

10. From Shelda Payne, "Ralph History in Ohio County Kentucky," April 22, 2008. https://www.ancestry.com/mediaui-viewer/collection/1030/tree/4699745/person/372111456145/media/16e24f47-0e3d-45dc-be13-7a2419277e2c?galleryindex=1&sort=-created.

11. Christopher Waldrep, *The Many Faces of Judge Lynch: Extralegal Violence and Punishment in America* (New York: Palgrave MacMillan, 2002), 24–25.

12. Equal Justice Initiative, *Lynching in America: Confronting the Legacy of Racial Terror*, 3rd ed. (2017), https://lynchinginamerica.eji.org/report/.

13. In the American Civil War (1861–65), the border states or the Border South were four, later five, slave states in the Upper South that primarily supported the Union. They were Delaware, Maryland, Kentucky, and Missouri, and, after 1863, the new state of West Virginia.

14. Imani Perry, *South to America: A Journey below the Mason-Dixon Line to Understand the Soul of a Nation* (New York: HarperCollins, 2022), 55.

15. Equal Justice Initiative, *Lynching in America*, chap. 1.

16. "Lockett Lynch Mob (Lexington, KY)," Notable Kentucky African Americans Database, September 2003, https://nkaa.uky.edu/nkaa/items/show/786.

17. Pitzulo, "Skirted Sheriff," 386.

18. Earl L. Brown, "Letter to the Editor," *Louisville Courier-Journal*, June 20, 1932, 4.

19. George C. Wright, *Racial Violence in Kentucky, 1865–1940: Lynchings, Mob Rule, and "Legal Lynchings"* (Baton Rouge: Louisiana State University Press, 1990), Kindle.

20. Three out of seven executed were Black while the census of this time reports 11 percent of Kentucky was Black.

21. Wright, *Racial Violence in Kentucky, 1865–1940*, 72–73.

22. In 1954, Anne and Carl Braden, a white couple, purchased a house in the Louisville suburb of Shively in order to sell it to a Black man, Andrew Wade. The Wade family was harassed, the Bradens were put on trial for sedition amid charges of a Communist conspiracy, and the house was bombed. For more information on the Bradens, see Kentucky History's historical marker text at https://explorekyhistory.ky.gov/items/show/298.

23. Ibram X. Kendi says, "A racist policy is any measure that produces or sustains racial inequity between racial groups. An antiracist policy is any measure that produces or sustains racial equity between racial groups. By policy, I mean written and unwritten laws, rules, procedures, processes, regulations, and guidelines that govern people. There is no such thing as a nonracist or race-neutral policy. Every policy in every institution in every community in every nation is producing or sustaining either racial inequity or equity between racial groups. . . . 'Racist policy' also cuts to the core of racism better than 'racial discrimination,' another common phrase. 'Racial discrimination' is an immediate and visible manifestation of an underlying racial policy. When someone discriminates against a person in a racial group, they are carrying out a policy or taking advantage of the lack of a protective policy. We all have the power to discriminate. Only an exclusive few have the power to make policy. Focusing on 'racial discrimination' takes our eyes off the central agents of racism: racist policy and racist policymakers, or what I call racist power." For more definitions on antiracism, see Ibram X. Kendi, "Ibram X. Kendi Defines What It Means to Be an Antiracist," Penguin, June 8, 2020, https://www.penguin.co.uk/articles/2020/06/ibram-x-kendi-definition-of-antiracist.

24. Pike also conducted private sessions with clients and gave speeches on her antiracism work (Elle Glenise Pike, *Getting Started in Antiracism* [formerly titled *The Antiracism Starter Kit*]).

25. According to data about police violence outcomes of police killings, Black victims are approximately three times more likely to be killed in comparison to their white counterparts ("Mapping Police Violence," 2022, updated February 17, 2025, www.mappingpoliceviolence.org). Additionally, it is worth noting that 97 percent of the killings occurred while a police officer was acting in a law enforcement capacity. These data do not include killings by vigilantes or security guards who are not off-duty police officers. Recent studies employing Mapping Police Violence data have found that the threshold for police killings of white people is much higher than those of Black people (R. T. DeAngelis, "Systemic Racism in Police Killings: New Evidence from the Mapping Police Violence Database, 2013–2021," *Race and Justice* 14, no. 3 [2024]: 413–422, https://doi.org/10.1177/21533687211047943). Similarly, other research finds that Black people are two times more likely to be killed by police "even when there are no other obvious circumstances during the encounter that would make the use of deadly force reasonable" (Jeffrey A. Fagan and Alexis D. Campbell, *Race and Reasonableness in Police Killings*, 100 B.U. L. Rev. 951 [2020], https://scholarship.law.columbia.edu/faculty_scholarship/2656).

26. Joni Mitchell, *Don Juan's Reckless Daughter*, 1977; *Silver Streak*, 1976; *The Tonight Show*, 1976.

27. By the time I was a young woman, Kentucky had made its state song more politically correct, replacing the racist term *darkies* with *people*, but not until 1986 and not until the state was confronted by Louisville's first African American representative, Carl Hines.

28. Emily Bingham, *My Old Kentucky Home: The Astonishing Life and Reckoning of an Iconic American Song* (New York: Alfred A. Knopf, 2022), xvii.

29. Barnes is also executive advisor to Henry Louis Gates Jr. for PBS's *Reconstruction: America After the Civil War* (Rhae Lynn Barnes, "The Birth of Blackface Minstrelsy and the Rise of Stephen Foster," U.S. History Scene, April 11, 2015, https://ushistoryscene.com/article/birth-of-blackface/).

30. Though there are no data confirming this information, only her own story conveyed to a family member, and then to my husband, it's possible that his mother, June, was unknowingly part of the horrific scientific experimentation conducted by Donald Ewan Cameron at the Allan Memorial Institute, affiliated with McGill University in Montreal. This program was later subsidized by the CIA, and the Canadian government also funded the project. In the 1950s and '60s, Cameron included sensory deprivation techniques in his treatment program, where patients were deprived of their senses by covering ears, eyes, and/or skin; were given little food, water, and oxygen; and injected with LSD to keep them in a paralyzed state. These patients suffered severely under conditions that violated human rights. The project conducted illegal human experimentation to determine whether drugs and psychological techniques could be used for the purposes of mind control. There

has been no apology on the part of the Canadian or US governments or institutions for any of these abuses, nor has there been any admission of responsibility.

31. Noel Ignatiev, "The Point Is Not to Interpret Whiteness but to Abolish It," talk at the conference "The Making and Unmaking of Whiteness," University of California, Berkeley, April 11–13, 1997.

32. I'm grateful to Paul C. Gorski for this notion: "I have come to believe that the white privilege brigade, with me among its chief enforcers, has been wrong to police the complexities of class (and, for that matter, other forms of oppression), out of conversations about white privilege. Worse, by doing so, we also have failed to interrogate the hierarchy of privilege among white people, including white people who are attempting to be anti-racists. And there is much to interrogate" ("Complicating White Privilege: Race, Poverty and the Nature of the Knapsack," January 1, 2012, http://www.edchange.org/publications/Complicating-White-Privilege.pdf).

33. White women have been part of white supremacy in America dating back to their role in slavery. That remained true after the Civil War, "through the birth and evolution of the Ku Klux Klan, and during the civil rights movement when white women were some of the most vocal opponents of school integration. And it remains true today, when women hold a key role in spreading QAnon ideology and sustaining white nationalist groups and movements. 'Like other parts of our economy and society, these movements would collapse without their labor,' Seyward Darby, author of *Sisters in Hate: American Women on the Front Lines of White Nationalism*," told Vox's correspondent Anna North, who writes, "And if we ignore the importance of women in the Capitol riot and the groups that backed and enabled it, we can't understand white supremacy in America—let alone dismantle it" (Anna North, "White Women's Role in White Supremacy, Explained," *Vox*, January 15, 2021, https://www.vox.com/2021/1/15/22231079/capitol-riot-women-qanon-white-supremacy).

34. North, "White Women's Role in White Supremacy, Explained."

35. Anne Merlan, "Peter Thiels Investment Firm Is Backing a Menstrual Cycle Focused Femtech Company," *Motherboard*, September 26, 2022, https://www.vice.com/en/article/4axnab/peter-thiels-investment-firm-is-backing-a-menstrual-cycle-focused-femtech-company.

36. Cassie Miller, "Male Supremacy Is at the Core of the Hard Right's Agenda," Southern Poverty Law Center, April 18, 2023.

37. The writer, educator, and social critic bell hooks expanded the concept of dominator culture as a model of society where fear and oppression uphold rigid interpretations of power and superiority within a hierarchical structure. A distinguished professor in residence at Berea College, hooks was born in Hopkinsville, Kentucky.

38. Eula Biss, "White Debt," *New York Times*, December 2, 2015.

39. Amber Periona, "U.S. Prison Population by Race," World Atlas (Society), July 18, 2019, https://www.worldatlas.com/articles/incarceration-rates-by-race-ethnicity-and-gender-in-the-u-s.html.

40. I would include in this group those in Kentucky who aided enslaved people on the Underground Railroad, like teacher, author, businesswoman, and abolitionist Delia Ann Webster; those who challenged the "colored school law" in the late 1800s, such as Edward Claybrook, Reverend C. Dabney, Reverend M. Harding, William Hunter, Giles Crump, Charles T. Jackson, Marshall "Chess" McLean, Henry Johnson, Walter Whitenhill, and O. G. K. Barrett (see chap. 4 of this volume, "How Could This Happen Here?"); those who tested the separate coach law by sitting in the white section of a train and later won a lawsuit against the railroad, Reverend William Hardin Anderson from Indiana and his wife, Sarah J. Steward Anderson; the founders of the town of Berea and Berea College, Kentucky's Cassius M. Clay and Reverend John G. Fee; the first Black person elected to the state Senate, Senator Georgia Davis Powers; expert on racism and the media Mervin Aubespin; University of Kentucky student organizer desegregating Lexington Abby Marlatt; University of Louisville student activist J. Blaine Hudson; civil rights organizer Audrey Grevious; National Urban League leader Whitney M. Young Jr.; lifelong activists charged with sedition in 1954, Anne and Carl Braden; the first female African American to be admitted to the White House, Congressional, and Supreme Court press corps, Alice Allison Dunnigan; and the 23,703 Black people in the federal service for the Union during the Civil War.

3. On Lynch Culture

1. Waldrep, *Many Faces of Judge Lynch*, 183.

2. During the trial, the defendants chewed gum and chuckled each time the victim was mentioned. At one point, the defense attorney likened Mr. Earle to a "mad dog" that deserved killing, and the white spectators laughed in support (Equal Justice Initiative, "White Mob Lynches Willie Earle Near Greenville, SC," A History of Racial Injustice (calendar), February 17, 1947, https://calendar.eji.org/racial-injustice/feb/17).

3. Equal Justice Initiative, "White Mob Lynches."

4. Here is a report of the case verdict.

> Gregory and Travis McMichael, the White father and son convicted in the killing of Ahmaud Arbery, were sentenced Monday to life in prison for their federal convictions on interference with rights—a hate crime—along with attempted kidnapping and weapon use charges.
>
> Their neighbor William "Roddie" Bryan Jr., the third man involved in Arbery's killing, was sentenced by US District Court Judge Lisa Godbey Wood to 35 years, which will be served at the same time as his state sentence. All three men are already serving life sentences for the convictions in state court on a series of charges related to the killing of the 25-year-old Black man, including felony

murder (Dakin Andone and Alta Spells, "McMichaels Sentenced to Life Terms, William 'Roddie' Bryan Gets 35 Years for Federal Hate Crime Convictions in Ahmaud Arbery's Killing," CNN, August 9, 2022, https://www.cnn.com/2022/08/08/us/ahmaud-arbery-hate-crime-federal-sentencing/index.html).

5. Joe Friesen, "Thousands Rally across Canada after Gerald Stanley Acquitted in Case of Colten Boushie," *Globe and Mail*, February 10, 2018; Shree Paradkar, "Our Reaction to Injustice Is a Reflection of Our Soul as Individuals and Canadians," *Toronto Star*, Opinion, February 10, 2018, https://www.thestar.com/opinion/star-columnists/2018/02/10/our-reaction-to-injustice-is-a-reflection-our-soul-as-individuals-and-canadians.html.

6. Dan Friedman, "Kyle Rittenhouse Didn't Break the Law. That's Terrifying," *Mother Jones*, November 19, 2021, https://www.motherjones.com/politics/2021/11/kyle-rittenhouse-verdict-aftermath-terrifying-stand-ground-copycat-kenosha/.

7. Historian Thomas Zimmer explains how institutions can amplify and bolster individual racist actions to systemically enforce a dominator ethos: "All strands of the Right—leading Republicans, the media machine, the reactionary intellectual sphere, the conservative base, the donor class—are openly and aggressively embracing rightwing vigilante violence," he wrote (as reported by Heather Cox Richardson, "Letters from an American," May 16, 2023, https://heathercoxrichardson.substack.com/p/may-15-2023).

8. "Trump to Far-Right Extremists: 'Stand Back and Stand By,'" AP News, September 30, 2020, https://apnews.com/article/election-2020-joe-biden-race-and-ethnicity-donald-trump-chris-wallace-0b32339da25fbc9e8b7c7c7066a1dbof.

9. Supremacy can manifest as white supremacy, male supremacy, straight supremacy, cis supremacy, ableist supremacy, and so on, and though each of these can justify harm and hoarding of resources, this book concerns itself with the violence of white supremacy and the lynch culture created from it.

10. "History of Lynching in America," NAACP, accessed September 29, 2021, https://naacp.org/find-resources/history-explained/history-lynching-america.

11. In 1792, when Kentucky became a state, those who were considered slaves in Virginia were also slaves in Kentucky, and a few years later, the Kentucky legislature enforced Slave Codes, which stated that all Black people of Kentucky, free or enslaved, were not entitled to the same status as white people.

12. George Yancy, *Black Bodies, White Gazes: The Continuing Significance of Race in America* (Lanham, MD: Rowman & Littlefield, 2016), 4.

13. "The Kentucky Slave Code of 1798 allowed for the slaveholder to be paid the value of any enslaved person who was executed. The process for payment was as follows: Once the enslaved person was taken into custody by the sheriff, he or she was to be assessed a value. The auditor of public accounts was authorized and required to issue a warrant to the treasury for the amount in favor of the slave owner. The owner was to produce the certificate of the clerk of the court that said the slave was condemned along with the sheriff's certificate that said the slave was

executed or perished before execution. The treasurer was then required to pay the owner the assessed value of the enslaved person" (William Littell and Jacob Swigert, "A Digest of the Statute Law of Kentucky . . .," Notable Kentucky African Americans Database, accessed June 13, 2019, https://nkaa.uky.edu/nkaa/items/show/300001815).

14. Bill, a twelve-year-old slave, was one of the first teens and the youngest teen to be executed in Kentucky; he was hanged for murder on July 30, 1791, in Woodford County. According to author Adalberto Aguirre, there were 1,161 slaves executed in the US between the 1790s and 1850s ("Slave Executions in the United States," *Social Science Journal* 36, no. 1 [1999]: 1–31, https:doi.org/10.1016/S0362-3319(99)80001-9).

15. M. Watt Espy's index of executions in the United States, better known as the Espy File, indicates executions of the enslaved correlated to punishment for slave revolts and prohibitions against miscegenation. Adalberto Aguirre says, "Espy's index reveals that criminal justice jurisdictions utilized a variety of other methods to execute blacks as well. Of the 1,098 blacks executed (including 1,035 slaves) before 1830, 990 were hanged, 60 were burned, eight suffered breaking on the wheel, three were hung in chains, three were gibbeted ["hanged on an upright post with projecting arm, so they slowly strangled rather than having their necks broken from a scaffold"], and fifty-one were put to death using some other method of execution or the execution method is unknown" (Adalberto Aguirre, Jr., "Slave Executions in the United States: A Descriptive Analysis of Social and Historical Factors," *Social Science Journal,* 1999, https://www.academia.edu/54066131/Slave_executions_in_the_United_States_A_descriptive_analysis_of_social_and_historical_factors; "Executions in the U.S. 1608–2002: The Espy File," Death Penalty Information Center, accessed October 4, 2024, https://deathpenaltyinfo.org/executions/executions-overview/executions-in-the-u-s-1608-2002-the-espy-file).

16. Capital offenses were declared for interracial sexual contact between Black men and white women. Rape offenses included any form of contact with white women, including writing letters to white women, proposing marriage to a white woman, eloping with a white woman, or simply paying attention to a white woman. Indeed, rape as a criminal category existed only for white women (Aguirre, "Slave Executions in the United States," 12).

17. Aguirre, "Slave Executions in the United States," 18.

18. Wright, *Racial Violence in Kentucky, 1865–1940*, 3.

19. Vanessa Sanchez, "Kentucky Newspapers Often Blamed Black Victims for Lynchings," Howard Center for Investigative Journalism, November 2, 2021, https://wordinblack.com/2021/11/kentucky-newspapers-often-blamed-black-victims-for-lynchings/.

20. Sanchez, "Kentucky Newspapers Often Blamed Black Victims for Lynchings."

21. "As voters and members of small-town elites, they pressured county sheriffs to uphold the law. As members of a far-flung communications network headquartered in Atlanta, they beamed a withering light of publicity on local affairs." Ames

campaigned for a lynch-free year (Jacquelyn Dowd Hall, "Second Thoughts: On Writing a Feminist Biography," *Feminist Studies* 13, no. 1 [1987]: 19–37, https://doi.org/10.2307/3177833).

22. My grandmother Ralph would have been in the group targeted by members of the educated, upper-class white women of the ASWPL, whose task it was to convince poor white women who might stand to gain through their husband's racial terror to instead stand against lynching. But Grandmaw was of the group of poorer white women who believed the lies of the dangerous Black male. Through her presence at the hanging of Rainey Bethea and in the use of racist words about the event, she participated in the cruelty and torture of lynch mobs. My family had been complicit with the southern indoctrination and cultural acceptance of lynching in the 1930s. Jessie Ames declared a second generation of lynchers had grown up with their mothers and fathers holding them, "balanced precariously on parents' shoulders in order to have a better view." The white women who resisted lynching were censored by their communities and partners; they were confronted by aggressive white men who preferred the status quo. The women of the ASWPL "attacked the traditional patriarchic order upon which the practice of lynching rested," and I expect formed another version of themselves in the process, one oriented to sovereignty, interdependence, and reversals of powerful myths that were formed to keep gender and race in line (Hall, "Second Thoughts," 19–37).

23. Upon investigation, the ASWPL found that of the 4,297 persons lynched since 1886, only 21 percent of the victims were charged with sexual assault or crimes against white women. In fact, the remaining 79 percent stemmed from interracial conflict over new forms of economic competition between poor white yeomen farmers who were threatened by Black men's growing socioeconomic power after emancipation. Some of the accounts on lynching incidents the women collected explicitly stated that "innocent Negroes were lynched on non-existent grounds at the instigation of white men who coveted the crops the Negroes had cultivated" (Rhae Lynn Barnes, "A Man Was Lynched Yesterday: Jessie Daniel Ames and the Association of Southern Women for the Prevention of Lynching, 1930–1942," U.S. History Scene, April 10, 2015, https://ushistoryscene.com/article/aswpl/).

24. Kentucky played a significant role in the NAACP; for example, the Louisville labor organizer William English Walling helped form the NAACP shortly after the Springfield Race Riot of 1908. Alberta Jones was the first woman prosecutor in Kentucky in 1964 and the first African American woman to pass the Kentucky Bar (1959). Journalist and essayist Walter White was the NAACP president at the time of the legal lynching of Bethea. In 1935, White protested President Roosevelt's silence at southern Democrats' blocking of antilynching legislation to avoid retaliatory obstruction of his New Deal policies.

25. Charles Ogletree points out that

> the members of a community who engaged in a lynching were often the same persons who, should the accused be tried, would sit on the

> grand and petit juries that would convict and sentence him. . . . Should such proceedings take place before a jury from which all African Americans have been excluded, either by law or custom; should the interval between that trial's beginning and end prove exceedingly brief . . . should that trial deny to the accused the right to self-defense . . . should that trial be presided over by a judge who acquiesced in these counterfeit proceedings, as was routinely the case, it is difficult to know what to call such incidents other than "legal lynchings" even though that phrase cannot help but appear oxymoronic from the standpoint of the social contract (*From Lynch Mobs to the Killing State: Race and the Death Penalty in America* [New York: New York University Press, 2006], 21–54).

Capital punishment took the place of spectacle lynchings because the spectacle became "less imperative once white dominance was assured by less transparent but more calculable means. . . . Perpetuation of the racial contract still required the coercive production of a class of subpersons, but no longer was it necessary to secure that end by visibly marking and publicly displaying the bodies of its members" (Ogletree, *From Lynch Mobs to the Killing State,* 21–54).

26. Robert L. Zangrando, *The NAACP Crusade Against Lynching, 1909–1950* (Philadelphia: Temple University Press, 1980), 18.

27. Brundage, *Under Sentence of Death,* 1–16. For the personal and familial ways whiteness promotes and creates lynch culture, see chap. 2 of this volume.

28. A Kentucky prisoner condemned before March 31, 1998, may choose to be electrocuted instead of death by lethal injection. Electrocution is also authorized if lethal injection is found unconstitutional by a court.

29. Giovanni Russonello, "How Many Americans Support the Death Penalty? Depends How You Ask," *New York Times,* June 2, 2021, https://www.nytimes.com/2021/06/02/us/politics/death-penalty-polls.html; statistics based on an August 2020 poll, "Most Americans Favor the Death Penalty Despite Concerns about Its Administration," Pew Research Center, June 2, 2021, https://www.pewresearch.org/politics/2021/06/02/most-americans-favor-the-death-penalty-despite-concerns-about-its-administration; "Death Penalty States," World Population Review, accessed March 26, 2025, https://worldpopulationreview.com/state-rankings/death-penalty-states.

30. The US Supreme Court did not ban the execution of children until 2005.

31. "State-by-State Death Row Populations by Race," Death Penalty Information Center, January 1, 2024, https://deathpenaltyinfo.org/death-row/overview/demographics. Also see Bright, "Discrimination, Death and Denial."

32. James W. Clarke, "Without Fear or Shame: Lynching, Capital Punishment and the Subculture of Violence in the American South," *British Journal of Political Science* 28, no. 2 (1998): 269–89, http://www.jstor.org/stable/194307.

33. Bright, "Discrimination, Death and Denial."

34. Liliana Segura, "The Stepchild of Lynching: Alabama's Lynching Memorial and the Legacy of Racial Terror in the South," *The Intercept*, June 17, 2018, https://theintercept.com/2018/06/17/lynching-museum-alabama-death-penalty/.

35. Clarke, "Without Fear or Shame."

36. Equal Justice Initiative, *Lynching in America*, 37.

37. Equal Justice Initiative, *Lynching in America*, 37.

38. John Gramlich, "From Police to Parole, Black and White Americans Differ Widely in Their Views of Criminal Justice System," Pew Research Center, May 21, 2019.

39. Bright, "Discrimination, Death and Denial." See also Austin Sarat, *From Lynch Mobs to the Killing State: Race and the Death Penalty in America* (New York: New York University Press, 2006), 214–15.

40. "For example, during the race riots of the Red Summer of 1919, Tulsa Oklahoma (1921), and Rosewood Florida (1923), law enforcement participated and/or stood aside as white mobs destroyed black lives and property. During the modern Civil Rights movement, episodes such as the police officers beating black civil rights activists in Birmingham and Selma, Alabama, also reflected the racist attitude of white local and state law enforcement in the United States" (Sandra E. Weissinger, ed., *Law Enforcement in the Age of Black Lives Matter: Policing Black and Brown Bodies* [Lanham, MD: Lexington Books, 2019], 20).

41. An ambulance had been on standby outside the apartment but, breaking a standard practice, left about an hour before the raid (Christina Carrega and Sabina Ghabremedhin, "Timeline: Inside the Investigation of Breonna Taylor's Killing and Its Aftermath," ABC News, November 17, 2020, https://abcnews.go.com/US/timeline-inside-investigation-breonna-taylors-killing-aftermath/story?id=71217247).

42. Ta-Nehisi Coates, "The Life Breonna Taylor Lived, in the Words of Her Mother," *Vanity Fair*, August 24, 2020, https://www.vanityfair.com/culture/2020/08/breonna-taylor.

43. That commando-raid style of policing began in politics, with the Nixon administration pushing police departments for behavior that would demonstrate being tough on crime and drugs. In Louisville during the protests following the murder of Taylor, the National Guard, in town to enforce a curfew, fatally shot Black restaurateur David McAtee, and in the aftermath of that killing, we learned that police had turned off their body cams during the incident, against department orders. The police chief was fired soon afterward. By June, Louisville banned no-knock warrants. One year later, Governor Andy Beshear signed Senate Bill 4, a bipartisan bill that partially bans no-knock warrants. Eventually, the public learned that the Louisville Police Department had originally received court approval for a "no-knock" entry, but the orders were changed before the raid to "knock and announce," meaning that the police had to identify themselves.

44. By August, the Louisville Metro Police Department had arrested six hundred protesters over seventy-five days. Only three of the arrests resulted in

trials being set up; the majority of the arrests were expunged from the protesters' records (Ed Pilkington, "UN Experts Condemn Modern-Day 'Racial Terror' Lynchings in US," *Guardian*, June 5, 2020, https://amp.theguardian.com/world/2020/jun/05/un-human-rights-monitors-us-modern-racial-terror-lynchings).

45. Richard A. Oppel Jr., Derrick Bryson Taylor, and Nicholas Bogel-Burroughs, "What to Know about Breonna Taylor's Death," *New York Times*, March 9, 2023, https://www.nytimes.com/article/breonna-taylor-police.html.

46. When the grand jury investigation came back, it found that Mattingly and Cosgrove were "justified in their use of force after having been fired upon by Kenneth Walker." The grand jury voted not to bring charges against the officers accused of participating in Taylor's killing. Instead, Hankison, a former Louisville detective fired after the incident, was charged with three counts of wanton endangerment for his role in the botched raid. What was most troubling about the grand jury announcement was that Hankison's charges are not for what he did to Taylor. Instead, the grand jury indicted Hankison because the bullets from his gun went through Taylor's walls and into her neighbor's apartment occupied by three people, none of whom were injured (Oppel, Taylor, and Bogel-Burroughs, "What to Know about Breonna Taylor's Death"). Brett Hankison is facing up to life in prison after being convicted of using excessive force. The verdict marks the first time any officer has been convicted in the deadly raid on March 13, 2020, that made Taylor's name a rallying cry during the racial justice unrest of that year ("Brett Hankison Found Guilty of Violating Breonna Taylor's Civil Rights," *Louisville Courier-Journal*, November 1, 2024, https://www.courier-journal.com/story/news/crime/2024/11/01/brett-hankison-verdict-in-breonna-taylor/75944338007/).

47. Senator Danny Carroll of Kentucky, a former police officer, also proposed a law that would "shield a large swathe of people from any disclosure by a public agency if they request it. It includes police officers, judges, prosecutors, public defenders, first responders, corrections officers, emergency call center employees, retired police, and their relatives. First Amendment attorney Michael Abate reckons it could cover half of Kentucky, if relative was defined broadly enough. As the bill is written, if someone wrote about these people anyway without knowing they were shielded, they could be prosecuted" (Linda Blackford, "Fever Dreams and the 1st Amendment, These Two Ky. Bills Are Downright Un-American," *Lexington Herald-Leader*, January 28, 2022).

48. Oppel, Taylor, and Bogel-Burroughs, "What to Know about Breonna Taylor's Death."

49. Jennifer L. Eberhardt, Phillip Atiba Goff, Valerie J. Purdie, and Paul G. Davies, "Seeing Black: Race, Crime and Visual Processing," *Journal of Personality and Social Psychology*, 87, no. 6 (2004): 876–93.

50. Northern journalist and muckraker Ray Stannard Baker asserted that "nearly all of the crimes committed by negroes are marked with an almost animal-like ferocity. . . . For the moment, under stress of passion, he [the Negro] seems to revert wholly to savagery." In 1905, white people could influence Baker to believe that poor law enforcement made lynching necessary (Ray Stannard Baker,

"What Is a Lynching? A Study of Mob Justice, South and North," McClure's Magazine, January 1905, https://journalismhistorycom.wordpress.com/2021/10/11/what-is-a-lynching/).

51. Gendered oppression arises from laws that target Black men almost exclusively as criminals, for example, the law that abolished public executions *except* in cases of rape (Pitzulo, "Skirted Sheriff").

52. Only twenty-two states have ever elected a Black woman to Congress. See Katherine Schaeffer, "22 States Have Ever Elected a Black Woman to Congress," Pew Research Center, February 16, 2023, https://www.pewresearch.org/short-reads/2023/02/16/22-states-have-ever-elected-a-black-woman-to-congress/.

53. Wood, *Lynching and Spectacle*, 263.

54. As Finoh and Sankofah explain,

> Black women, girls, and non-binary people are seldom seen as victims. Instead, they are seen as deserving of harm or unable to be harmed. This perpetuates a long legacy of impunity for violence against Black women, girls, and non-binary people.
>
> Because Black women and girls have historically been dehumanized, considered unrapeable, and left without legal recourse, they become easier targets for abuse and are more reluctant to come forward. Daniel Holtzclaw, a former Oklahoma City police officer convicted of sexual violence in 2015, specifically targeted low-income Black women because he thought they were less likely to be believed.
>
> The silencing of and structural biases against Black women, girls, and non-binary people can have devastating consequences—including the incarceration of survivors themselves (Maya Finoh and Jasmine Sankofah, "The Legal System Has Failed Black Girls, Women and Non-binary Survivors of Violence," ACLU, January 28, 2019, https://www.aclu.org/blog/racial-justice/race-and-criminal-justice/legal-system-has-failed-black-girls-women-and-non).

55. Donald Yacavone, *Teaching White Supremacy: America's Democratic Ideal and the Forging of our National Identity* (New York: Pantheon, 2022), Kindle.

56. Sabrina Strings, *Fearing the Black Body: The Racial Origins of Fat Phobia* (New York: New York University Press, 2019), 6.

57. Yacavone, *Teaching White Supremacy.*

58. As anthropologist Aihwa Ong has said "modern medicine is the prime mover, defining and promoting concepts, categories and authoritative pronouncements on hygiene, health, sexuality, life and death. . . . The medical gaze . . . establishes the normative identity and behavior of individuals, and populations" ("Making the Biopolitical Subject: Cambodian Immigrants, Refugee Medicine and Cultural Citizenship in California," *Social Science Medicine*, 40, no. 9 [June 1995]: 1244).

59. One example lies in the systemic discriminatory features (and not an individual police officer's bigotry) that underlie law enforcement practices and

policies. According to Sandra E. Weissinger, author of *Law Enforcement in the Age of Black Lives Matter: Policing Black and Brown Bodies* (Lanham, MD: Lexington Books, 2019), the "federal statute which prohibits government authorities or agents acting on their behalf from engaging in a pattern or practice of conduct by law enforcement officers that deprives persons of their Constitutional rights. . . . Under President Obama, the Department of Justice opened 25 pattern or practice investigations of police departments across the country, including Baltimore, Chicago, and Ferguson Missouri" (51).

60. Brundage, *Lynching in the New South: Georgia and Virginia, 1880–1930* (Champagne: University of Illinois Press, 1993), 8–16.

61. Brundage, *Lynching in the New South*, 13.

62. From the author's interview with Perry Ryan, August 18, 2021.

63. From my interview with Ryan.

64. From the author's interviews with Kentucky archivists and a police records manager, June 2019.

65. Confirmation bias is a tendency to selectively search for and emphasize information that is consistent with a preferred hypothesis, whereas opposing information is ignored or downgraded. This bias is rampant in policing and justice systems. For more, see M. Lidén, "Confirmation Bias in Criminal Cases" (PhD diss., Department of Law, Uppsala University, Sweden, 2018), https://www.diva-portal.org/smash/get/diva2:1237959/FULLTEXT01.pdf.

66. Black people who are later exonerated are 60 percent more likely to be sentenced to life imprisonment than their white peers and spend an average of 4.4 years longer in prison before being exonerated, according to the Innocence Project (Daniele Selby, "8 Facts You Should Know about Racial Injustice in the Criminal Legal System," Innocence Project, February 5, 2021, https://innocenceproject.org/news/facts-racial-discrimination-justice-system-wrongful-conviction-black-history-month/).

67. Charlotte Wolf, "Constructions of a Lynching," *Sociological Inquiry* 62 (Winter 1992): 83–97, https://doi.org/10.1111/j.1475-682X.1992.tb00184.x.

68. Arthur F. Raper, *The Tragedy of Lynching* (Chapel Hill: University of North Carolina Press, 1933); W. Fitzhugh Brundage, Larry J. Griffin, Paula Clark, and Joanne C. Sandberg, "Narrative and Event: Lynching and Historical Sociology," in Brundage, *Lynching in the New South*, 9.

69. According to Campaign Zero, police killed 1,134 people in the US in 2021. Black people are almost three times more likely to be killed than white people. A study published in 2017 by the Equal Justice Initiative found that 4,084 Black men, women, and children were lynched in twelve southern states between 1877 and 1950, while 300 lynchings took place in other states.

70. I owe a debt of gratitude to author Camonghne Felix, who presented these ideas in "Don't Blame Alice Sebold," *The Cut*, December 8, 2021, https://www.thecut.com/2021/12/dont-blame-alice-sebold.html, and in her work elsewhere.

71. Christina Zhao, "'BBQ Becky,' White Woman Who Called Cops on Black BBQ, 911 Audio Released: 'I'm Really Scared! Come Quick!'" *Newsweek*, September 4, 2018, https://www.newsweek.com/bbq-becky-white-woman-who-called-cops

-black-bbq-911-audio-released-im-really-1103057; Sarah Maslin Nir, "How 2 Lives Collided in Central Park, Rattling the Nation," *New York Times*, May 26, 2020, https://www.nytimes.com/2020/06/14/nyregion/central-park-amy-cooper-christian-racism.html. For racist calls to dispatchers, see Rachael Herron, "I Used to Be a 911 Dispatcher. I Had to Respond to Racist Calls Every Day," *Vox*, October 31, 2018, https://www.vox.com/first-person/2018/5/30/17406092/racial-profiling-911-bbq-becky-living-while-black-babysitting-while-black.

72. Matt Berical, "What Is the Male Version of Karen?," *Fatherly*, June 8, 2020, https://www.fatherly.com/life/male-version-of-karen-meme.

73. Equal Justice Initiative, *Lynching in America*.

74. Over the last fifty years, defendants chose trial in less than 3 percent of state and federal criminal cases—compared thirty years ago when 20 percent of those arrested chose trial. The remaining 97 percent of cases were resolved through plea deals (Innocence Project Staff, "Report: Guilty Pleas on the Rise, Criminal Trials on the Decline," August 7, 2018, https://innocenceproject.org/guilty-pleas-on-the-rise-criminal-trials-on-the-decline/).

75. Two-thirds of people executed in the 1930s were Black, and the trend continued for a generation. By 1950, the Black share of the South's population fell to just 22 percent, but 75 percent of people executed in the South were Black (Clarke, "Without Fear or Shame").

76. George C. Wright reports on the June 1880 case of *Commonwealth v. Johnson*, which ruled that "no one can be lawfully excluded from a jury due to race or color." But *Virginia v. Rives* before the Supreme Court ruled that the burden of proof for proving discrimination rested with Black individuals. In 1938, the NAACP carried a case to the Supreme Court for a death penalty by Kentucky on James Hale, which received a new trial. In 1986, the Supreme Court again ruled on the composition of juries in *Batson v. Kentucky*, but Wright says, "This ruling has had little effect because prosecutors are astute enough to resort to other tactics, such as the manner of questioning black potential jurors, to accomplish the same goal of all-white juries for sensitive cases" (George C. Wright, "Legal Executions of Kentucky Blacks," in Brundage, *Under Sentence of Death*, 267).

77. There exist community beliefs in the sacrifice of the scapegoat, whereby the sacrifice of the victim purges the community of its own disorder (Jenna Gericke, "The Strangers, The Crowd, and The Lynching: Using Mimetic Theory to Explore Episodes of Human Violence," *Apollon* 7 (2017): 16–32, http://www.apollonejournal.org/apollon-journal/the-strangers-the-crowd-and-the-lynching).

78. From the *Washington Post* on the success of the long Southern strategy, still in play: "Despite the long-standing national gender gap, where more women vote for the Democratic Party than men, Southern white women remain firmly in the Republican camp. In 2016, while Hillary Clinton captured the support of white women outside of the South 52 to 48, Trump bested her among white women who live in the South, 64 percent to 36 percent. And this result was not unusual: In 2018, only 25 percent of white women voted for Democrat Stacey Abrams in Georgia's gubernatorial race" (Angie Maxwell, "What We Get Wrong about the

Southern Strategy," *Washington Post*, July 26, 2019, https://www.washingtonpost.com/outlook/2019/07/26/what-we-get-wrong-about-southern-strategy/).

79. According to one report,

> Further complicating Kentucky's situation, nearly half its state inmates are housed in local jails, many of which are badly overcrowded, rather than state prisons that offer a full array of vocational and educational programs and addiction treatment. Jails are much smaller facilities in county seats that are meant to hold people awaiting trial or serving short sentences, not felons incarcerated for years. Kentucky expects to spend $628 million on its Department of Corrections in the fiscal year that begins July 1, up 17 percent from four years earlier in a state budget already struggling to pay for pension contributions and Medicaid (John Cheves, "Prison Populations Are Falling in Most States but Ballooning in Kentucky. Here's Why," *Lexington Herald-Leader*, April 26, 2019, https://www.kentucky.com/news/politics-government/article229666564.html).

80. The Stô:lô (pronounced "Staw-low"), or "River People," are Coast Salish people whose mother language is Halq'eméylem. They continue to live along the lower Fraser River and its tributaries.

81. John Vaillant, "The Lynching of Louie Sam," *The Walrus*, December 12, 2008.

82. Vaillant, "Lynching of Louie Sam."

83. Shari Narine, "Lack of Action at Truckers' Blockades Shows Racist Intent of Alberta's Critical Infrastructure Defense Act, Says Chief," *Toronto Star*, February 3, 2022, https://www.thestar.com/news/canada/2022/02/03/lack-of-action-at-truckers-blockades-shows-racist-intent-of-albertas-critical-infrastructure-defence-act-says-chief.html.

84. Jillian Kestler-D'Amours, "Canada: Day for Truth and Reconciliation Spurs Calls for Action," AlJazeera, September 30, 2021, https://www.aljazeera.com/news/2021/9/30/canada-national-day-truth-and-reconciliation-spurs-calls-for-action.

85. While aboriginal women represent just 4.3 percent of Canada's female population, they represent 16 percent of female murder victims and 11 percent of missing persons cases involving women (Mali Ilse Paquin, "Unsolved Murders of Indigenous Women Reflect Canada's History of Silence," *The Guardian*, June 25, 2015).

86. Michelle Cyca, "Tanya Talaga Is Telling the Stories Canada Needs to Hear," *Maclean's*, December 14, 2021. Murray Sinclair says that evidence about children dying in the schools and being improperly handled after death was revealed in a report done in 1907, by Peter Bryce (Marie-Danielle Smith, "Murray Sinclair on Reconciliation, Anger, Unmarked Graves, and a Headline for This Story," *Maclean's*, August 18, 2021).

87. "White Supremacist Groups Are Thriving on Facebook," Tech Transparency Project, May 21, 2020, https://www.techtransparencyproject.org/articles/white-supremacist-groups-are-thriving-on-facebook.

88. The victims were Tywanza Sanders, twenty-six; Reverend Clementa Pinckney, forty-one; Cynthia Hurd, fifty-four; Reverend DePayne Middleton-Doctor, forty-nine; Ethel Lance, seventy; Myra Thompson, fifty-nine; and Reverend Daniel Simmons Sr., seventy-four.

89. Devan Cole, "Graham Denies Systemic Racism Exists in the US and Says, 'America's Not a Racist Country,'" CNN, April 25, 2021.

90. "Year In Hate: New SPLC Analysis Shows Extremists Leveraging Little-Known and Encrypted Technology to Spread Dangerous Messages, Plot Violence," Southern Poverty Law Center, February 16, 2021, https://www.splcenter.org/news/2021/02/16/year-hate-new-splc-analysis-shows-extremists-leveraging-little-known-and-encrypted.

91. Modifies the law relating to unlawful discrimination, SS#2 SCS SB 43, June 30, 2017 (signed by the Governor), https://www.senate.mo.gov/17info/BTS_Web/Bill.aspx?SessionType=R&BillID=57095378.

92. Across the country, states instituted new laws that have forced teachers to cut and alter lessons addressing Black history, impacting student access to inclusive, accurate education about the country's history of racism. A wave of anti-LGBTQ demonstrations and harassment campaigns resulted in increased security measures at drag shows, library story hours, and Pride celebrations; in many cases, organizers this year canceled queer community events out of safety concerns. A historic number of antitrans bills now restrict the rights of trans people and, often, their ability to seek crucial gender-affirming medical care. And, because of the Supreme Court's *Dobbs* decision, people in thirteen states cannot seek abortions where they live and face the loss of personal autonomy, injury, and even death ("The Year in Hate and Extremism 2022," Southern Poverty Law Center, accessed March 26, 2025, https://www.splcenter.org/resources/guides/year-hate-extremism-2022/).

93. Jess Clark, "Kentucky Bill Would Make It Illegal to Teach about Institutional Racism," Louisville Public Media, February 15, 2022, https://wfpl.org/ky-bill-would-make-it-illegal-to-teach-about-institutional-racism/.

94. Elizabeth A. Harris and Alexandra Alter, "Book Ban Efforts Spread across the U.S.," *New York Times*, January 30, 2022, https://www.nytimes.com/2022/01/30/books/book-ban-us-schools.html.

95. Hate groups hold beliefs or practices that attack or malign an entire class of people, typically for their immutable characteristics, while antigovernment groups see the federal government as an enemy of the people and promote baseless conspiracy theories. These groups often work together, can hold shared beliefs, use similar strategies, and negatively impact the same communities. Hate and antigovernment groups make up the extreme edge of America's hard right, an inherently antidemocratic movement that rejects pluralism and equity. The movement instead strives to build a society dominated by hierarchy, where people whom far rightists deem threatening—women, Black and Brown people, LGBTQ people, non-Christians, and others—are socially and politically subjugated. The hard right has the advantage of building on already existing structural white

supremacy, as well as its persistent and regular manifestations in everyday life and in politics ("The Year in Hate and Extremism 2022").

96. Sherrilyn A. Ifill, *On the Courthouse Lawn: Confronting the Legacy of Lynching in the 21st Century*, rev. ed. (Boston, MA: Beacon, 2018), 15.

97. Brundage, *Lynching in the New South*, 40.

98. As reported by Heather Cox Richardson, "Letters from an American," May 21, 2023, https://heathercoxrichardson.substack.com/p/may-21-2023, as well as Cathryn Stout and Thomas Wilburn, "CRT Map: Efforts to Restrict Teaching Racism and Bias Have Multiplied across the U.S.," Chalkbeat, February 1, 2022, https://www.chalkbeat.org/22525983/map-critical-race-theory-legislation-teaching-racism "America's Censored Classrooms 2024," https://pen.org/report/americas-censored-classrooms-2024/.

4. How Could This Happen Here?

Epigraph Sources: Meara Sharma, "Bryan Stevenson: Walking With the Wind," March 17, 2014, https://www.guernicamag.com/walking-with-the-wind/; S. C. Foster and E. M. Favor, *My Old Kentucky Home* (New York: E. Berliner's Gramophone, 1897); Mary Wollstonecraft, *A Vindication on the Rights of Women* (London: J. Johnson, 1792); Frederick Douglass, "Address . . . January 9th, 1894, on the Lessons of the Hour—Folder 1 of 8," January 9, 1894, courtesy of Library of Congress.

1. The Confederate monument in Owensboro was located at the southwest corner of the lawn, at the intersection of Third and Frederica Streets. In April 2021, the Kentucky Division of the United Daughters of the Confederacy sued the members of Daviess County Fiscal Court in Daviess County District Court. Kentucky UDC claimed ownership of the monument and requested—and were granted—a temporary restraining order preventing the monument from being moved until the ownership issue was resolved in court. In March 2022, with the case still unresolved, the Southern Poverty Law Center joined the Owensboro branch of the NAACP in placing a billboard on Owensboro's central thoroughfare with the message: "Show [heart symbol] for all. REMOVE Owensboro–Daviess County's Confederate Monument." On April 29, 2022, Daviess Circuit Court judge Lisa Payne Jones granted Daviess Fiscal Court's motion for a summary judgment. In her sixteen-page judgment, Jones ruled that the Confederate monument is owned by the fiscal court, and she vacated the earlier temporary restraining order. Nearly 122 years after the monument was dedicated in September 1900, it was dismantled in 2022, beginning with the removal of the sculpture in May 2022. The pedestal was removed in August 2022 and given to the Kentucky United Daughters of the Confederacy, who relocated it to a Civil War battle site in Daviess County that they own. In November 2022, the sculpture was relocated to Owensboro's City Cemetery, aka Potter's Field, with ownership transferred to the Owensboro Museum of Science and History.

2. Jonathan B. Pritchett, "Demographic Causes and Consequences of the Interregional Slave Trade: The Slave Breeding Hypothesis" (Department of Economics, Tulane University, New Orleans, LA, October 2017).

3. Matthew Salafia, "Searching for Slavery: Fugitive Slaves in the Ohio River Valley Borderland, 1830–1860," *Ohio Valley History* 8, no. 4 (2008): 46.

4. Lee A. Dew and Aloma W. Dew, *Owensboro, The City on the Yellow Banks: A History of Owensboro, Kentucky* (Bowling Green, KY: Rivendell, 1988), 43.

5. In 1855 with other members of Union Church, Fee founded Berea College, the first college in the state that was interracial and coeducational. Cassius M. Clay, a Kentucky landowner and leader in the movement for gradual emancipation, provided land and funds for Berea. They modeled the school on Oberlin College, an antislavery stronghold in Ohio. In 1859, Fee and the Berea teachers were driven from Madison County by southern proslavery sympathizers. By 1865, following the Civil War, they'd returned to start a school for ninety-six Black and ninety-one white students. Berea's interracial education was overturned in 1904 by the Kentucky legislature's passage of the Day Law, which prohibited education of Black and white students together, and it wouldn't be amended until 1950, when Black students were allowed to return.

6. The two Black schools were housed in inadequate buildings and operated only three or four months per year, while the white schools were in good buildings and had a ten-month year. Only taxes collected from African Americans were to be used for educating African American children in the city. For white children, the sum of $9,400 was available for two well-built schools, eighteen teachers, and the nine- to ten-month school session. For African American children, $700 provided the one inferior school, three teachers, and a school session of about three months. In 1883, US Circuit judge John Barr ruled that the method of distributing school funds was unfair. "If I am correct in my conclusion, all that colored children in Owensboro are entitled to is the equal protection of the laws, in that a fair share of this fund be applied toward the maintenance of the common schools especially provided for colored children. In this view the only remedy is in equity. . . . United States courts have heretofore enjoined state officers from obeying state laws which were declared to be unconstitutional." For more see CLAYBROOK and others v. CITY OF OWENSBORO and others, District Court, D. Kentucky, 16 F.297 U.S. Dist. 1883, and *Claybrook v. Owensboro* by L. A. Coghill (thesis), https://law.resource.org/pub/us/case/reporter/F/0016/0016.f.0297.pdf; "Claybrook v. Owensboro," Notable Kentucky African Americans Database, accessed June 19, 2023, https://www.ukscrc001.net/nkaa/items/show/376.

7. W. H. Anderson was a Civil War veteran, having served in the Thirteenth Regiment US Colored Infantry. He was the minister of McFarland Chapel in Evansville, Indiana, in 1889 when he became the first minister in the state to receive an honorary doctor of divinity from State University in Louisville, Kentucky ("Anderson, William Hardin," Notable Kentucky African

Americans Database, accessed June 19, 2023, https://nkaa.uky.edu/nkaa/items/show/1).

8. John Eligon and Will Wright, "In Louisville, Looking to Protests of the Past to Move Forward," *New York Times*, October 6, 2020, https://www.nytimes.com/2020/10/06/us/louisville-protests-civil-rights.html.

9. Heather Cox Richardson, *How the South Won the Civil War: Oligarchy, Democracy and the Continuing Fight for the Soul of America* (Cary, NC: Oxford University Press, 2020), 49.

10. Dew and Dew, *Owensboro*, 41.

11. For a short time in the mid-nineteenth century, the American Party, or the Know Nothings, formed a political coalition known for its unapologetic nativism, and it took the place of the Whigs of Kentucky.

12. Lincoln's birthplace refused to ratify the Thirteenth Amendment in 1865, one month after the US House of Representatives passed it. Kentucky did not move to ratify the Thirteenth Amendment until state representative Mae Street Kidd, D-Louisville, one of three Black Americans then in the Kentucky legislature, filed a resolution to do so in 1976.

13. The Night Riders were a group of tobacco farmers in Kentucky and Tennessee who used vigilante justice to coerce tobacco farmers to band together against industrial monopolies who were fixing tobacco prices.

14. James C. Klotter and Craig Thompson Friend, *A New History of Kentucky* (Lexington: University Press of Kentucky, 2018), 206–22.

15. Anne E. Marshall, *Creating a Confederate Kentucky: The Lost Cause and Civil War Memory in a Border State* (Chapel Hill: University of North Carolina Press, 2010), 2.

16. Marshall, *Creating a Confederate Kentucky*, 4.

17. Wright, "Legal Executions of Kentucky Blacks," 253.

18. "How a Racist Film Helped the Ku Klux Klan Grow for Generations," *The Economist*, March 27, 2021, https://www.economist.com/graphic-detail/2021/03/27/how-a-racist-film-helped-the-ku-klux-klan-grow-for-generations.

19. Adam McCann, "Most and Least Diverse States in America," Wallet Hub, September 17, 2024, https://wallethub.com/edu/most-least-diverse-states-in-america/38262.

20. "Poverty in Kentucky," *Welfare Info*, 2023, https://www.welfareinfo.org/poverty-rate/kentucky/; Jeff Desjardins, "Visualizing the Poverty Rate of Each U.S. State," *Visual Capitalist*, November 25, 2018, https://www.visualcapitalist.com/visualizing-poverty-rate-u-s-states/. In 2017, nearly a third of Black and Hispanic populations are notably poor. Kentucky is the fifth most poor state.

21. In 2001, the Library of Congress digitized this collection, and it's now available in sound recordings, manuscripts, and photographs.

22. George C. Wright, *A History of Blacks in Kentucky: In Pursuit of Equality, 1890–1980* (Lexington: University Press of Kentucky, 2009).

23. Luther Adams, "'Headed for Louisville': Rethinking Rural to Urban Migration in the South, 1930–1950," SIAS Faculty Publications, 2006, 1, https://digitalcommons.tacoma.uw.edu/cgi/viewcontent.cgi?article=1000&context=ias_pub.

24. Habeas Corpus Hearing, Rainey (Railey) Bethea v. Commonwealth of Kentucky, District Court of the United States for the Western District of Kentucky Owensboro Division, August 5, 1936. Also reported by Ryan, *Last Public Execution in America*, chap. 20.

25. Brent Staples, "How the White Press Wrote Off Black America," Opinion, *New York Times*, July 10, 2021, https://www.nytimes.com/2021/07/10/opinion/sunday/white-newspapers-african-americans.html.

26. Interview with Keith Lawrence by the author.

27. "Eighty Years after Last Public Hanging in America, Some Owensboro Residents Still Impacted by Event," WKU Public Radio, August 11, 2016, https://www.wkyufm.org/post/eighty-years-after-last-public-hanging-america-some-owensboro-residents-still-impacted-event#stream/0.

28. Ifill, *On the Courthouse Lawn*, xxi.

29. Ifill, *On the Courthouse Lawn*, xvi.

30. According to Yacavone's research,

> Rather than Southern slavery, however, it was *Northern* white supremacy that proved the more enduring cultural binding force, planted along with slavery in the colonial era, intensely cultivated in the years before the Civil War, and fully blossoming after Reconstruction. Inculcated relentlessly throughout the culture and in school textbooks, it suffused Northern religion, high culture, literature, education, politics, music, law, and science. It powerfully resurfaced after the Civil War and Reconstruction to assert control over the emancipated slaves to become the basis for national reconciliation, exploded in intensity with renewed immigration in the 1920s and '30s and endured with diminishing force to the present day (Yacavone, *Teaching White Supremacy*).

31. Wolf, "Constructions of a Lynching," 83–97.

32. "Eighty Years after Last Public Hanging in America."

33. Here is an account from *Lynching in America*.

> As attendees and participants in lynchings, Southern white children were taught to accept and embrace traumatic violence and the racist narratives underlying it. At one Kentucky lynching, young white children between six and ten years old brought wood and tended to the fire in which the victim was burned. Boys especially were expected to actively engage in lynching; their roles expanded as they got older until, as young adults, they took on a direct role in the torture and murder. Lynching was characterized as a civic duty of white Southern

men that brought praise rather than sanctions from community elders and institutions (Equal Justice Initiative, *Lynching in America*, 37).

34. Ezra Klein, "Bryan Stevenson on How America Can Heal," *Vox*, July 20, 2020.

5. Canada's Lynch Culture

1. A Quinnipiac poll conducted in January 2018 after Trump's Oval Office comments about immigration showed that 58 percent of American voters found the comments to be racist, while 59 percent said that he does not respect people of color as much as he respects white people.

2. In September 2016, fifteen signatories of the Buffalo Treaty requested the Geographical Board of Canada to officially change the name of Tunnel Mountain to Sacred Buffalo Guardian Mountain (https://www.buffalotreaty.com/flux/buffalo-mountain-banff).

3. Jason Warick, "Catholic Church's Reconciliation Fund Draws Mixed Reaction from Residential School Survivors," CBC, June 13, 2023, https://www.cbc.ca/news/canada/saskatoon/catholic-church-s-reconciliation-fund-draws-mixed-reaction-from-residential-school-survivors-1.6875522. The pope issued an apology on behalf of the Catholic Church on July 25, 2022. The full text of it can be found in Canadian Press, "'I Am Deeply Sorry': Full Text of Residential School Apology from Pope Francis," CBC, July 25, 2022, https://www.cbc.ca/news/canada/edmonton/pope-francis-maskwacis-apology-full-text-1.6531341.

4. What became Banff National Park was primarily the hunting and gathering grounds for the Stoney Nation. The groups they engaged with on these and other lands included the Ktunaxa (Kutenai), Secwépmc, and Cree people. The Blackfoot Nations were believed to have traveled through the area as well, though their hunting territories were more likely to be where the bison roamed on prairie lands. Stoney people also had relationships with the Tsuu'tina and Métis, who are also included in the Treaty 7 Nations. As of the date of this publication, I do not have access to the Stoney name for the landform later known as Mt. Rundle. I personally used the name "House Mountain" because it appears as one to me.

5. Theodore (Ted) Binnema, and Melanie Niemi, "'Let the Line Be Drawn Now': Wilderness, Conservation, and the Exclusion of Aboriginal People from Banff National Park in Canada," *Environmental History* 11, no. 4 (2006): 724–50, http://www.jstor.org/stable/3985800.

6. Much of the interpretation around Banff National Park is framed by statements that insist on seeing Indigenous groups in the region as "traveling through" and "gathering together." If writers might instead center oral histories of local Indigenous Nations as evidence, for example, in interviewing Elders, then there could be perspectives beyond academic discourse, which leans toward colonialist and white-based perspectives.

7. Binnema and Niemi, "Let the Line Be Drawn Now."

8. Graeme Hamilton, "The Shady Past of Parks Canada: Forced Out, Indigenous People Are Forging a Comeback," *National Post*, August 25, 2017, https://nationalpost.com/news/canada/the-shady-past-of-parks-canada-forced-out-indigenous-people-are-forging-a-comeback.

9. Robert Jago, "Canada's National Parks Are Colonial Crime Scenes," *The Walrus*, June 10, 2020, https://thewalrus.ca/canadas-national-parks-are-colonial-crime-scenes.

10. Mark David Spence, *Dispossessing the Wilderness: Indian Removal and the Making of the National Parks* (New York: Oxford University Press, 1999), 2–119.

11. Including utilizing seasonality, fuel characteristics, weather, return interval, and knowing the consequences of not burning.

12. Binnema, and Niemi, "Let the Line Be Drawn Now," 730.

13. Binnema, and Niemi, "Let the Line Be Drawn Now," 728.

14. Banff National Park is 6,641 square kilometers today, so this was substantially larger territory than at present.

15. In December 1883, at a site near Medicine Hat, railway workers drilled for water. Instead of finding groundwater, however, the workers stumbled upon a rich reservoir of natural gas. John George Brown learned from the Kootenay and Stoney Indians that oil oozed along what is now Cameron Creek, Alberta. In the 1880s, he publicized the presence of oil in the Waterton Lakes region. Alberta was explored for oil from 1894 to 1898, on recommendation from the Geological Survey of Canada. When they failed to locate the source pool of the oil, exploration was suspended until 1913. The notion of identity transference in the national parks is credited to the influence of Mark David Spence.

16. Spence says that something similar had happened at Yosemite with Indian Field Days, an event that "often degenerated into little more than an excuse for tourists and park officials to pose in buckskin and feathered headdress . . . [confirming] popular white conceptions of how Indians were supposed to look and behave" (Mark David Spence, *Dispossessing the Wilderness: Indian Removal and the Making of the National Parks*, 117; "Banff Indian Days Affirmed Stereotypes, Reinforced Culture," *Rocky Mountain Outlook*, April 3, 2014, https://www.rmoutlook.com/local-news/banff-indian-days-affirmed-stereotypes-reinforced-culture-1565423).

17. Elder Roland Rollinmud resurrected the annual multiday event in 2005 as a celebration mostly closed to the public, a space for Stoney Elders to pass along cultural practices and traditions (Jenna Dulewich, "Nakoda Banff Indian Days Returns to Traditional Land," *Cochrane Today*, August 7, 2019, https://www.cochranetoday.ca/local-news/nakoda-banff-indian-days-returns-to-traditional-land-1626354).

18. Courtney W. Mason, "The Banff Indian Days Tourism Festivals," *Annals of Tourism Research* 53 (2015): 77–95.

19. This understanding was offered by Dagny Dubois, Archives and Special Projects and Support for Indigenous Initiatives at the Whyte Museum of the Canadian Rockies in Banff, Alberta. It's important to note the resilience that the Stoney Nation showed in making Banff Indian Days an opportunity for connection and sustenance.

20. The "Indian pass system" was meant to be a temporary emergency measure to quell Indigenous resistance in the Northwest Rebellion but became permanent

policy from the 1880s to the 1950s under successive federal governments and the Department of Indian Affairs.

21. Jago, "Canada's National Parks Are Colonial Crime Scenes."

22. Foodways are systems of knowledge and expression related to food at the intersection of culture, tradition, and history.

23. For example, on the coast of British Columbia, Heiltsuk Guardian boats monitor fisheries, Kitasoo/Xai'xais Guardians fend off grizzly poachers, and Haida Watchmen halt souvenir collection at their World Heritage Site (Frank Brown and Calvin Sandborn, "Support for Indigenous Guardians Can Be the Key to Meaningful Reconciliation," *Globe and Mail*, Opinion, September 26, 2020).

24. Graeme Hamilton, "The Shady Past of Parks Canada: Forced Out, Indigenous People Are Forging a Comeback," *National Post*, August 25, 2017.

6. Truth, Grief, and Reconciliation

1. Zoe Todd and AM Kanngieser, "Attending to the Environment as Kin Studies," in *Constellations: Indigenous Contemporary Art from the Americas*. This event was organized by the Hyundai Tate Research Centre: Transnational and The Museo Universitario Arte Contemporáneo (MUAC) October 2020. For more of Zoe Todd's work go to https://zoestodd.com/. Kanngieser's CV with links to projects can be found at https://amkanngieser.com/.

2. Consider the ways that the state breaks the kinship ties of migrants, as well as the examples noted in this book on the ways that Indigenous and Black kinship bonds have been broken through North America's refusal to recognize the harm of lynch culture. It was slavery that made the enslaved kinless. Hortense Spillers has stated features that engendered "new forms of affinity and solidarity. . . . Brothers, othermothers, honorary aunties: even ostensibly heterocentric Black communities have always had a vocabulary that exceeds the state's imaginary" (Tyler Bradway and Elizabeth Freeman, *Queer Kinship: Race, Sex, Belonging, Form* [Durham, NC: Duke University Press, 2022], 16). Philosopher and gender theorist Judith Butler notes that in America and other countries, "sexual orientation and marital status are preconditions for adoption or even access to reproductive technology. And sometimes, as we know, people lose their children when their gender status changes, or when their sexual orientation becomes known" ("Breaks in the Bond: Reflections on Kinship Trouble," UCL Housman lecture, University of California at Berkeley, February 8, 2017).

3. Joseph M. Pierce, "In Good Relations," in Bradway and Freeman, *Queer Kinship: Race, Sex, Belonging, Form* (Durham, NC: Duke University Press, 2022), 97.

4. bell hooks, *Yearning: Race, Gender, and Cultural Politics* (Boston: South End Press, 1999), 213.

5. Anja Kanngieser and Zoe Todd, "From Environmental Case Study to Environmental Kin Study," *History and Theory* 59, no. 3 (2020): 385–93, https://doi.org/10.1111/hith.12166; Isabel Scheur, "Environmental Kin Study, Reparation

After Science, Nature and Settler Colonialism," *Afternatures: The Politics of Race, Science and Nature,* Fall 2021, https://afternatures.com/environmental-kin-study/.

6. Suzanne Simard has noted that communication between plants through mycorrhizal networks has been shown to involve the transmission of water, carbon, macronutrients, micronutrients, biochemical signals, allelochemicals, or hormones from one plant to another, usually from a sufficient plant to a plant in need. Recognition of kin is also evident between established and regenerating trees linked in a mycorrhizal network, leading us to consider hub trees as "mother trees." We have found that the mother trees can distinguish their kin from stranger seedlings, shuttling more microelements and supporting vaster mycorrhizal networks to close relatives, thus providing a competitive edge for kin seedlings. However, mother trees also share small amounts of resources with strangers, suggesting mechanisms exist not just for species but also community-level selection (Suzanne Simard, "Conversations in the Forest: The Roots of Nature's Equanimity," *Land Lines* [blog], Nature Conservancy of Canada, March 10, 2015, https://www.natureconservancy.ca/en/blog/archive/conversations-in-the-forest.html).

7. I'm specifically choosing to use the language that author and Indigenous scholar Robin Wall Kimmerer and others have suggested to sustain our awareness of interspecies relatedness and kinship (Willow Defebaugh, "Embracing the More-Than-Human Through Law and Language," *Atmos,* March 14, 2025, https://atmos.earth/embracing-the-more-than-human-through-law-and-language/; Robin Wall Kimmerer, "Nature Needs a New Pronoun: To Stop the Age of Extinction, Let's Start by Ditching 'It,'" *Yes!,* March 30, 2015, https://www.yesmagazine.org/issue/together-earth/2015/03/30/alternative-grammar-a-new-language-of-kinship).

8. Although the visual confirmation of microorganisms present in the blood of healthy individuals requires further examination, evidence confirming the presence of microbial genetic material in the blood-circulatory system is accumulating (Sandrine Païssé et al., "Comprehensive Description of Blood Microbiome from Healthy Donors Assessed by 16S Targeted Metagenomic Sequencing," *Transfusion* 56, no. 5 [2016]: 1138–47. https://doi.org/10.1111/trf.13477; Diego J. Castillo, Riaan F. Rifkin, Don A. Cowan, and Marnie Potgieter, "The Healthy Human Blood Microbiome: Fact or Fiction?" *Frontiers in Cellular and Infection Microbiology* 9 (2020): 148, https://doi.org/10.3389/fcimb.2019.00148).

9. Kim TallBear, "The US-Dakota War and Failed Settler Kinship," *Anthropology News* 57, no. 9 (2016), also at *Unsettle* online, https://kimtallbear.substack.com/p/the-us-dakota-war-and-failed-settler.

10. Ezra Klein, *Why We're Polarized* (New York: Simon & Schuster, 2020.)

11. Alexis Shotwell, "Claiming Bad Kin: Solidarity from Complicit Locations," *Bearing,* Society for the Diffusion of Useful Knowledge, no. 3 (March 2019): 7–11.

12. Shotwell, "Claiming Bad Kin."

13. adrienne marie brown, *We Will Not Cancel Us, and Other Dreams of Transformative Justice,* Emergent Strategy Series (Chico, CA: AK Press), 8.

14. Christina Sharpe, "Lose Your Kin," *New Inquiry*, November 16, 2016, https://thenewinquiry.com/lose-your-kin/.

15. Sarah Sentilles, *Stranger Care: A Memoir on Loving What Isn't Ours* (New York: Random House, 2021) 21.

16. Shotwell, "Claiming Bad Kin."

17. Billy Kobin, "LMPD Officer Shot, Woman Killed during Drug Investigation Off St. Andrews Church Road," *Louisville Courier-Journal*, March 13, 2020, https://www.courier-journal.com/story/news/crime/2020/03/13/louisville-police-officer-shot-suspect-killed-springfield-drive/5040349002/.

18. Nick Cave, "The Red Hand Files," no. 6, October 2018, https://www.theredhandfiles.com/communication-dream-feeling/.

19. Adrian Miller, *Black Smoke: African Americans and the United States of Barbecue* (Chapel Hill: University of North Carolina Press, 2021), 11.

20. For the northerners: a meat and three might include the selection of a meat, like fried chicken or catfish, along with a selection of three sides from a list of up to a dozen specialties of vegetables and starches, like collards, green beans, and mashed potatoes, and is often served with iced tea and cornbread. John T. Edge, director of the Southern Foodways Alliance at the University of Mississippi, says the meat and three came from the transition from the farm to urban life in cities of the South: "Those dishes represent two of the many influences commonly found in Southern food: the cuisine of enslaved West Africans forcibly brought to the South and the 'country food' common among predominantly white farmers" (Adam Rhew, "How the Meat and Three Celebrates Southern Bounty," *Eater*, December 27, 2016, https://www.eater.com/2016/12/27/13990844/meat-and-three-north-carolina-alabama-georgia).

21. The Pendennis Club has hosted a stag boxing night, with a boxing ring set up in the club's grand Georgian ballroom. On February 19, 1960, Muhammad Ali, then Cassius Clay, participated in this event, in which he scored a third-round technical knockout over Ronnie Craddock, whom he had also just beaten in the recent Golden Gloves heavyweight final. The story of the address change is found in Raad Cawthon's story "Louisville, Ali Setting Things Right," *Philadelphia Inquirer*, November 27, 1999, A1.

22. Melvin McLeod, "There's No Place to Go But Up—bell hooks and Maya Angelou in Conversation," Lion's Roar, January 1, 1998, https://www.lionsroar.com/theres-no-place-to-go-but-up/.

23. Jonathan M. Metzl, *Dying of Whiteness: How the Politics of Racial Resentment Is Killing America's Heartland* (New York: Basic Books, 2019), 7.

24. Bessel van der Kolk, *The Body Keeps the Score: Brain, Mind and the Body in the Healing of Trauma* (New York: Penguin Books, 2015).

25. bell hooks states,

> I began to use the phrase in my work "white supremacist capitalist patriarchy" because I wanted to have some language that would

actually remind us continually of the interlocking systems of domination that define our reality and not to just have one thing be like, you know, gender is the important issue, race is the important issue, but for me the use of that particular jargonistic phrase was a way, a sort of short cut way of saying all of these things actually are functioning simultaneously at all times in our lives and that if I really want to understand what's happening to me, right now at this moment in my life, as a black female of a certain age group, I won't be able to understand it if I'm only looking through the lens of race. I won't be able to understand it if I'm only looking through the lens of gender. I won't be able to understand it if I'm only looking at how white people see me. (From bell hooks, "Cultural Criticism and Transformation," Media Education Foundation interview, accessed March 26, 2025, https://www.mediaed.org/transcripts/Bell-Hooks-Transcript.pdf; see also bell hooks and George Yancy, "Buddhism, the Beats and Loving Blackness," Opinionator, *New York Times*, December 10, 2015, https://archive.nytimes.com/opinionator.blogs.nytimes.com/author/bell-hooks/)

In the 1980s, Kimberlé Crenshaw had identified intersecting social identities that relate to oppression and domination and had said, "Intersectionality is a metaphor for understanding the ways that multiple forms of inequality or disadvantage sometimes compound themselves and create obstacles that often are not understood among conventional ways of thinking" ("Demarginalizing the Intersection of Race and Sex: A Black Feminist Critique of Antidiscrimination Doctrine, Feminist Theory and Antiracist Politics," *University of Chicago Legal Forum* 1989, no. 1 [1989]: Article 8, https://chicagounbound.uchicago.edu/uclf/vol1989/iss1/8).

26. Shotwell, "Claiming Bad Kin."

27. For an in-depth analysis of the relationship of body schema to reciprocity, see K. Romdenh-Romluc, "Fanon, the Body Schema, and White Solipsism," *Southern Journal of Philosophy* 62, no. 1 (2024): 110–23, https://doi.org/10.1111/sjp.12556.

28. Justin Michael Williams and Shelly Tygielski, *How We Ended Racism: Realizing a New Possibility in One Generation* (Boulder, CO: Sounds True, 2023), 103.

29. The Truth and Reconciliation Commission of South Africa attracted global attention and was the first to include both victims and perpetrators. Authorized by President Nelson Mandela under the leadership of former Anglican Archbishop Desmond Tutu, the commission's goal was to uncover the truth about human rights violations during apartheid in that country. South Africa showed the importance of public participation in the process, but the government was slow to implement the recommendations, a problem in other countries with reconciliation processes too. The Truth and Reconciliation Commission of Canada (2008–2015) investigated the human rights abuses in the Canadian residential school system, which was funded by the government and operated by Christian

churches, which used forced enfranchisement, disconnection from families, sexual and physical abuse, deprivation of language and culture, malnutrition, and starvation to remove these children's identities as Indigenous people. Since the commission's formal close, and the release of its ninety-four Calls to Action, Canada's commitment to change has been mixed. Eight years after Prime Minister Trudeau promised to implement them, eighty-one calls remain unfulfilled, according to the Yellowhead Institute. In the US, only two local reconciliation efforts have ever been attempted, one by Greensboro, North Carolina, for the 1979 KKK/American Nazi Party's murder of demonstrators marching to advance social, economic, and racial justice, and the other by the Maine Wabanaki-State Child Welfare Truth and Reconciliation Commission (2012–2015), whose findings in the wake of rights abuses by the state child welfare system included that aboriginal children were five times more likely to be put into foster care than other children and that federal reviews indicated that over 50 percent of aboriginal children did not have their native ancestry verified.

30. David Graeber and David Wengrow, *The Dawn of Everything: A New History of Humanity* (London: Allen Lane, 2021), 208.

31. "On 6 January, thousands of Trump supporters gathered at a 'Save America' rally organized to challenge the result of last November's presidential election. They listened as Mr. Trump spoke to them on the National Mall, near the White House in Washington, DC. In a 70-minute address, Mr. Trump exhorted them to march on Congress where politicians had met to certify Democrat Joe Biden's win. The attack began moments after he took the applause. Those words have now played a central part in his second impeachment, which lawmakers voted in favor of last month" ("Capitol Riots: Did Trump's Words at Rally Incite Violence?" BBC, February 13, 2021, https://www.bbc.com/news/world-us-canada-55640437).

32. Brown-Forman is widely known as being based in nepotism and autocratic rule. Those employees who are outliers don't tend to do well in its very conservative environment. More recently, Brown-Forman has dropped its DEI initiatives. For more, see Conor Reynolds, "Brown-Forman Drops Diversity and Inclusion Programmes, Leaves LGBT Equity Index," Yahoo!Finance, August 23, 2024, https://finance.yahoo.com/news/brown-forman-drops-diversity-inclusion-132338451.html.

33. Tanya Talaga, "Tanya Talaga Opens Up about the State of Reconciliation in Canada," CTV, *The Social*, https://www.theloop.ca/watch/news/canada/tanya-talaga-opens-up-about-the-state-of-reconciliation-in-canada/6138027175001/1660173970673870600/the-social.

34. Maud Newton, "My Father's Family Kept Slaves—And He Defended It. Acknowledging It Matters," *Guardian*, September 14, 2022, https://www.theguardian.com/world/2022/sep/14/slavery-family-racist-history-ancestors-wrongdoing.

35. Reparations4Slavery, "Reparative Geneaology," accessed March 26, 2025, https://reparations4slavery.com/reparative-genealogy.

36. George Yancy and Judith Butler, "What's Wrong with 'All Lives Matter'?" *New York Times*, January 12, 2015.

Selected Bibliography

Abdurraqib, Hanif. *A Little Devil in America: Notes in Praise of Black Performance*. New York: Random House, 2021.

Backhouse, Constance. *Colour-Coded: A Legal History of Racism in Canada, 1900–1950*. Toronto: University of Toronto Press, 1999.

Bingham, Emily. *My Old Kentucky Home: The Astonishing Life and Reckoning of an Iconic American Song*. Lexington: University Press of Kentucky, 2024, New York: Knopf, 2022.

Biss, Eula. *Having and Being Had*. New York: Riverhead Books, 2020.

Bradway, Tyler, and Elizabeth Freeman. *Queer Kinship: Race, Sex, Belonging, Form*. Durham, NC: Duke University Press, 2022.

brown, adrienne maree. *We Will Not Cancel Us: And Other Dreams of Transformative Justice*. Chico, CA: AK Press, 2020.

Brundage, W. Fitzhugh. *Lynching in the New South: Georgia and Virginia, 1880–1930*. Champagne: University of Illinois Press, 1993.

Brundage, W. Fitzhugh. *Under Sentence of Death: Lynching in the South*. Chapel Hill: University of North Carolina Press, 1997.

Buck, Pem Davidson. *The Punishment Monopoly: Tales of My Ancestors, Dispossession, and the Building of the United States*. New York: Monthly Review Press, 2019.

Buck, Pem Davidson. *Worked to the Bone: Race, Class, Power & Privilege in Kentucky*. New York: Monthly Review Press, 2001.

Casper, Monica, and Eric Wertheimer, eds. *Critical Trauma Studies: Understanding Violence, Conflict and Memory in Everyday Life*. New York: New York University Press, 2016.

Catte, Elizabeth. *What You Are Getting Wrong about Appalachia*. Cleveland: Belt Publishing, 2018.

Chee, Alexander. *How to Write an Autobiographical Novel: Essays*. New York: Mariner Books, 2018.

Coates, Ta-Nehisi. *We Were Eight Years in Power: An American Tragedy*. New York: One World, 2017.

Cooper, Brittney. *Eloquent Rage*. New York: St. Martin's Press, 2018.

Coulthard, Glen Sean. *Red Skin White Masks: Rejecting the Colonial Politics of Recognition*. Minneapolis: University of Minnesota Press, 2014.

Daschuk, James. *Clearing the Plains: Disease, Politics of Starvation, and the Loss of Indigenous Life*. Regina, Saskatchewan: University of Regina Press, 2019.

Dederer, Claire. *Monsters: A Fan's Dilemma*. New York: Knopf, 2023.

Dew, Lee A., and Aloma W. Dew. *Owensboro, The City on the Yellow Banks: A History of Owensboro, Kentucky*. Bowling Green, KY: Rivendell, 1988.

DuRocher, Kristina. *Raising Racists: The Socialization of White Children in the Jim Crow South*. Reprint ed. Lexington: University Press of Kentucky, 2018.

Federal Writers' Project. *Slave Narratives: Kentucky*. Bedford, MA: Applewood Books.

Harkins, Anthony, and Meredith McCarroll, eds. *Appalachian Reckoning: A Region Responds to* Hillbilly Elegy. Morgantown: West Virginia University Press, 2019.

hooks, bell. *Belonging: A Culture of Place*. New York: Routledge, 2008.

Hunter, Daniel. *Building a Movement to End the New Jim Crow*. Arlington, VA: Hyrax Publishing, 2015.

Hyde, Lewis. *A Primer for Forgetting: Getting Past the Past*. New York: Farrar, Straus and Giroux, 2019.

Ifill, Sherrilyn A. *On the Courthouse Lawn: Confronting the Legacy of Lynching in the 21st Century*. Boston, MA: Beacon, 2007.

Ignatiev, Noel. *How the Irish Became White*. Milton Park, UK: Routledge, 2008.

Johnson, Lacy M. *The Reckonings: Essays on Justice for the Twenty-First Century*. New York: Scribner, 2018.

Kendi, Ibram X. *How To Be An Antiracist*. Updated ed. New York: One World, 2023.

Laymon, Kiese. *How to Slowly Kill Yourself and Others in America*. New York: Scribner, 2020.

Lorde, Audre. *The Selected Work of Audre Lorde, by Roxane Gay*. New York: Norton, 2020.

Marshall, Anne E. *Creating a Confederate Kentucky: The Lost Cause and Civil War Memory in a Border State*. Chapel Hill: University of North Carolina Press, 2010.

Marzano-Lesnevich, Alex. *The Fact of a Body: A Murder and A Memoir*. New York: Flatiron Books, 2017.

Mason, Courtney. *Spirits of the Rockies: Reasserting an Indigenous Presence in Banff National Park*. Toronto: University of Toronto Press, 2014.

Maza, Sarah. *Thinking about History*. Chicago: University of Chicago Press, 2017.

McFeely, William S., and C. Vann Woodward. *The Strange Career of Jim Crow*. Oxford: Oxford University Press, 2001.

McWhorter, Diane. *Carry Me Home: The Climactic Battle of the Civil Rights Revolution*. New York: Simon & Schuster, 2001.

Menakem, Resmaa. *My Grandmother's Hands, Racialized Trauma and the Pathway to Mending Our Hearts and Bodies*. Las Vegas, NV: Central Recovery Press, 2019.

Metzel, Jonathan M. *Dying of Whiteness: How the Politics of Racial Resentment Is Killing America's Heartland*. New York: Basic Books, 2019.

Milloy, John S. *A National Crime: The Canadian Government and the Residential School System 1879–1986*. Winnipeg: University of Manitoba Press, 2001.

Moreton-Robinson, Aileen. *The White Possessive: Property, Power, and Indigenous Sovereignty*. Minneapolis: University of Minnesota Press, 2015.

Morrison, Toni. *Playing in the Dark: Whiteness and the Literary Imagination*. Cambridge, MA: Harvard University Press, 1992.

Morrison, Toni. *The Source of Self-Regard: Selected Essays, Speeches, and Meditations*. New York: Knopf, 2019.

Newton, Maud. *Ancestor Trouble: A Reckoning and a Reconciliation*. New York: Random House, 2022.

Ogletree, Charles, Jr., and Austin Sarat. *From Lynch Mobs to the Killing State: Race and the Death Penalty in America*. New York: New York University Press, 2006.

Perry, Adele. *On the Edge of Empire: Gender, Race, and the Making of British Columbia 1849–1871*. Toronto: University of Toronto Press, 2001.

Perry, Imani. *South to America: A Journey below the Mason-Dixon to Understand the Soul of a Nation*. New York: HarperCollins, 2022.

Phillips, Steve. *Brown Is The New White: How the Demographic Revolution Has Created a New American Majority*. New York: New Press, 2016.

Purnell, Derecka. *Becoming Abolitionists: Police, Protests and the Pursuit of Freedom*. New York: Astra Publishing House, 2021.

Richardson, Heather Cox. *How the South Won the Civil War: Oligarchy, Democracy and the Continuing Fight for the Soul of America*. Cary, NC: Oxford University Press, 2020.

Saslow, Eli. *Rising Out of Hatred: The Awakening of a Former White Nationalist*. New York: Doubleday, 2018.

Savoy, Lauret. *Trace: Memory, History, Race and the American Landscape*. Berkeley: Counterpoint Press, 2015.

Segrest, Mab. *Memoir of a Race Traitor*. New York: New Press, 2019.

Sentilles, Sarah. *Stranger Care*. New York: Random House, 2021.

Shotwell, Alexis. *Knowing Otherwise: Race, Gender and Implicit Understanding*. University Park: Pennsylvania State University Press, 2011.

Smith, Clint. *How the Word Is Passed: A Reckoning with the History of Slavery across America*. New York: Little, Brown, 2021.

Spence, Mark David. *Dispossessing the Wilderness: Indian Removal and the Making of the National Parks*. New York: Oxford University Press, 1999.

Strings, Sabrina. *Fearing the Black Body*. New York: New York University Press, 2019.

Talaga, Tanya. *The Knowing*. New York: Harper Collins, 2024.

Tallbear, Kim. *Unsettled Podcast and Substack Newsletter.* https://kimtallbear.substack.com/.
Tolnay, Stewart E., and E. M. Beck. *A Festival of Violence: An Analysis of Southern Lynchings, 1882–1930.* Urbana: University of Illinois Press, 1995.
Treaty Seven Elders and Tribal Council, with Walter Hildebrandt, Dorothy First Rider, and Sarah Carter. *The True Spirit and Original Intent of Treaty 7.* Montreal: McGill-Queens University Press, 1996.
Tyson, Timothy. *The Blood of Emmett Till.* New York: Simon & Schuster, 2017.
Waiser, Bill. *Park Prisoners: The Untold Story of Western Canada's National Parks, 1915–1946.* Markham: Fifth House, 1995.
Waldrep, Christopher. *The Many Faces of Judge Lynch: Extralegal Violence and Punishment in America.* New York: Palgrave MacMillan, 2002.
Ward, Jesmyn. *Let Us Descend.* New York: Scribner, 2023.
Weathersby, Irvin, Jr. *In Open Contempt: Confronting White Supremacy in Art and Public Space.* New York: Viking, 2025.
Weissinger, Sandra E. *Law Enforcement in the Age of Black Lives Matter: Policing Black and Brown Bodies.* Lanham, MD: Lexington Books, 2019.
Wilkerson, Isabel. *Caste: The Origins of Our Discontents.* New York: Random House, 2020.
Wilkerson, Jessica. *To Live Here, You Have To Fight: How Women Led Appalachian Movements for Social Justice.* Urbana: University of Illinois Press, 2019.
Williamson, Joel. *The Crucible of Race: Black-White Relations in the American South since Emancipation.* New York: Oxford University Press, 1984.
Wright, George C. *Racial Violence in Kentucky: Lynchings, Mob Rule and "Legal Lynchings."* Reprint ed. Baton Rouge: Louisana State University Press, 1996.
Yacovone, Donald. *Teaching White Supremacy: America's Democratic Ideal and the Forging of Our National Identity.* New York: Pantheon, 2022.
Yancy, George. *Black Bodies, White Gazes: The Continuing Significance of Race in America.* 2nd ed. Lanham, MD: Rowman & Littlefield, 2016.

About the Author

Sonya Lea is the author of *Wondering Who You Are,* a memoir that became a finalist for the Washington State Book Award and garnered praise from *Oprah Magazine* and the BBC, who named it a "top ten book." Her essays and interviews have appeared in *Salon, The Southern Review, Brevity, Guernica, Ms. Magazine, The Los Angeles Review of Books, The Rumpus,* and more. She teaches at workshops and creates writing retreats in the US and Canada. Lea is the recipient of an Artist Trust Award, two Canada Council Awards, and a grant from the Alberta Foundation for the Arts. She lives in the Pacific Northwest with her kin.